Global Real Estate Investment

Global Real Estate Investment
Trends and Experinces

Edited by

B Sujatha

2010

Icfai Books
The Icfai University Press

Global Real Estate Investment: Trends and Experinces

Editor: B Sujatha

First Edition: 2010
Printed in India

Published by

The Icfai University Press
52, Nagarjuna Hills, Punjagutta
Hyderabad, India – 500 082
Phone: (+91) (040) 23430–368, 369, 370, 372, 373, 374
Fax: (+91) (040) 23352521, 23435386
E-mail: info@icfaibooks.com, icfaibooks@icfai.org, ssd@icfai.org

ISBN: 9788131408766

Editorial Team: Sushuma G and Aditya Ghosh
Quality Support: R Kalyani and Battu Yugandhar

Contents

Section II

Country Experiences

OVERVIEW

With economies around the world becoming more integrated as a result of increased trade in goods and services, global capital markets have become more interconnected. Global real estate investment has definitely come of age, and the industry is continuing to advance. It is expected to become more sophisticated, mature, innovative, transparent, disciplined, and accountable to investors, and even better positioned to compete with stocks and bonds for capital. For a number of years, larger investors in Canada, Germany, Ireland, Netherlands and the US have pursued active global real estate investment strategies. More recently, these larger investors have been joined by a broader range of investors seeking to invest in global markets, including those from Scandinavia, the Middle East, Australia, Hong Kong, Japan, South Korea, Spain and the UK. Global real estate has generated around 10% annual total returns, compared with 3% for equities in the year 2005.

Investors are attracted towards global real estate investment because of its advantage of low risk and steady returns. Many countries have also realized the growth of global real estate investment and have enacted laws to remove barriers to international investment. Capital is becoming more global. Investors around the world are thinking globally and have become more willing and even eager to own foreign assets. Many compelling reasons exist for investors to consider real estate as an important component of their portfolios. In the global context, the relatively more stable income streams in the form of cash flow from property operations or dividends from listed real estate securities are becoming more appealing to both individual retirees and pension funds. Both the private and the public global real estate investment areas have experienced a substantial increase in the value over the last few years. The global public real estate market has grown by more than 27% in 2005 to USD644 billion.

As the importance of global real estate investment is increasing, this book focuses on the global trends relating to real estate funds as an investment option. It gives an overview of the current scenario of the global real estate sector, the players in the global securities market in this segment and the various investment vehicles available. It also highlights the advantages of investing in a global real estate portfolio and the issues involved.

The book is presented in two sections. The first section brings out the significance of real estate as a distinct asset class and why it has become an important component in an efficient portfolio. It also covers what factors should be considered when deciding where to invest. It traces the growth and trends in the global real estate securities market.

The second section of the book deals with the existing trends in various countries across the globe. It analyses the REIT market in Germany, UK, Japan, US and Switzerland. It also highlights the capital flows into the real estate market of the Middle East and China and the lessons for the developing markets.

Section I: Emerging Trends

The transformation of the global public real estate market in recent years reveals that it has been accepted as a separate asset class. Investor's interest is attracted to REIT because of its less risk and high yield. Global real estate investment has increased to $900 billion in 2006, with nearly 40%[1] increase compared to the previous year. The first section of the book highlights the trends prevailing in the global market.

The first article "**Global Real Estate Investment – Trends and Outlook**" by *B Sujatha* traces the evolution, growth and development of the global real estate securities market. It highlights the benefits of investing in a global real estate portfolio, and recent developments in a global real estate portfolio. The author concludes that the outlook for the global REIT markets is positive with tremendous growth potential.

With the proliferation and growth of REIT and REIT-like structures around the world, the sophistication of real estate investment continues to increase. The second article "**Global Real Estate Investment – The World is Becoming Flatter**" written by *Lijian Chen* and *Thomas I Mills* describes three basic styles of real estate ownership in the context of investment and lists the benefits of global real estate investment in terms of stability of income, diversification and a wider spectrum of investment strategies. It further brings out the reasons for the success of REITs and the strategic considerations for international real estate investment.

The third article "**Why Invest in International Real Estate?**" sourced from *www.aiggig.com,* examines how international real estate can increase portfolio diversification and mitigate risk. The author says that in addition to the evolution in vehicles and markets, an evolution of investor attitudes is also serving to shape the real estate investment landscape.

---

[1] $900bn Invested in Global Real Estate during 2006, *http://www.joneslanglasalle.com/en-GB/news/2007/Global_capital_flows.htm*

IV

The fourth article "**Global REITs: A New Platform of Ownership**" authored by *Philip Conner* and *Youguo Liang* examines the trends in the listed property sector, the key drivers of the recent REIT market growth and the implications of a vibrant global REIT market for real estate capital, space markets and investors. The article also brings to light that for investors the growth of the public markets creates more opportunities to access the attractive return characteristics of property investments, while helping to mitigate many of the risks that historically have made investors avoid the asset class.

REIT shares derive a great part of their value from tangible, hard assets and provide benefits of balance, diversification and greater risk/reward efficiency to a broad range of investment portfolios. The article "**The Investor's Guide to Real Estate Investment Trusts (REITs)**" sourced from *www.investinreits.com*, analyses the returns from REITs vis-a-vis other stocks and bonds and highlights the advantages of real estate investment. It shows how REITs have a diverse investment allocation across a broad range of specific real estate sub-sectors like industrial parks, warehouses, apartment communities, regional malls, healthcare facilities, hotels and resorts.

The real estate private equity fund market has matured into one of the most significant sources of equity financing for real estate transactions. The sixth article "**Trends in the Real Estate Private Equity Industry**" sourced from *www.ey.com*, covers market and capital trends, fund performance and reporting, tax considerations, and infrastructure and technology trends in the real estate private equity fund market. Because of its yield and appreciation potential, real estate is attracting more investment capital flows and the number of funds being created has increased significantly. Fund sponsors are increasing their investment allocations to other markets outside the United States, including Asia-Pacific, Eastern and Western Europe and Canada.

The next article "**Globalization of Real Estate Capital Flows**" by *Raj Bhandari* and *Tim Morris* brings to light the transformation taking place in international real estate markets. It is shifting from non-traditional real estate owners and moving in bulk to organizations dealing with real estate funds. The author also discusses the growth of public real estate market in India and the market conditions in various countries like Japan, Russia, China, Europe, Mexico and Spain.

The eighth article "**Global Real Estate Securities – Where do they Fit in the Broader Market?**" written by *Fraser Hughes* and *Jorrit Arissen* estimates the size of the investment grade, or high quality commercial global real estate market and analyzes the trends and developments therein. The value addition "**Global Real Estate Investment Trends**" compiled from *www.rreef.com*, traces the performance of the global real estate market.

Section II: Country Experiences

Since its inception from 1960s, REITs operations were confined to US and Australia. In recent years, there is a rapid expansion of REIT in other countries. Investment in real estate markets other than US and Australia has increased. Many countries have enacted laws to set up REIT and in a few countries they are in the process. The second section discusses the real estate markets in US, Europe and Asia Pacific.

The first article "**What can Europe Learn from US REITs: Lessons from the Ivory Towers**" penned by *Tobias Just* gives an overview of REIT market in US, its growth and development and how its success can be emulated by other countries. The article recommends that the European REIT laws be amended over time to meet the market demands which will in turn, accelerate growth. The consolidation in the REIT sector is happening through mergers and market delisting. Going private will be the correcting force for the REIT market.

The German Real Estate Investment Trust or G-REIT is in the center of interest in Germany these days and is expected to be introduced in the beginning of 2007. A swift introduction of G-REITs would fill a national gap in the international range of real estate investments, to vitalize the business location Germany, and to professionalize the German real estate economy.

The next article "**The Introduction of the Real Estate Investment Trusts (REITs) in Germany**" penned by *Constantin M Lachner* and *Rafael von Heppe* discusses G-REIT legislation, corporate structure and requirements of G-REITs. It elaborates upon taxation of G-REITs. The G-REIT requires a free float of at least 15% of the shares or, in the moment of listing in the organized market, of at least 25%, in order to allow small investors to participate in fungible real estate investments.

The third article "**Swiss Issues Real Estate: Real Estate Market 2007 – Facts and Trends – Real Estate an Investment**" authored by *Ulrich Braun, Fredy Hasenmaile, Martin Neff, Thomas Rieder* and *Yves-Denis Schönenberger,* talks about real estate funds in Switzerland. Real estate funds remain attractive to medium and long- term investors as rising interest rates and strong economic activity would increase the rental income from residential and office buildings. There are only marginal differences between indirect investments in Switzerland and continental Europe. Apart from the waiver of tax at the company level, Swiss-law real estate funds and real estate investment companies are very similar to American REITs. Most of them have a high dividend yield.

The fourth article "**Regulatory Impact Assessment for Real Estate Investment Trusts (UK-REITS)**" throws light on UK-REITs, their requirements and costs incurred by the companies elected to join UK-REITs. Around 80% are large companies, 17% medium-sized companies, and the remaining small companies will be directly affected by the legislation of UK-REITs. The property investment market is the principal market that would be affected by the measure, though there might be some associated impact on developmental activity. The article concludes with the effect of a breach of a regime condition. The effect will depend on the size of the breach, the nature of the condition and the number of times that a breach has occurred.

The next article "**Asian REITs: A New Dimension for Investors**" by *Philip Conner* and *Marc Halle,* examines the growth and development of the Asian REIT market. The evolution of the new REIT vehicles in Asia is likely to mirror the development of the Australian and US markets in many respects. REITs promise to improve transparency, liquidity and the industry's access to capital, while creating a more dynamic and competitive property market that should encourage more professionalism and best practices throughout the industry is heartening. The potential for further growth in the Asian REIT market is significant. Asian economies are expected to continue expanding at a healthy pace over the next two years, with very strong growth in China and India.

Japan, the first REIT market to emerge in Asia, has grown exponentially over the five years since it inception, contributing to the upturn in the Japanese real estate market. The sixth article "**Real Estate Investment Trusts in Japan**" sourced from London Stock Exchange briefly outlines the J-REIT market in Japan, describes the J-REIT structure and their listing requirements. Japan has rapidly advanced to be the third largest REIT market in a few years, in asset terms behind US and Australian listed property trusts. The J-REIT market is likely to continue growing in the medium term. "**Lessons for Japan from US REITs**" by *G Sushuma,* is a value addition to this article. It tells us that the current restrictive system of Japanese REITs can by no means effectively help expand the size of REITs industry. Japan would need some basic research and major revisions of REIT rules, if they want REIT to be an effective public policy instrument.

The seventh article "**China – Many Opportunities, Unique Risks**" written by *Youguo Liang* and *M Shayne Arcilla* discusses the various risks in China's real estate market. The abolition of the state-sponsored housing system in the '90s and the introduction of land-lease rights helped spur an investment market for real estate over the past 10 years. China holds many risks for real estate investors, including the lack of legal tradition, judicial independence, government corruption, underdeveloped banking and capital markets, currency control and an opaque market. China also has unique risks arising from state monopoly on land ownership, and uncertainties associated with evolving rules and regulations.

The final article "**Middle East Capital Flows and the Allure of Real Estate**" by *Anwar Elgonemy* highlights that the interest in Middle East real estate investment is starting to flow from traditional destinations like Europe and the US to look at opportunities closer home. The property market in the Middle East is worth an estimated $150 billion. Domestic real estate assets are expected to become more attractive channels for citizens and national investment groups. The majority of the real estate investment products are aimed at HNWIs, and the funds are used to finance assets for capital appreciation, or for the development or acquisition of income-generating assets.

This book should be of interest to all major stakeholders – real estate developers, players in the mutual fund industry, students, researchers, analysts, investors and the general public.

Section I

Emerging Trends

1

Global Real Estate Investment – Trends and Outlook

B Sujatha

Investment in real estate has always been attractive to investors both in terms of yield and diversification of portfolio. High entry costs, long gestation periods and legal complexities have been the deterrents to direct investment in property, especially for small investors. The development of a listed property sector internationally has made real estate a popular asset class among investors allowing them to participate in the benefits with a much lower stake and the advantage of liquidity as well.

"Ninety percent of all millionaires become so through owning real estate. More money has been made in real estate than in all industrial investments combined. The wise young man or wage earner of today invests his money in real estate."

– Andrew Carnegie.

Land or real estate property, as it is more popularly referred now, is an inextensible and imperishable asset that always appreciates in value. Land provides security to mankind. Prior to the age of industrial revolution, ownership of land used to be a measure of wealth or status of an individual or family. Investment in land has been traditionally favored for centuries. To quote Theodore Roosevelt, "Every person who invests in well-selected real estate in a growing section of a prosperous community adopts the surest and safest method of becoming independent, for real estate is the basis of wealth." However, participation in the benefits of real estate investment was the domain of the rich and wealthy and the elite class due to the high investment outlay, long holding periods and cumbersome legal formalities involved. But today, the advent of securitization has brought real estate investment to the reach of the common man. New products and investment vehicles have made it possible for even small investors to invest in the profitable options of significant real estate projects like shopping malls, office complexes, technology parks, hotels and healthcare facilities. Real Estate Investment Trusts (REITs) connote the induction of commercial real estate into mainstream capital market. The proliferation of REIT-like structures worldwide has been a catalyst for capital appreciation opportunities.

What is REIT?

Real Estate Investment Trust (REIT) is a company that owns and manages income generating real estate. The income may arise out of commercial or residential property. The inherent advantage of REIT lies in exemption from corporate tax for the income that gets distributed as dividends. REIT thus paves the way for securitizing real estate investment in a tax efficient way, benefiting both corporate players and the investors. It is an investment vehicle that enables property companies to raise capital through the stock market on the one hand, and on the other hand allows easy access to property as an asset class in the investor's portfolio. High proportion of dividend adds to their attraction from the investor viewpoint.

Factors Driving the Shift to REITs

- Enables small investors to participate in a diversified investment portfolio.
- Helps to decrease the gap between net asset value and market value for listed companies.
- Improved access to real estate as an asset class for investors with a long-term horizon.
- Greater liquidity and improved efficiency of the property market from the investment perspective.

The growth of REIT structures around the world has provided a new mode of investment in global real estate markets, thereby contributing significantly to the increase in market capitalization of global real estate securities from $110 billion in 1997 to $1.2 trillion[1] in 2006, as seen from Figure 1.

Figure 1: Growth of Global Real Estate Securitization on December 31, 2006 ($ billions)

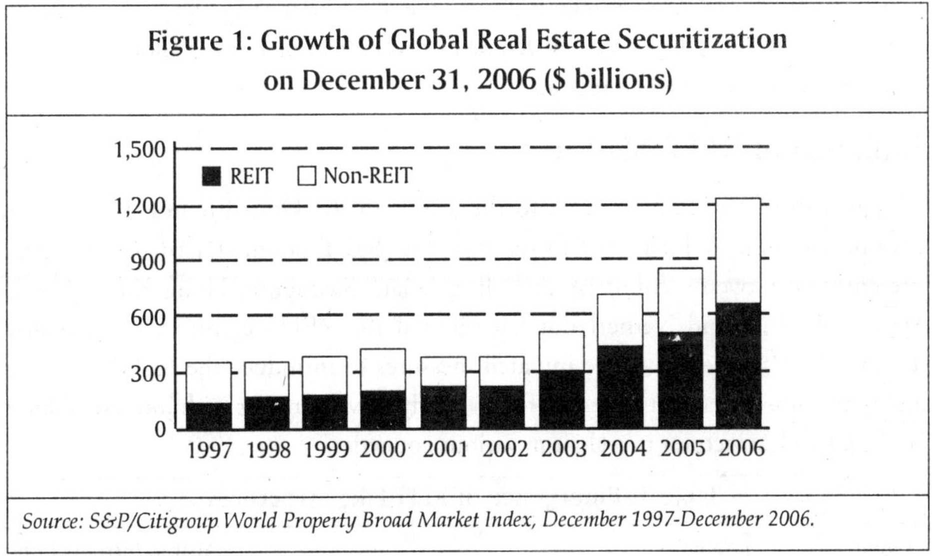

Source: S&P/Citigroup World Property Broad Market Index, December 1997-December 2006.

Benefits of REIT to Investors

REITs are investments that provide high dividends plus long-term capital appreciation. Long-term returns on REIT stocks usually exceed that of transitional investment classes like equity stocks and bonds. REITs are tax efficient investment vehicles that not only prevent double taxation, but also bring with them the advantages of professional management of the real estate portfolio. REITs are similar to stocks traded in major markets, so the investor has the ease of investing or divesting, giving utmost liquidity to his capital. The low investment threshold enables him to participate even in large scale realty projects and gain proportionate benefits. In view of the high pay out prospects, the investor can enjoy high and stable income streams that are often backed by long-term lease agreements. Over and above the regular returns fetched by rental incomes, the investors stand to gain by appreciation in land value, which in turn gets reflected as increase in share price.

[1] "REITs: A Global Perspective, The Emergence and Growth of Global REITs, 2007", *www.cohenandsteers.com*

Risks Associated with REITs

Most of the REITs focus on specific segments of real estate such as technology parks, shopping malls and healthcare facilities to name a few. This makes them vulnerable to downward trends in that sector. Similarly, concentration of projects or investments in one geographic location or region also exposes them to the vagaries of the economy or region. However, this can be overcome by diversification of asset allocation across segments, property types or regions.

Evolution of REIT Market

The growth of REITs dates back to the 1960s in the United States. It, however, became a popular vehicle only in the 90s. The REIT boom started in 1991, and presently over twenty countries including Japan, Singapore, Hong Kong, Korea, France, Belgium and Netherlands have joined the REIT regime. UK, Germany, Taiwan, Mexico and Italy have initiated measures to introduce the REIT structure, and many other Asian countries are following the developments with interest. Table 1 lists the REIT structures prevalent in various countries.

Table 1: Emergence of REIT-Like Structures

Country	Name	Year of Introduction
New Zealand	Property Trust	1956
United States	Real Estate Investment Trust	1960
Netherlands	Fiscale Beleggingsinstelling	1969
Australia	Listed Property Trust	1971
South Africa	Property Unit Trust	1981
Brazil	Fundos de Investimento Imobiliario	1993
Malaysia	Real Estate Investment Trust	1993
Canada	Real Estate Investment Trust	1994
Italy	Fondi di Investimento Immobiliare	1994
Belgium	Societe d'Investissement a capital fixe	1995
Turkey	Gayrimenkul Yat	1998
Singapore	Singapore Real Estate Investment Trust	2002
Japan	Japanese Real Estate Investment Trust	2000
South Korea	Korean Real Estate Investment Trust	2001
Austria	Immobilien – Investmentfonds[gesetz] (ImmoInv FG)	2003

Contd...

Contd...		
France	Societe d'Investissements immobiliers cotees	2003
Hong Kong	Hong Kong Real Estate Investment Trust	2003
Taiwan	Real Estate Investment Trust	2003
Puerto Rico	Real Estate Investment Trust	
United Kingdom	UK Real Estate Investment Trust	2007
Germany	German Real Estate Investment Trust	1972/2000
Compiled from various sources		

United States

The origin of the real estate investment trust or REIT can be traced back to the 1880s when investors were shielded from double taxation as trust income was exempt from corporate tax if distributed to beneficiaries. However, this tax advantage was reversed in the 1930s and stayed so until president Eisenhower signed the 1960 real estate investment trust tax provision and re-established the special tax considerations qualifying REITs as pass through entities. The 1980s witnessed an increase in REIT investment, which was further strengthened by the reform trend. The Tax Reform Act of 1986 permitted REITs to manage their properties directly, and REIT investment barriers to pension funds were eliminated in 1993.

The property market gradually witnessed a shift from private ownership to public equity and debt and finally publicly listed vehicles. REITs as an investment vehicle took off successfully in the US only when the legislation permitted creation of unlisted REITs and brought down the distribution requirements to 90%. The legislation required 100 shareholders and 75% of the income be derived as rentals or interest on debts secured by real estate property. The number of publicly traded REITs has grown from 53 in 1974 to over 200 as on October 2006, holding assets valued at over US$475 billion[2]. About one fifth[3] of investment grade commercial real estate property is owned by REITs in the US, and their reach extends across borders to Asia, Europe and Latin America. The inclusion of REITs in the US S&P 500[4] index from the year 2001, acknowledges their significance in the public capital markets.

---

2 "Real Estate Update", October 2006, Deloitte, *http://www.deloitte.com/dtt/cda/doc/content/uk_re_realestateupdate_oct06.pdf*

3 FTSE EPRA/NAREIT Global Real Estate Index Monthly Bulletin, November 2005.

4 Standard & Poor's 500 index is an index consisting of 500 stocks designed to be a leading indicator of US equities meant to reflect the risk/return characteristics of the large-cap universe. *http://www.investopedia.com*

The long-term performance of US Equity REITs stood testimony to their success in terms of compound annual returns that surpassed the S&P 500 and Dow Jones Industrial Indices for a sustained period of three decades – from December 1971 to December 2002.

Figure 2: Equity Market Capitalization of Listed US REITs

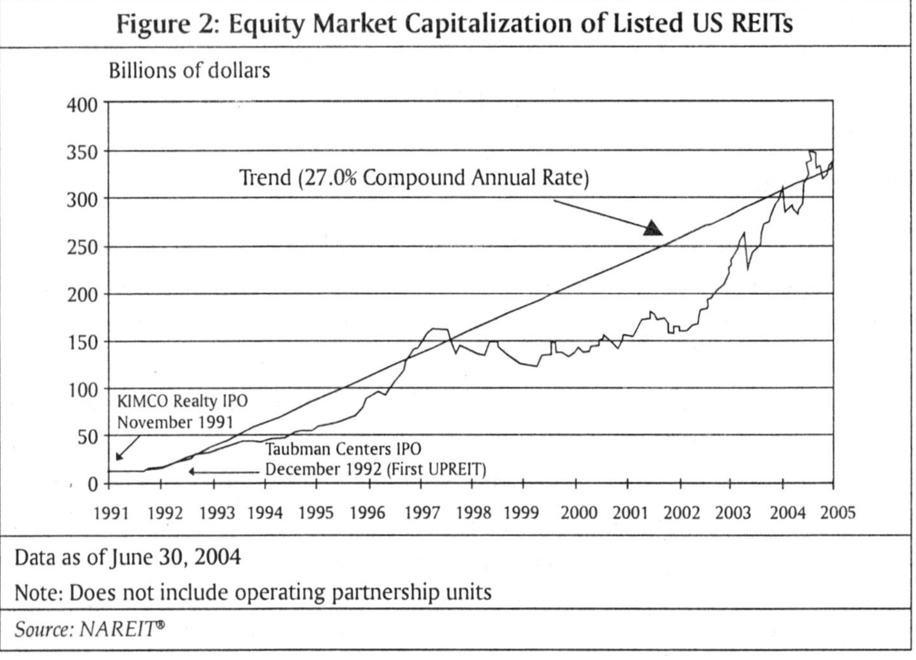

Data as of June 30, 2004

Note: Does not include operating partnership units

Source: NAREIT®

Asia Pacific

Australia

Following the US, Australia was also quick to follow suit with pioneering initiatives in structuring tax efficient investment vehicles for the realty sector. Like the US REITs, they came up with their investment structure called the Listed Property Trust (LPT) established in 1971. Australia is the second largest listed property market in the world constituting 11% of the FTSE EPRA/NAREIT Global Real Estate Index[5]. Over 800000 investors are reported to operate in the Australian LPT segment with over 50 LPTs having a market capitalization of US$50 billion. LPTs indicate 40% lesser volatility as compared to other stocks and constitute about 8.5% of the total Australian stock market. Almost 50% of the investment grade real estate is estimated to be owned by LPTs, while the US market holds about 12.5%. The Australian LPT is considered to

[5] FTSE EPRA/NAREIT Global Real Estate Index Monthly Bulletin, November 2005.

be one of the most open REIT regimes with no restrictions on leverage or development. The entire income of the trusts must be distributed as dividends.

Japan

J-REITs were introduced in Japan in 2000 modelled along the lines of the US REITs. In the five years since inception, J-REITs have grown from 2 issuers to 40 with a market capitalization growth from JPY260 billion ($2.2 billion) to JPY4.7 trillion[6] (approximately $40 billion). The J-REITs are highly regulated and may be established as a contract or company type investment trust. At least 75% of the assets should be invested in real estate and 90% of profits must be distributed. J-REITs have grown to occupy a significant place in the real estate securitization and investment market in Japan as substantiated by the Ministry of Land Infrastructure and Transport (MLIT) reports indicating that 25% of the real estate assets securitization that happened in 2005 were done through J-REITs. The yield advantage of J-REITs over the Japanese Government bonds has been a major factor driving the impressive growth of J-REITs. It is expected that the proposal to introduce J-UPREITS[7] (Umbrella Partnership REITs) and capital gain deferral on transfer of assets to REITs will help to revive the non-metropolitan areas of Japan.

Singapore

The S-REIT structure was introduced in Singapore in 2002 and is administered by the Monetary Authority of Singapore (MAS) and the Singapore Stock Exchange (SGX-ST). The $6.4 billion S-REIT market has about 8 listed REITs, which constitute 3.1% of the total market capitalization of the SGX-ST and is the third largest in the region next to Australia and Japan. S-REITs allow offshore investments, and require 90% of profits to be distributed.

Hong Kong

Hong Kong REIT rules were introduced in 2003, and the REIT market has been expanding fuelled by high demand and investor interest. As of May 2006, there are four listed REITs in Hong Kong with a total market capitalization of

---

6 "The IFLR Guide to Japan 2007", *http://ommtokyo.jp*

7 UPREIT was introduced in 1992 by the US as a vehicle that allows companies to convert interests in one entity to another entity with no tax implications.

$6.2 billion[8]. REITs constitute 0.3%[9] of the total market capitalization of the Hong Kong Stock Exchange.

India

In March 2005, the Government of India relaxed its policy guidelines governing foreign investment in real estate sector, which stimulated the interest of offshore REITs. In June 2006, the Securities and Exchange Board of India approved guidelines for Real Estate Mutual Funds in India. The recent policy changes are expected to attract institutional and retail investment in the realty sector and transform it into a more organized one. Among the other Asian markets, South Korea already has an established REIT structure in the form of RETF and CR-REIT (Corporate Restructuring REIT), though not listed. Malaysia is also in the process of reviewing its REIT guidelines, and other countries like Taiwan, Thailand and Philippines are also working on joining the REIT revolution.

South Africa

REITs in South Africa are structured in the form of Property Unit Trusts (PUTs). PUTs are subject to stringent regulation and governed by the Collective Investment Schemes Act. These vehicles are allowed to invest in property companies or in immovable property. Capital profits cannot be distributed and have to be reinvested. Gearing limit of 30% is fixed. There are no minimum distribution requirements specified. However, the income earned by PUTs is exempt from tax only to the extent of distribution to unit holders.

Europe

Netherlands

It has one of the oldest regimes of REIT systems, which was introduced since 1969, as Fiscale Beleggingsinstelling (BI). Offshore investments are allowed under the BI structure, while leverage is restricted to 60% of the book value of real estate property and 20% of other property. BIs are required to distribute 100% of their operating income. The Netherlands market has around seven major listed BI stocks with a market capitalization of US$16.5 billion. Modifications to the existing BI structure known as the "luxury version" to render it more flexible are on the cards.

---

8 Michele Lerner, Investor Appetite Grows for Hong Kong REITs, July/Aug 2006, *http://www.nareit.com*

9 John Sullivan and Hayden Flinn., Lessons from Australia as Asian REITs thrive, IFLR, March 2006.

Belgium

Belgium introduced the SICAFI (Société d' Investissement à Capital Fixe Immobilière) structure in 1995. A SICAFI is defined as "a listed property fund, with a fixed amount of corporate share capital, whose role is to provide tax neutrality for collecting and distributing the rental income"[10]. Belgian SICAFI market has seven listed companies with a market capitalization of US$4.0 billion. Offshore investment is not permitted for Belgian SICAFIs and a leverage limit of 50% is imposed. 80% of the earnings need to be distributed as dividends. Reports indicate possible changes to the SICAFI structure including a rise in the gearing limits and exclusion of transfer tax from portfolio valuations.

France

Société d'Investissement Immoblier Côtée (SIIC) was introduced in France in 2003 with passive investment in real estate as main activity. Other activities are allowed but limited to being ancillary to the main activity. The SIIC regime is considered fairly lenient with no leverage limitations and distribution requirement of 85% of profits and 50% of capital gains. The SIIC sector has about 9 companies with a market capitalization of US$23.8 billion.

Italy

FIIs (Fondi di investimento immobiliare) are special funds that were introduced in 1994 in Italy, but not pure REITs. They are exempt from tax and have no obligation as regards distribution. They are managed by "Società di gestione del risparmio" (SGR) and subject to a leverage of 60% of the value of the real estate and 20% of the value of other assets.

United Kingdom

The introduction of REITs in January 2007 in UK has been the culmination of a decade long consultation between the Government and the industry in a bid to have a tax efficient investment vehicle and also to align UK with other markets in Europe. The UK REIT must be a fully listed company and resident in UK. At least 90% of the profits must be distributed to shareholders. Existing property companies can opt

---

10 "Epra Global REIT Survey. A comparison of the major REIT regimes in the world", EPRA, September 2004.

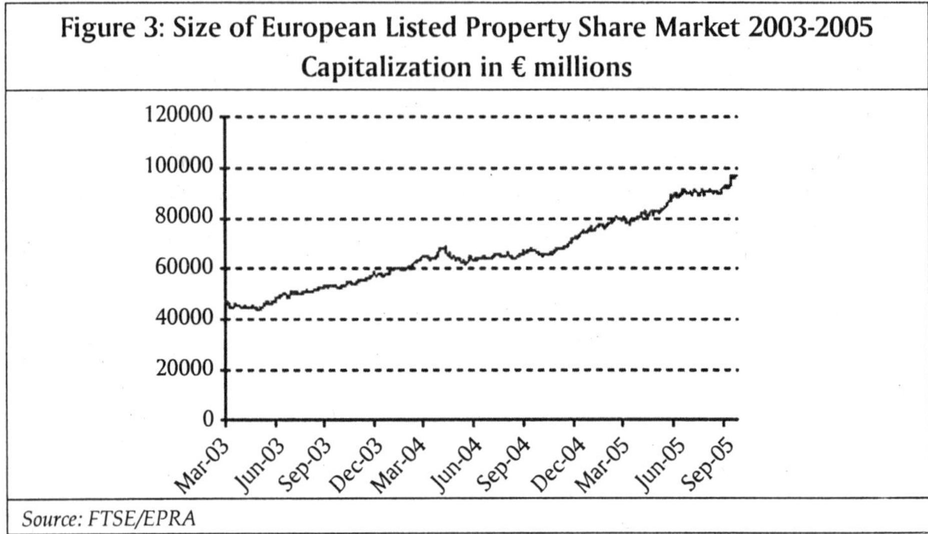

Figure 3: Size of European Listed Property Share Market 2003-2005 Capitalization in € millions

Source: FTSE/EPRA

for UK REIT status subject to a conversion charge of 2% of the market value of their rental properties. Nine public companies have opted to convert to REITs immediately after introduction of REITs in UK.

Germany

The German Government is working on introduction of G-REITs as a tax efficient investment vehicle. It is proposed that G-REITs will be formed as joint stock corporations and listed in the EU or EEC stock exchanges. "Topic REITs" dedicated to specific segments are also planned to be permitted. G-REITs shall be exempt from tax subject to distribution of 90% of its profits, and a withholding tax of 25% shall be levied on the distribution.

Performance of REIT Markets

The globalization trend of the real estate economy is vividly reflected by the proliferation of REIT structures around the world. The introduction of the tax efficient REIT structure has led to substantial reduction in NAV discounts, in markets like France and UK, driving the strong performance of REIT markets globally. The Global REIT Survey 2006 report published by Ernst & Young provides a snapshot of the performance of REITs around the world through an analysis of relative returns among thirteen established REIT markets using various criterias such as market size

Table 2	
Global Region	**Country**
North America	United States
	Canada
Europe, Middle East and Africa ("EMEA")	France
	Belgium
	Netherlands
	South Africa
Pacific	Australia
	New Zealand
Asia	Hong Kong
	Japan
	Malaysia
	Singapore
	South Korea
Source: Global REIT Report 2006, Ernst & Young.	

and depth, total return over one- and three-year periods, and volatility. Table 2 shows the region-wise list of countries that have been examined in this report.

According to Ed Psaltis, one of the main authors of the report and a partner of Ernst & Young Australia in the real estate segment, "The REIT sector is well established in most major regions of the world and is fast becoming a significant factor in molding world economies and investment choices."

Key Findings of the Report

The report tracks the market capitalization of 484 public REITs around the world at $608 billion, holding an asset value of over $890 billion including gearing. United States is the market leader with a predominant share of 253 public REITs and market capitalization of $395 billion. Smaller players outperformed their high profile peers in terms of rate of return over a one/three year period. New Zealand's market with just six REITs returned an average of 24.6% over the last year, while South Africa topped the three year average with 34% with just seven public REITs. South Africa also returned a strong performance over the last year at 23%, and ranked lowest in volatility and second lowest in gearing. Hong Kong matched the United States in average trading volume per REIT, while Japan topped the list of Asian players in total volume of REIT trading, coming third in the overall list. Most of the REITs in

Asian and EMEA[11] markets are trading at a premium of 5.8% to 14.6% on their assets. The US and Canadian REITs had the highest volatility indicating movement in line with the wider equities market. The report highlights financial comparability as the major challenge in the global REIT industry, in view of the different accounting practices and distribution regulations prevalent.

REIT Market Trends and Outlook

Globalization and Consolidation are the two major trends ruling the global REIT market. The case for global REIT allocation is driven by the demand from Australia, Japan, Netherlands and Belgium, while the US REIT market is setting new benchmarks in consolidation through M&A activity. A global portfolio offers more diversification opportunities and hedges the industry against economic or geopolitical risks. The correlation between countries for real estate securities is much lower than bonds and stocks, which further strengthens the case for global real estate portfolios.

The significant differences in the REIT structures in various countries stem from the variation in focus, conversion taxes, distribution requirements and whether they are internally or externally managed. While most of the public REITs are structured as equity REITs, mortgage REITs are also permitted in the US, Canada, Singapore and Netherlands. Further there are certain regional differences worth noting. European realty players prefer to invest in office and retail over apartments or industrial properties. Japanese REITs invest predominantly in office properties, and in Hong Kong and Singapore, the preference is for office and for-sale housing property. The US REIT markets are inclined towards a diversified holding rather than specific segments.

The REIT sector is expected to grow further driven by the expanding REIT markets in Australia, France, Canada, Netherlands, Japan, Hong Kong and Singapore. Its market capitalization is anticipated to grow further driven by the conversion trend to public ownership from private portfolios in established markets, and the enactment of legislations for REIT-like structures in UK, Germany, and other emerging economies. The Asian region including the South Korean and Malaysian REIT markets is expected to hold most potential for growth with low or negative premiums to net asset value. The true impact of REITs lies in creating a global brand for property investment. Like any other industry, the ultimate challenge for REITs

11 Europe, Middle East and Africa.

would be to maintain growth through innovation and new development, consolidation or international expansion. It is a matter of consensus that REITs are on the road to become mainstream investment and a safe bet for even conservative investors. To quote Marshall Field[12], "Buying real estate is not only the best way, the quickest way, the safest way, but the only way to become wealthy."

(B Sujatha is a Consulting Editor at Icfai Business School Research Center, Chennai. She can be reached at suja1209@gmail.com).

References

1. "Epra Global REIT Survey: A comparison of the major REIT regimes in the world", EPRA, September 2004.
2. *European Quarterly*, January 2006, *http://www2.prudential.com/*
3. FTSE EPRA/NAREIT Global Real Estate Index Monthly Bulletin, November 2005.
4. "REITs: A Global Perspective, The Emergence and Growth of Global REITs, 2007", *www.cohenandsteers.com*
5. "Global REITs – Development and Outlook", *http://uk.standardlifeinvestments.com*
6. Global REIT Report 2006, Ernst & Young.
7. John Sullivan and Hayden Flinn., "Lessons from Australia as Asian REITs thrive", IFLR, March 2006.
8. José Luis Suárez and Amparo Vassallo, INDIRECT INVESTMENT IN REAL ESTATE: LISTED COMPANIES AND FUNDS, WP No 602 July, 2005, *www.iese.edu*
9. Linda McDonald, "The Case for Global Real Estate Securities", *www.rogerscasey.com*
10. Michele Lerner, "Investor Appetite Grows for Hong Kong REITs", July/Aug 2006 *http://www.nareit.com*
11. "Real Estate Update", October 2006, Deloitte
12. "REITs 101: The History of REITs", *http://www.reitnet.com*
13. Robert C. Lee, "The Globalization of the REIT Industry".
14. The IFLR Guide to Japan 2007, *http://ommtokyo.jp*

---

[12] Founder of Marshall Field's, an iconic Chicago, Illinois, department store that grew to become a major chain under the name Macys.

2

Global Real Estate Investment – The World is Becoming Flatter*

Lijian Chen and Thomas I Mills

With economies around the world becoming more integrated as a result of increased trade in goods and services, global capital markets have become more interconnected. Certainly, the world's equity and debt markets have moved much more closer to becoming a single global market, and thus it is a flatter world in many senses. For global real estate investment, the world has also become flatter as well. The time has come for real estate to become a truly global industry. Barriers to international real estate investment are coming down. Capital is becoming more global. Investors around the world are thinking globally and have become more willing and even eager to own foreign assets.

Since 2004, global real estate investment has become even more widely accepted by investors and effort has been made to increase transparency in real estate investment. The continued strong performance of real estate has only

* This is an extract from "Global Real Estate Investment – Vol. II: The World is Becoming Flatter". The complete paper can be accessed at *www.ubs.com/realestate*. The title of this paper is inspired by the bestseller book *The World is Flat: A Brief History of the Twenty-First Century,* by Thomas L Friedman.

helped to emphasize the asset class' attractiveness further. Private real estate has delivered solid results, often generating returns above historical averages. Public real estate has also stood out in terms of performance. The overall market capitalization for real estate securities has significantly increased and tax-transparent REIT-like structures have been adopted by an increasing number of countries. Many large institutional investors have become convinced that they must have an international outlook on real estate investment.

Major Benefits of International Real Estate Investment

Many compelling reasons exist for investors to consider real estate as an important component of their portfolios. The three main benefits of global real estate investment are increased stability of aggregate income stream, diversification of returns for a mixed-asset portfolio, and a greater market size for attractive real estate investments, both public and private.

In the global context, the relatively more stable income streams to investors in the form of cash flow from property operations or dividends from listed real estate securities should appeal to both individual retirees and pension funds. Furthermore, significant diversification potential exists, given the low correlation of both private and listed real estate with other asset classes, such as equities and bonds. Finally, by expanding the investment universe to cover a growing list of more mature, developed real estate markets, investors can access a much wider spectrum of investment strategies and a broader selection of real estate ownership forms.

Losses Not as Severe in Poor Performance Cycles

From a return perspective, operating income from real estate varies through different rent and vacancy cycles. Because these cycles are not synchronized across countries, holding real estate in different countries tends to smooth out fluctuations in yields. For example, the correlation across regions is considerably lower for real estate securities than it is for stocks and bonds. Private real estate correlations across countries are also quite low. This suggests that the benefit of holding a globally diversified portfolio of real estate securities is higher than for bonds or broad equities.

History shows that compared to the other major asset classes, real estate, in general, appears to endure less severe losses when the down cycle inevitably strikes.

However, as today's investors are constantly warned, past performance is not indicative of future results. That brings us to the next important benefit of investing in real estate on a global basis.

Diversification: A Prudent Strategy

When considering the merits of investing in international real estate, compared to purely domestic real estate, the benefits of diversification cannot be overemphasized. Global diversification of a real estate portfolio can help protect investors from economic and political uncertainty, particularly when an investor is based in a relatively small or less developed nation. Even for investors in the US, where we estimate the real estate market offers the largest stock of institutional grade real estate in the world, the domestic market still comprises only about 40% of the global real estate universe, and thus it pays to diversify beyond national borders.

There are a variety of ways to diversify a real estate portfolio. Commonly employed approaches include diversification by investment style, product cycle, manager, geography, and property sector. Diversification across property sectors also suggests another benefit of investing globally in real estate. In some countries, there may be fewer opportunities available to invest in institutional-quality real estate in certain sectors than in other countries, or the lack of a credible index to track performance, as is the case with the multifamily sector in Ireland, might cause certain institutions to be reluctant to invest. As a result, the best way to gain additional exposure to those sectors may be to invest in them in other countries.

Size Matters

The third most important benefit of investing globally is the size of the investible universe of international real estate. Exhibit 1 illustrates that the size of private real estate markets in regions around the globe as of the end of 2005 was approximately USD8.0 trillion. Though US's investible real estate universe is approximately USD3.1 trillion, or nearly 40% of the global figure, it is clear that even a US investor would be missing a considerable opportunity by investing only domestically. For investors from smaller countries, the opportunity set is increased even more by going global. In the arena of publicly listed real estate, it is also true that the global opportunities exceed those available domestically in any single country.

Exhibit 1

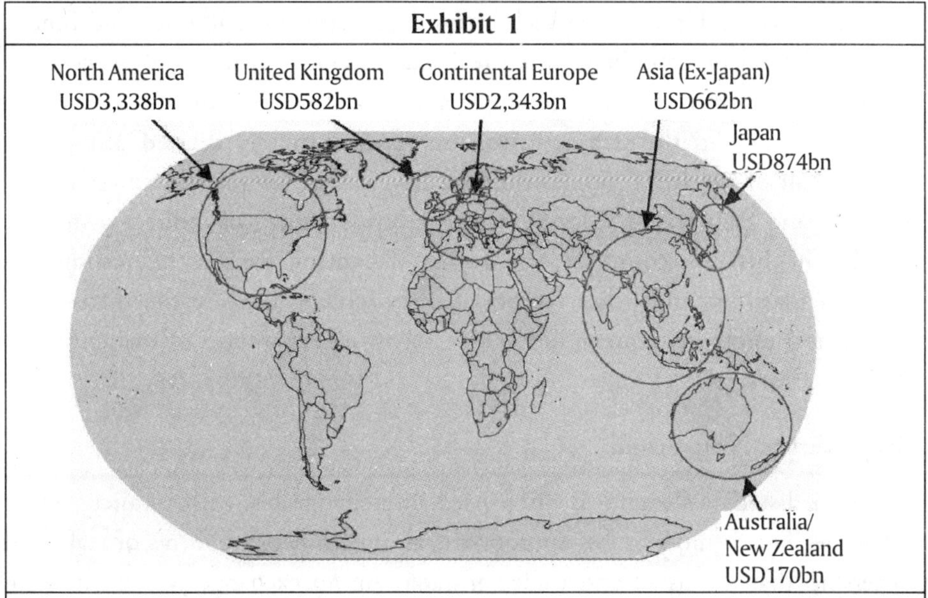

Source: UBS Global Asset Management Real Estate Research as of 31 December 2005. This data does not include single-family homes.

Private Versus Public Real Estate

The main purpose of this section is to discuss whether public real estate can be considered a good substitute for private real estate. Three basic ways to describe styles of real estate ownership in the context of investment: direct versus indirect, listed versus non-listed, and private versus public.

Direct Versus Indirect

Direct ownership of real estate involves investors acquiring and managing a portfolio of real estate assets by themselves, either executing their strategy with in-house capabilities and personnel or hiring a dedicated investment management team to do so (e.g., separate accounts). Due to lack of size and expertise, and the cost of setting up and running an internal group, direct private ownership is simply not a practical option for many investors. However, in many countries, this is still the most widely employed investment style for financially successful individuals owning real estate.

Indirect ownership can take such forms as investment in an open-end fund, a closed-end fund or a publicly-traded real estate stock. When investors choose to invest in REITs on their own, seemingly a direct investment, the management of the real estate and the strategy decisions are ultimately carried out by the management of the REIT. Some countries have rather unique structures, such as Germany and Switzerland. Clearly, with the various forms of indirect ownership available in different countries, the degree of control, fee structures, liquidity, NAV calculations, and other factors all vary widely. Despite the differences, indirect real estate investment still is a very cost-effective form of ownership for many investors.

Listed Versus Non-Listed

The term 'listed real estate' is often used interchangeably with publicly-traded real estate. This is more or less appropriate, although there are forms of real estate ownership that are listed and traded intraday on an exchange, yet are in some ways similar to non-listed real estate. The Swiss real estate mutual funds, for instance, are listed funds investing directly in real estate. There are also funds that are marketed to institutional investors and not listed on an exchange, but which invest in publicly traded real estate. Those funds, therefore, are non-listed, but invest in listed real estate.

In general, listed real estate is traded on exchanges and priced by its markets on the basis of supply and demand for shares in the companies. Non-listed real estate includes everything else that is not listed on a stock exchange. It is generally true that listed real estate offers greater liquidity than non-listed concerns. In addition, to be listed, a company needs to comply with various rules and policies governed by regulatory agencies. Hence, they are generally more transparent in their operations than non-listed companies. For most of the major listed real estate companies, analysts regularly estimate their NAVs and score their performance potential, which is an attempt to value the underlying real estate they own.

Public Versus Private

Public real estate includes all exchange-traded companies whose primary businesses are real estate related, and whose shares are readily available for all investors, whether institutions or individuals, to purchase. Private real estate can take the form of direct ownership of buildings, or indirect investment through vehicles, such as open-end and closed-end funds, that invest directly in properties.

Another major difference between public and private real estate is the valuation methodology. While the value of public real estate is decided through the demand and supply mechanism on an exchange, the determination of value for private real estate is much more complex. In the case of open-end funds in the US, the value of the units depends on appraised values of the properties, rather than the achievable sales price of the buildings in the portfolio.

One example that might further clarify some of the differences in the styles of ownership mentioned above is the variety of US REIT structures that exist. A publicly-listed REIT is what typically comes to mind when we think of REITs: they are registered with the Securities and Exchange Commission (SEC), and trade on an exchange such as the New York Stock Exchange. A public non-listed REIT refers to a REIT which has registered with the SEC as a public offering but which is not publicly traded on an exchange. A private REIT typically refers to a REIT in which the shares are privately placed to accredited investors or qualified purchasers, and therefore exempt from having to register under SEC regulations. All three of these vehicles must comply with the various REIT rules in the US regarding such issues as income distribution and ownership concentration.

Although both public and private real estate have low correlations with large-cap stocks and bonds, they also have low correlations with each other. Sector concentration is another important aspect to be considered when analyzing the difference between public and private real estate. In some markets or sectors, REITs have come to own a fairly large share of the higher quality properties that exist, and have achieved significant market shares. By some estimates, REITs owned approximately 50% of all enclosed malls in the US by the middle of 2003, and their share of ownership has increased since then. Furthermore, ownership forms between public and private real estate can change. A large number of private companies have become public companies for a variety of reasons, including access to capital. Conversely, several companies have recently gone in the opposite direction. In the US, a number of public REITs have been taken private, and the total transaction volume of such public-to-private deals rose from USD3.8 billion in 2004 to USD13.0 billion in 2005.

Tax considerations also factor into the choice of an optimal ownership structure for investors, particularly when international investment is involved. Differences between both of these forms of real estate and the other major asset classes, are sufficiently significant that they both should play a role in an investor's optimal real estate portfolio. For the past few years, however, propelled by the rapid growth of REITs, the public real estate universe has been expanding at a greater pace than that of private real estate.

Growing Market Size

In the last few years, both the private and public global real estate investment universes have experienced substantial increase in the value. In most of the countries private real estate prices have been rising. The performance of real estate investments has contributed to the increase of market value worldwide. Apart from the increase in prices of real estate and the size of the investable universe of core, institutional-quality property, there is an increase in the market capitalization of publicly-traded real estate and the proliferation and growth of REIT-like structures around the globe. Exhibit 2 summarizes the update of our estimate for the global investable universe of core real estate.

Exhibit 2

	Investable real estate universe (USD billions)	Population (millions)	GDP (current USD billions)	GDP per capita (USD thousands)	Average annual GDP growth (%) (2000-2005)
World		5,999.3	44,025.5	7.3	2.7
United States	3,097	296.4	12,479.5	42.1	2.5
Japan	874	127.4	4,571.3	35.9	1.4
United Kingdom	582	60.0	2,192.4	36.5	2.3
Germany	537	82.5	2,826.6	34.3	0.7
France	426	60.6	2,114.1	34.9	1.5
Italy	354	58.1	1,709.3	29.4	0.7
Spain	245	43.5	1,110.3	25.5	3.1
Canada	241	32.2	1,124.0	34.9	2.5

Contd...

Contd...					
South Korea	216	48.5	800.6	16.5	4.5
Hong Kong	181	6.9	176.5	25.6	4.2
Taiwan	150	22.6	349.8	15.5	3.0
Australia	148	20.4	690.3	33.9	3.1
Netherlands	128	16.3	626.7	38.4	0.8
Singapore	115	4.3	116.4	27.2	3.3
Hungary	103	10.0	110.7	11.1	4.1
Belgium	77	10.4	370.0	35.7	1.4
Sweden	64	9.1	356.1	39.4	2.2
Austria	63	8.2	309.1	37.8	1.5
Switzerland	60	7.4	366.7	49.8	1.0
Greece	49	11.0	217.3	19.8	4.2
Norway	47	4.6	289.7	62.9	2.1
Portugal	42	10.5	177.7	17.0	0.5
Denmark	41	5.4	255.5	47.2	1.4
Finland	37	5.2	190.0	36.4	2.2
Ireland	37	4.2	195.4	46.9	5.1
Czech Republic	34	10.2	123.4	12.1	3.4
New Zealand	22	4.1	107.7	26.2	3.5
27 core markets subtotal/average	7,970	979.9	33,957.1	32.3	2.5
Core markets as percent of world (%)		16.3	77.1		

Source: UBS Global Asset Management Real Estate Research based on data obtained from EIU as of 31 December 2005.

Exhibit 3 depicts the dramatic increase of public real estate's market capitalization. In 2006 alone, the total free-float market capitalization of the FTSE EPRA/NAREIT global listed real estate index (comprised of 338 companies at the end of 2006) rose 40.5% from USD644 billion to USD905 billion. Out of the USD939 billion universe as of the end of April 2007, 35.6% is in Asia, 21.9% in Europe and 42.5% in North America.

Existing REITs have been acquiring properties, and their properties have gone up in value as private real estate prices have increased. In some markets, new

Exhibit 3

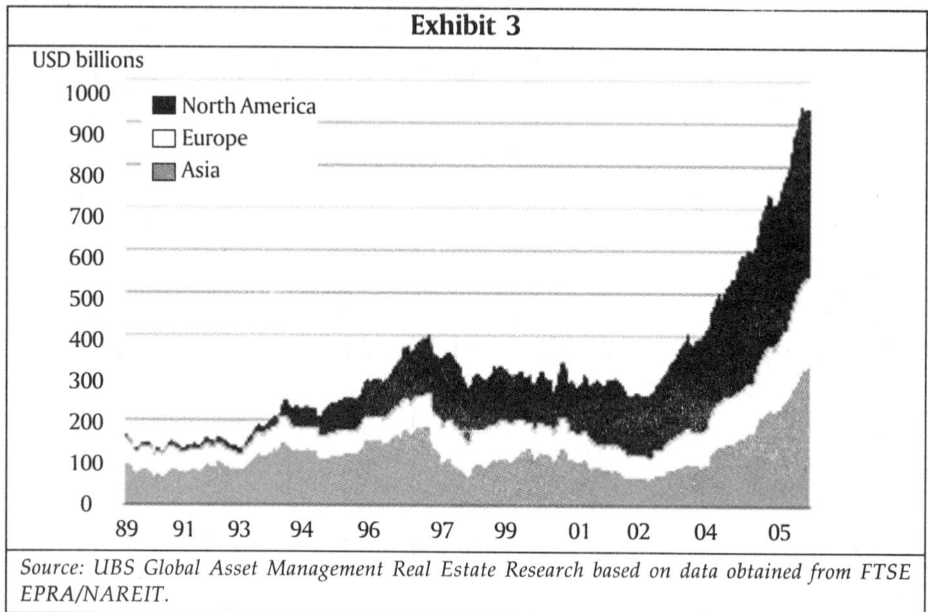

Source: UBS Global Asset Management Real Estate Research based on data obtained from FTSE EPRA/NAREIT.

public real estate companies have been created. For example, in Japan, where the J-REIT market did not exist until September 2001, it has grown to a sizable REIT sector of 41 J-REITs and a market capitalization of JPY 6.4 trillion (roughly USD55 billion) by the end of April 2007, a dramatic increase from 28 J-REITs and a market capitalization of JPY 2.8 trillion at the end of 2005.

There are other important trends emerging other than the overall growth trend of the global public real estate universe. Most of the REIT markets are still rapidly evolving, adding new sectors and changing the sector mix. Many REITs started with portfolios representing multiple property types (i.e., diversified across sectors), but increasingly REITs today are more specialized, focusing on a single property sector.

The larger markets are generally characterized by higher daily trading volume, hence providing higher liquidity. In contrast, smaller, yet growing, REIT markets tend to have only limited liquidity. Several REIT markets remain small and have yet to show much potential for scalability. For example, with ten REITs listed thus far, Bulgaria has a total market capitalization of approximately USD66 million as of October 2005. Thus far the sectors in South Korea and Taiwan have not seen significant growth since inception. However, despite recent rapid expansion, there is still room for considerable growth in many listed real estate markets around the world.

Another important trend to note in Exhibit 4 is that the property-sector compositions of these five REIT markets are very different. The US market is the only one that is relatively evenly composed of several key property sectors, including office, industrial, retail, and residential. All four remaining REIT markets shown are dominated by either the office or retail sectors. It is clear that most REIT markets are still rapidly evolving.

Exhibit 4

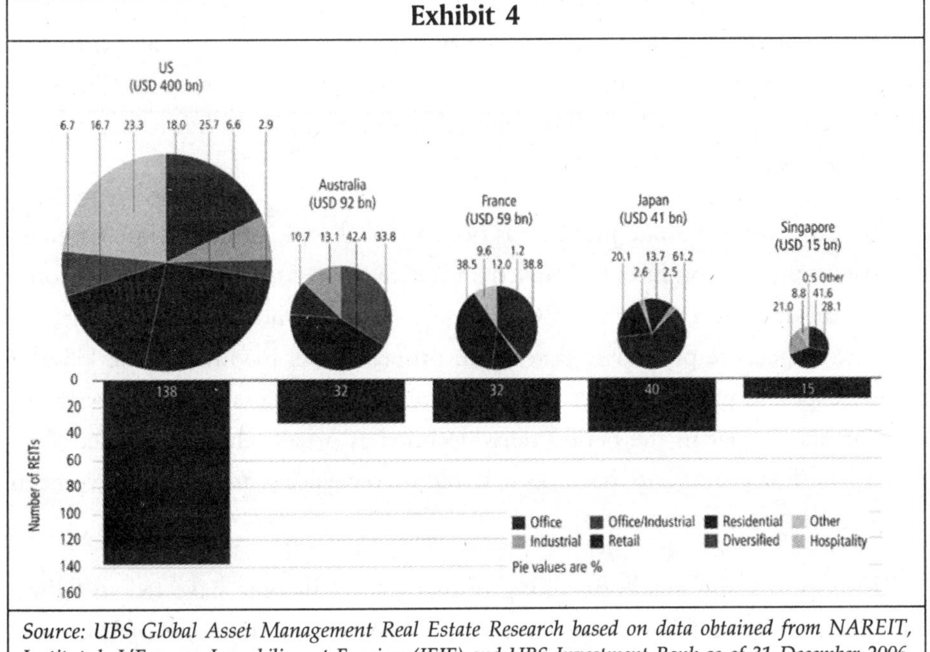

Source: UBS Global Asset Management Real Estate Research based on data obtained from NAREIT, Institut de L'Epargne Immobiliere et Fonciere (IEIF) and UBS Investment Bank as of 31 December 2006.

The public real estate market is still in the early phase of the growth cycle. Real estate as a separate asset class with several attractive characteristics has only recently begun to gather wider recognition from institutional and private investors worldwide, especially many large institutional investors in emerging economies. Second, from the perspective of optimal asset allocation, many investors are still significantly under-allocated to real estate in their mixed-asset portfolios.

The proliferation and growth of REIT and REIT-like structures around the world has still only utilized a small share of the potential pool of securitizable real estate assets in many countries. The debate on the optimal allocation mix between public and private real estate investment will likely continue for a long time. It is widely expected that the global expansion of the two real estate investment platforms is just getting started.

Private Real Estate: Steady Income Attractive Amidst Some Pricing Concerns

In 2006, all of the IPD private real estate indices around the world reported as of April 2007 showed positive total returns, even in Germany which experienced a capital value decline. This is because the income component of total return was sufficiently large to offset the drop in capital value that occurred. This illustrates that real estate generates high and stable income returns in addition to potential capital appreciation.

Concern over real estate pricing has been a global topic of discussion. In many countries capitalization rates have fallen and prices have risen significantly. Income returns can drop as a result of falling property-level income, as rents decline, for example, or because prices rise faster than property-level income. In the US and Europe over the past five years the phenomenon has generally been a result of both factors. Earlier in the period rents declined as prices remained stable, while in the past few years rents have been stable or recovering and prices have been rising steadily.

Rising prices and stable or falling property-level income have led to falling capitalization rates for several years. It can be argued that one of the most influential forces driving global cap rates down is the sustained interest in the real estate asset class and the resulting continuous and substantial inflow of capital into the real estate sector. The weight of capital attempting to move into real estate from pension funds and other investors seeking attractive risk-adjusted returns relative to the other asset classes is likely to continue and it is expected to put a downward pressure on cap rates. Real estate open-end funds in Europe and the US have billions of dollars in their queues that they are striving to invest in a disciplined manner. Also, Asian institutional investors represent huge pent-up demand for real estate investment products.

Given that pension funds and most other institutional investors have long investment horizons, their capital tends to be more patient and less likely to be shifted from one asset class to another in the short term. This tendency should bode well for the stability of capital in the property sector. Other factors that are likely to support pricing stability are stronger economic growth and the subsequent recovery or further improvement of real estate fundamentals around the world. Fundamentals such as vacancy rates and rents are in the process of recovering in many countries and property sectors, which should cause property-level incomes to rise, adding to capital value increases even with stable cap rates.

REITs Going Global

Why have REITs Succeeded?

Interest in listed real estate has continued to grow over the past year. The number of countries adopting REIT structures has increased and more countries are entering the debate and planning phase of adopting them. In countries where REIT structures already exist, their market capitalizations have generally been increasing. It should be noted that while listed real estate does not necessarily have to be in the form of a REIT, the trend reflects investors' preferences for REIT-like vehicles. Investors seeking exposure to real estate favor the high payout ratio of property operating income that REITs must distribute in the form of dividends. Investors also like it that REITs must invest nearly exclusively in real estate. Another attraction of investing in REITs is the benefit of tax transparency that virtually all REITs offer.

There are other benefits from investing in listed real estate *vis-à-vis* private real estate. Listed real estate and REITs in particular are attracting more investors globally as the investment in REIT shares can be executed in a timely manner and shifting allocations from one property sector or country to another can be made quickly and at reasonable low cost.

The tremendous demand for REITs and REIT-like products has led to substantial declines of dividend yield spreads of REITs over 10-year government bond yields over the past three years. The future evolution of REITs globally is likely to continue benefiting from two trends. First, investors are increasingly drawn to the high dividend yields relative to general equities and the stability of the underlying asset class. Second, governments around the world are seeing REITs as a way to improve the relative competitiveness of their listed real estate markets. The REIT sector will likely enjoy a strong tailwind for at least a few more years to come.

REIT Proliferation

REITs and REIT-like structures continue to spring up around the world. In 2005, Hong Kong successfully delivered the Link REIT, which became the largest REIT IPO in the world when it issued shares with an aggregate value of HKD22 billion (USD 2.8 billion). Besides the most recent success in Hong Kong, REITs have succeeded in France. Since its introduction in 2003, the French Sociétè d'Investissement Immobilier Cotee (SIIC) structure has fostered a sector that has grown to a market capitalization of more than EUR45 billion (USD59 billion) as of the end of 2006. The French experience also appears successful in terms of its pricing of listed property companies relative to the value of the real estate they own.

Not every REIT market in the world has experienced rapid growth. In a number of countries, REIT structures currently exist, but for various reasons the development of those markets has been limited. In South Korea, for example, the REIT market has existed since 2001. However, it remains notably small and underutilized, largely due to regulatory hurdles obstructing the setting up and operation of REITs, such as restrictions on the use of debt to acquire properties and high minimum capital requirements. South Korea has, however, recently made changes to improve the attractiveness of its structures for investors, operators, or both.

In the case of the Netherlands, the proliferation of REIT structures around the world is pressuring its financial authorities to modify its existing REIT regime in order to maintain competitiveness. The Netherlands, which has had a REIT structure since 1969, is discussing ways to increase flexibility and attractiveness for foreign investors.

Two major markets in which the creation of REIT structures occurred in 2007 are the UK and Germany. The governments of both countries were initially concerned about structuring the market so that tax revenues are not reduced. If a foreign entity acquires real estate in either the UK or Germany, taxes would be paid on the rental income stream. If that entity were to invest through a REIT, the income stream would become a dividend income stream and often taxed at a lower rate under withholding tax agreements, possibly at 0%. Potential loss of future tax revenue is something that concerns most governments, and is impacting on discussions of new REIT regime introductions in some countries. Such losses of future tax revenue can be in part offset by taxes on capital gains upon conversion of an existing property to a REIT, as was the case in France.

Cross-Border Investing and Off-Shore Listing

REITs have become a global phenomenon not only in terms of the increasing number of countries that have adopted REIT regimes and created REIT markets, but also in terms of the growing number of REITs implementing growth strategies on a global basis. REITs' global expansion strategy has thus far taken the forms of cross-border acquisition and off-shore listing.

Cross-border activity by listed real estate companies has been on the rise. Some of this activity has been in the form of one listed company acquiring shares in another in outright mergers. Investment in foreign properties by listed real estate companies is becoming increasingly common. There has also been a dramatic increase over the past five years in the number of vehicles that are listed on the exchange of one country while the real estate in the vehicle is located in another.

More existing listed real estate companies and REITs are expanding their real estate investment across borders. As increasingly more and more real estate assets become securitized worldwide, it is expected to become significantly more attractive to design and implement real estate investment strategies with a global scope. Judging from numerous reports on international investment funds and mandates being created, it seems that investors have become less sensitive to international borders in exploring investment opportunities.

Strategic Considerations for International Real Estate Investment

Currency Risk

Currency movements can add or subtract from an investor's gain significantly. Investors holding assets outside of their domestic currency zone must consider their exposure to the adverse risk of foreign currency movements. Many investors perceive currency fluctuations as an obstacle to investment in foreign real estate, and the associated risks from currency losses may in some cases exceed the investor's level of risk tolerance.

Foreign exchange volatility has been found to be comparatively high relative to the volatility of private real estate returns. Unless investors have a clear view on future exchange rates, which are notoriously difficult to predict, currency fluctuations primarily lead to increased risk without changing the expected return of cross-border investments.

Various hedging instruments are available to mitigate the impact of currency fluctuations. The simplest hedge is the use of local debt also known as a natural hedge. Derivative instruments commonly used to hedge currency risk include Forwards and Options.

- Options: In the event of a large, unfavorable movement in the currency of the foreign country relative to the US dollar, the option value should increase to partially offset the loss on the investment. Some investors are reluctant to use options, however, because they generally involve an upfront cost to purchase.
- Forwards: Generally involve no upfront cost, and in theory can eliminate the currency risk on the cash flows from an investment. While an option allows the investor to take advantage of favorable currency movements and only limits the impact of downside movements, forwards have an offsetting loss if the currency moves to give the investor additional returns on the investment. Conversely, there is an offsetting gain if the currency moves in the other direction.

Hedging too much income also has its risks. If the amount hedged using a forward exceeds the actual amount of income that the property produces, the investor is still subject to some level of currency risk. Depending on each investor's risk profile, currency hedging should be considered when managing the risk of non-domestic currency exposure. The method used to hedge currency risk will not be the same for all investors, and natural hedges, currency derivatives, or a combination of both may be appropriate.

Taxation

Considerable effort is expended to structure investments to minimize tax leakage as taxes can significantly reduce the final return to investors. Some investors, no doubt, believe that the best tax strategy, summed up by a participant at a European conference in 2005, is to "hire expensive lawyers!" Expert structuring can certainly reduce the tax leakage, but expertise costs money and adds complexity.

Particularly for tax-exempt real estate investors, there tends to be a fairly strong home bias. The most favorable taxation status that tax-exempt investors can achieve overseas is equivalent to their domestic treatment, or paying no tax on gains or income. However, a no-tax scenario is often not possible, or it would take a Herculean effort to achieve tax-exempt treatment. Thus, from a taxation point of view, investors generally fare worse when investing abroad.

Governments usually understand that they can either hinder or encourage investment in their countries through tax policies. While many countries realize the need for, 1) lower tax rates to encourage capital investment, 2) simpler tax systems, 3) mutually beneficial tax treaties to make their economies and financial markets more competitive, and 4) an increase in cross-border investment opportunities for pension funds, it is difficult to reconcile with the loss of tax revenue. Governments in general are working to reduce tax burdens for foreign institutional investors buying their real estate. The US continues to expand and update its network of tax treaties, trying to encourage more investment from foreign investors, and is particularly focusing on lowering taxes for foreign pension funds. With the increasing interest in global real estate investment, movement in this direction will be welcomed by investors around the world and should help to create a flatter world with respect to taxes for real estate investment.

Property Derivatives

Derivatives add to the completeness of the real estate capital market and offer flexibility in gaining or reducing certain property exposures. A derivatives market allows the swapping of exposure to the property market without any physical transfer of assets. For example, investors can use derivates to reduce exposure to the office sector while increasing exposure to the apartment sector, as long as there are other investors intending to achieve the opposite exposure. It is well known that the liquidity in private real estate investment markets is limited. Transactions could take months to complete and transaction fees can take a significant bite out of returns. By employing derivatives, investors and funds can nearly instantly increase or decrease positions in property in a more cost-effective fashion, free of complications of actual property transfer. Moreover, derivatives present an effective way for investors and funds to achieve exposures to foreign markets without the need to hire local professionals to manage physical assets. For instance, international swaps could be developed to exchange Hong Kong retail returns with New York apartment returns. From the perspective of portfolio strategy, one might argue that property derivatives offer a more effective approach towards optimal portfolio management.

Further development of this market will probably be helped by an increase in the number of participants and in the total amount of the swaps transacted. Greater liquidity should, in theory, make it easier to locate parties for both sides of a swap. Potentially, banks could take a position, rather than find counterparty for a swap, and could then securitize this position by selling bonds based on it to investors (for example, a bond backed by the IPD UK Index return). With every successful completion of a property derivative contract, a global property derivatives market advances closer to reality. The property derivatives market is expected to continue to grow and develop new types of contracts to meet investors' needs. As of today, the property derivatives market, with limited scale and liquidity, must be considered to be still in its infancy.

Conclusion

With economies around the world becoming more integrated as a result of the increased trade of goods and services, the global capital markets have become more interconnected. Certainly, the world's equity and debt markets have moved much closer to become a single global market, and thus it is a flatter world in many senses. For global real estate investment as well, the world has also become flatter. The time has come for real estate to become a truly global industry.

In general real estate continues to be an attractive investment and in times when performance was not strong, real estate losses were less severe than the other asset classes. The sophistication of real estate investment continues to increase, and the development of property derivatives based on private real estate indices is an example of how the asset class is becoming more mature and flexible. With the rising prices that real estate in most areas has experienced, investors are concerned that a downturn might be looming. However, the reasons for the price increases have been largely structural, driven by lower risk premiums demanded by investors and the investors should consider holding both types of real estate in their portfolios, enabling them to achieve greater diversification benefits than by choosing to hold one or the other.

The proliferation of REIT structures in regions where they did not exist before, and their explosive growth in many regions where they do, are a sign of increasing investor interest in real estate. Barriers to entry are coming down. Hedging all or part of an equity investment in real estate can mitigate the risks, and more governments are encouraging tax-transparent REIT-like structures and often eliminating withholding tax on ordinary dividends for foreign private REIT investors, leveling the playing field.

Global real estate investment has definitely come of age, and the industry is continuing to advance. It is expected to become more sophisticated, mature, innovative, transparent, disciplined and accountable to investors, and even better positioned to compete for capital with stocks and bonds.

(Lijian Chen, Global Head of Research, UBS Global Asset Management. He can be reached at lijian.chen@ubs.com

Thomas I Mills, Head of Research – Asia, UBS Global Asset Management. He can be reached at tom.mills@ubs.com).

3

Why Invest in International Real Estate?

Real estate investment has been strengthened by the proliferation of investment vehicles and the growth of emerging markets. In addition to the evolution in vehicles and markets, an evolution of investor attitudes is also serving to shape the real estate investment landscape. As a lower-risk, higher-performing asset class, the level of real estate investment will most likely continue to increase for the next two decades. This article examines how international real estate can increase portfolio diversification and mitigate risk.

You may wonder, why invest in real estate at all? After all, real estate is not directly traded on public exchanges, and the physical asset is characterized by lack of liquidity, lumpiness, high transaction costs, and geographic idiosyncrasies. Despite all of these drawbacks, real estate, both domestic (US) and international, has produced solid returns that have outpaced the domestic stock market over the last five years, is collateralized, and in the case of institutional-grade assets, typically yields a consistent income stream.

Real estate offers benefits through potentially higher returns, risk reduction and portfolio diversification. International real estate can extend these benefits

---

Source: www.aiggig.com © AIG Global Real Estate Investment Corp. Reprinted with permission. This article was published in 2006, 2005.

and increase portfolio diversification, which can potentially reduce overall portfolio risk. At the same time, a number of studies have shown that international real estate has historically distributed higher-than-average income compared to other types of international equities, which can help mitigate stock market fluctuations.

The US has traditionally been the main destination for real estate investment. Over the past 20 years, a host of factors has made international markets more interesting and potentially highly profitable, including deregulation, high economic growth, integration of financial markets, economic and political reforms, and accelerating globalization.

Potentially Higher Returns

International real estate can help increase returns by investing in international properties with prospects for better financial performance than domestic assets. For example, had US investors, during the period 1985-1995, invested in office properties in the UK, Australia and Canada, rather than domestic assets, they would have earned a significantly higher return. During this period, the US office market's average annual return was 0%, while these markets averaged 12.4%, 8.1% and 4.5%, respectively.[1]

Risk Reduction and Portfolio Diversification

Risk can be reduced by investing in markets that are less volatile. Some real estate markets – Canada, for example – demonstrate less volatility in the office sector than the US. To put it in the language of stocks, they exhibit lower betas. Investors can reduce risk simply by diversifying their portfolios with the inclusion of foreign assets whose performance is likely to be minimally correlated with the performance of domestic assets. Such low correlations are attributed to differences in behavior over time stemming from different market regimes and idiosyncratic economic shocks. Despite increasing global integration of economies, there is still significant country and continent divergence in real estate market and property performance.

In addition to these general benefits, investors in international real estate can also take advantage of the growth of emerging markets and of a growing number of global investment vehicles to expand their investment options and enhance potential returns.

---

1 Torto, Raymond, "Benefits and Issues in Global Real Estate," *Journal of Real Estate Portfolio Management*, 2002.

Expanded Choice through a Growing Number of Global Investment Vehicles

More and more investment vehicles and products are now gaining ground throughout the global markets, both public and private. Such investments include new REITs (real estate investment trusts) and REIT-like vehicles, the global expansion of the CMBS (commercial mortgage backed securities) market, and a growing number of private investment products (funds, individual deal investments). With a greater array of products and strategies from which to choose, an investor is more likely to find a better fit for his particular return/risk tolerance.

There is an increasing number of sophisticated financial products beyond the domain of equity investments. Public debt investing, predominantly in the form of CMBS, has emerged as a strong global trend. Liquidity, as well as the ability to securitize large income streams and to tranche loans into various risk profiles, has made this asset class increasingly attractive. CMBS and other investment products may have the potential to grow faster than the US due to country-specific factors. The Japanese CMBS market emerged as a result of the steep decline in real estate prices during the 1990s. Financial institutions stressed increased securitization to repair balance sheets. Japan and mature markets of Australia and Europe are also expected to see CMBS grow much faster than the US market. The growth rate of CMBS issuance in countries other than the US has mostly outpaced that of the US during the last few years.

Another key trend in the industry is the rapid expansion of global real estate investment options in terms of quantity and variety of nonlisted private investment vehicles. In addition to non-listed property investment vehicles in US, there are a large number of established vehicles with various strategies, specialized sectors and return targets (i.e., core, value-added, opportunistic, etc.) available to investors. According to INREV, the number of non-listed real estate funds (excluding German open-ended funds) has grown from 40 in 1994 to more than 400 in 2005. The gross asset value funds of these funds for the same period has expanded from EUR40 billion to more than EUR160 billion, a four-fold figure in just a decade. A similar trend can be discerned in Asia.

As a result of the growth in quantity and diversity of real estate investment vehicles globally, and of public and private markets, we have seen beneficial by-products of increased transparency, credibility, and liquidity, which, in turn, is attracting more real estate investment capital.

Riding the Emerging Market Growth Wave

Economic growth rates tend to be higher in emerging markets than in developed economies. In other words, emerging markets are in the early phases of their growth cycles. High GDP growth rates are typically composed of population, employment, and investment growth—all of which drive real estate returns. Countries in Asia, South America, and even several countries in the Middle East and Africa are showing much higher rates of growth than developed countries in recent years. As a result, real estate markets in these countries are expected to experience proportionate expansion in the real estate sector (new and renovated buildings of all types) to accommodate the growing demand for a larger quantity and quality of assets at a faster pace than in developed countries.

The lowering of entity barriers in many countries has been facilitating emerging market investment. For example, as recently as the late 1990s, foreign investors could not invest directly in South Korea. The same was true for Taiwan as recently as a few years ago. India only this year liberalized its FDI laws with respect to real estate. Today more real estate markets than ever are open, with the trend continuing towards greater openness, transparency, and increasing capital flows.

In short, there is more room for achieving alpha in the globalized real estate investment market. Due to the unique risks of international investing, attaining excellent risk-adjusted returns is not always an easy task.

Risk-Averse Investing in an Aging Population

In addition to the evolution in vehicles and markets, an evolution of investor attitudes is also serving to shape the real estate investment landscape.

In the late 1990s, there was a strong bias against "bricks and mortar" companies. It was believed that hard assets only served to weigh companies down, slowing their ability to maneuver deftly in high growth markets. This bias has been reversed to favor not only "bricks and mortar" companies, but *the bricks and mortar themselves.* The comparatively tame performance of the US stock market and the hesitation surrounding investment in the intangible products of technology, biotechnology, service and dot.com companies have led many institutions to favor investments that have strong tangible value.

Moreover, in the post-Enron world, investors are attracted to real estate investments and operating companies that employ more straightforward accounting practices, with a high percentage of their value derived from current cash flow. Real estate investment is thus less susceptible to creative accounting and financial legerdemain.

The hard tangibility and the comforting transparency of real estate may explain why many investors are drawn to real estate on a human, emotional level. However, real estate's qualitative "bricks and mortar" appeal is also supported by its ability to reduce volatility and enhance returns through income and appreciation, which is derived from the diversification and stability that it offers. These attributes make real estate an especially appealing investment for those nearing retirement.

The stock market decline of five years ago has served to remind investors of the utility of portfolio diversification, and has enhanced the attractiveness of stable, income-producing investments.

Real estate values are relatively stable compared to stocks; recent empirical studies assessing volatility of private and direct real estate show a range of 6.5-9% annualized standard deviation.[2] The boom and bust real estate cycles of the 1980s have been tempered by a number of trends that have been emerging since the 1990s, which include increased securitization, improved transparency, better market coverage and information, and increased investor sophistication.

In terms of stability, real estate's current income has been as good as or better than any major investment class over the last five years.[3] The income derived from leasing and rental properties provides investors with a comparatively high yield level. The income component of real estate returns have not been negatively

---

2 CISDM Research Department, "The Benefits of Real Estate Investment 2005 Update", June 2005.

3 Ibid, 2005.

Past performance is not indicative of future results.

Diversification does not ensure against market loss.

affected by the recent influx of investment capital, even though cap rates have declined.

Real estate's appeal is not just due to its relatively lower risk and its complementarity with other investments, but also in its longevity and stability, which is particularly appealing to the "Baby Boomer" demographic. This group, which in the US refers to Americans who were born between 1945 and 1962, is the wealthiest demographic segment in history, and currently represents about 27% of the US population.

Empirical data support the "lifecycle risk aversion hypothesis," which predicts that the older a person becomes, the more risk averse he becomes. This is a result of a shorter income earning horizon in which an investor has few income earning years to offset any potential poor investments.

Thus, as Baby Boomers near retirement, they will shift to less risky investments. Because real estate continues to gain visibility as a lower-risk, higher-performing asset class, the level of real estate investment will most likely continue to increase for the next two decades.

In the post-technology bubble era, with a large aging demographic becoming increasingly risk averse, investors should continue to favor the stability, diversity, and income-producing attributes of "bricks and mortar" investments.

(AIG Global Real Estate Investment Corp., a member company of American International Group, Inc. ("AIG"), is a part of AIG Global Real Estate, a group of international real estate companies that actively invests in and manages real estate for clients and AIG member companies in over 50 countries around the world. AIG Global Real Estate owns, manages, or has under development approximately US $14.6 billion in equity[4] in more than 53 million square feet of all property types in major global markets. AIG Global Real Estate is affiliated with AIG Global Investment Group. Additional information on the company can be found at www.aigglobalrealestate.com

AIG Global Investment Group comprises a group of international companies which provide investment advice and market asset management products and services to clients around the world.

---

4 As of 31 March 2007.

Certain information may be based on information received from sources AIG Global Investment Group (AIGGIG) considers reliable; AIGGIG does not represent that such information is accurate or complete. Certain statements contained herein may constitute "projections," "forecasts" and other "forward-looking statements" which do not reflect actual results and are based primarily upon applying retroactively a hypothetical set of assumptions to certain historical financial information. Any opinions, projections, forecasts and forward-looking statements presented herein are valid only as of the date of this document and are subject to change. AIGGIG is not soliciting or recommending any action based on any information in this document.)

4

Global REITs: A New Platform of Ownership

Philip Conner and Youguo Liang

The success and impressive growth of the REIT and Listed Property Trusts (LPT) markets in the US and Australia, and in various other markets with tax-transparent vehicles, is helping to drive the proliferation of REIT-like vehicles worldwide. The article examines the trends in the listed property sector, the key drivers of the recent REIT market growth and the implications of a vibrant global REIT market for the real estate capital and space markets and for investors.

The global public real estate market is undergoing a transformation today. In countries throughout Asia, Europe and Latin America, authorities are introducing or considering new tax-transparent property investment vehicles similar to US real estate investment trusts (REITs) and Australian listed property trusts (LPTs). In markets where these vehicles have been introduced, and where they already existed, investors' demand for safety and yield has caused share prices to rise sharply over the last few years. As a result, the equity market capitalization of the global public property market has grown significantly since 2001, and tax-transparent vehicles (hereafter generically referred to as "REITs") have accounted for the lion's share of the growth.

The growth of the global REIT market stems from the confluence of powerful demand and supply forces: short- and long-term demand for stable, income-oriented investments and an expanding universe of real estate investment opportunities that offer relatively attractive yields and modest opportunities for capital growth. But the expanding global REIT market also means that real estate has gained acceptance as an asset class, which accounts for the demand side, and that the market infrastructure, the supply side, is developing rapidly to satisfy (and foster) increasing investor demand. This report examines the trends in the listed property sector, the key drivers of the recent REIT market growth and the implications of a vibrant global REIT market for the real estate capital and space markets and for investors.

Global Property Universe and Public Ownership

The global commercial real estate market is large and quite diverse. Although these obvious features make it difficult to measure the exact size of the investable universe of institutional-quality properties, we estimate the total size of the global commercial real estate market was about $14 trillion as of year-end 2003, or

Exhibit 1: Regional Distribution of Commercial Real Estate[1]

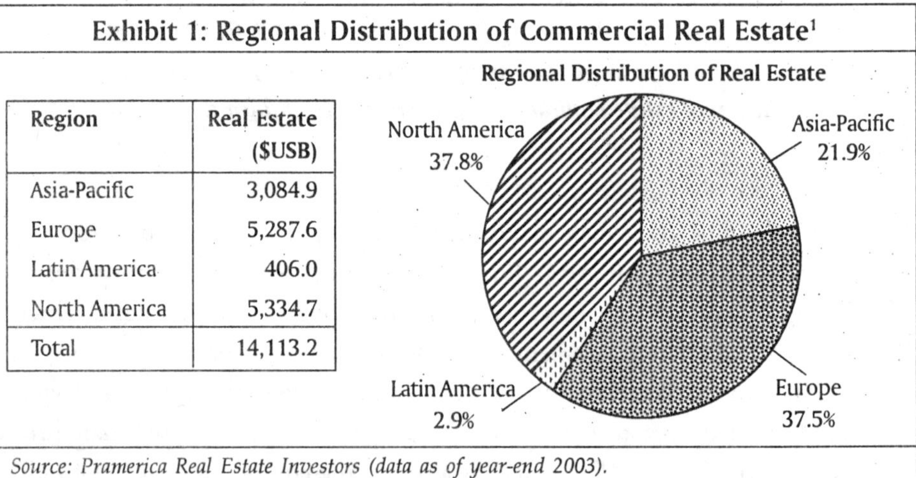

Region	Real Estate ($USB)
Asia-Pacific	3,084.9
Europe	5,287.6
Latin America	406.0
North America	5,334.7
Total	14,113.2

Source: Pramerica Real Estate Investors (data as of year-end 2003).

[1] The estimated size of the global market and individual market value estimates for the 50 countries in our coverage universe are based on each country's economic output (GDP) as a measure of the size and maturity of the economy, and on relative wealth, for which we use GDP per capita as a proxy. For more information, see "A Bird's Eye View of Global Real Estate Markets," Pramerica Real Estate Investors, March 2003.

roughly 12% of the global investment universe including stocks, bonds and property (see Exhibit 1). Europe and North America each accounted for about $5.3 trillion of the commercial real estate universe, or nearly 38% each, followed by Asia-Pacific's roughly $3 trillion (22%) and Latin America's $406 billion, or 3% share.

Despite the large size and diversity of the global economy and property markets, the investable universe of institutional real estate is concentrated in the major property markets. Exhibit 2 shows the top-15 countries in terms of higher-grade commercial real estate and their respective market shares in our 50-country universe. Together, the top-15 markets account for nearly 88% of all commercial real estate in the 50 countries we track, and a slightly smaller share, about 84%, of the total economic output.

Private ownership has always dominated the real estate industry, in part because the underlying assets, the individual properties themselves, trade in the private

Exhibit 2: Top-15 Commercial Property Markets

Rank	Country	Population (million)	Higher-Grade Real Estate ($USB)	Global Share	Cumulative Share
1	United States	290.3	4,944.5	35.0%	35.0%
2	Japan	127.2	1,934.7	13.7%	48.7%
3	Germany	82.3	1,084.9	7.7%	56.4%
4	United Kingdom	60.3	807.7	5.7%	62.2%
5	France	60.2	793.9	5.6%	67.8%
6	Italy	58.0	663.4	4.7%	72.5%
7	Canada	31.6	390.1	2.8%	75.2%
8	Spain	40.8	378.6	2.7%	77.9%
9	China	1,295.2	240.5	1.7%	79.6%
10	South Korea	47.9	233.5	1.7%	81.3%
11	Netherlands	16.2	230.9	1.6%	82.9%
12	Australia	19.9	227.5	1.6%	84.5%
13	Mexico	103.3	189.2	1.3%	85.9%
14	Switzerland	7.3	144.0	1.0%	86.9%
15	Belgium	10.3	136.2	1.0%	87.9%

Source: Pramerica Real Estate Investors (data as of year-end 2003).

transaction market and, in most cases, are financed with private equity and/or debt. As a result, private investors (institutions and individuals) and owner-users (mostly large corporations) own most of the commercial properties that make up the investable universe. However, most countries with well-developed real estate investment markets also have publicly listed companies or funds that own property and offer investors an alternative indirect approach to investing in real estate.

Exhibit 3 shows the regional distribution of the listed property sector by available equity market capitalization (i.e., relatively liquid, publicly tradable shares). While equity market capitalization is not directly comparable to the aggregate market value estimates in the first two exhibits, the listed property sector clearly represents a small fraction of the total commercial property universe. Using the S&P/Citigroup BMI World Property Index, North America dominates the public real estate market with a 50% share, followed by Asia (32%) and Europe (18%).[2]

Exhibit 3: Listed Property Equity Market Capitalization by Region

Region	Real Estate ($USB)
Asia-Pacific	169.2
Europe	101.1
North America	266.0
Total	536.3

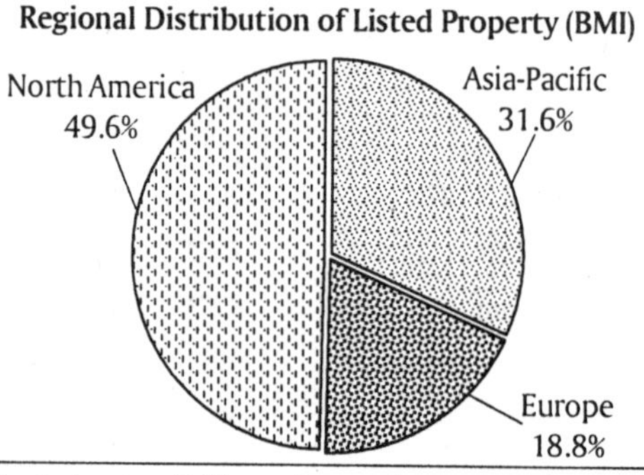

Regional Distribution of Listed Property (BMI)

North America 49.6%
Asia-Pacific 31.6%
Europe 18.8%

Sources: S&P/Citigroup BMI World Property Index (available equity market capitalization as of January 3, 2005); Pramerica Real Estate Investors.

The listed property market, not surprisingly, is also highly concentrated. The top-15 markets account for more than 99% of the sector's available equity market capitalization (see Exhibit 4). Logically, considerable overlap exists between the countries with the largest real estate markets and those with the largest listed property markets. Eleven of the top-15 listed property markets are among the 15 largest commercial real estate markets. The US, which accounts for about 35% of the global real estate market, represents about 48% of the listed property sector's

[2] The S&P/Citigroup BMI World Property Index is a free-float weighted index comprised of public real estate companies that meet certain free-float market capitalization, trading volume and other criteria.

available equity market capitalization, while Japan, with the second-largest real estate market, ranks 5th by equity market capitalization.

A few exceptions are noteworthy. For example, Australia has the second-largest listed property market (based on available equity market capitalization), but ranks 12th based on property market size. Hong Kong and Singapore rank 4th and 9th, respectively, based on listed property market capitalization, yet neither country appears in the 15-largest commercial property markets. Germany, however, falls near the bottom of the ranking by listed property market capitalization with less than 1% of the global listed property market, despite having the 3rd-largest commercial real estate market.[3]

The structural features of the different listed property investment vehicles around the world are nearly as diverse as the markets in which they exist. At one

Exhibit 4: Top-15 Listed Property Markets

Rank	Country	Equity Market Capital ($USB)	Global Share	Cumulative Share
1	United States	255.1	47.6%	47.6%
2	Australia	63.3	11.8%	59.4%
3	United Kingdom	52.1	9.7%	69.1%
4	Hong Kong	50.6	9.4%	78.5%
5	Japan	45.4	8.5%	87.0%
6	France	12.4	2.3%	89.3%
7	Netherlands	12.1	2.2%	91.5%
8	Canada	10.9	2.0%	93.6%
9	Singapore	9.1	1.7%	95.3%
10	Sweden	5.2	1.0%	96.2%
11	Austria	4.1	0.8%	97.0%
12	Spain	4.2	0.8%	97.8%
13	Belgium/Luxembourg	2.9	0.5%	98.3%
14	Germany	2.6	0.5%	98.8%
15	Italy	2.5	0.5%	99.3%

Sources: S&P/Citigroup BMI World Property Index (available equity market capitalization as of January 3, 2005); Pramerica Real Estate Investors.

[3] The BMI Property Index does not include the big German open-end and closed-end funds that represent a large share of individual (retail) and institutional property investment activity in the German market in recent years.

end of the spectrum are vertically integrated operating companies that resemble non-real estate corporations except that their primary business is somehow related to property (e.g., development, financing, management, etc.). At the other end are relatively passive vehicles that own one or more assets and often are externally managed by a team that may also advise other, similar investment funds.

Many of these vehicles, though not all, are tax-transparent, which means that most or all of the company or trust's revenues are exempt from corporate taxes as long as they are distributed to shareholders. As a result, and because of other common structural features (e.g., minimum distribution requirements), tax-transparent vehicles usually pay attractive, stable cash yields. The trade-off for this feature, however, is that REITs' ability to retain capital for reinvestment in existing assets and new acquisitions is somewhat limited.

Small Sector, Big Growth

Although the global listed property sector is still relatively small compared with the global commercial property universe, it has grown significantly over the last decade. Since January 1994, the sector's equity market capitalization has more than quadrupled from about $130 billion to more than $536 billion (see Exhibit 5). Much of this growth has occurred within the last two to three years and has been

Exhibit 5: Robust Growth in Listed Property Sector

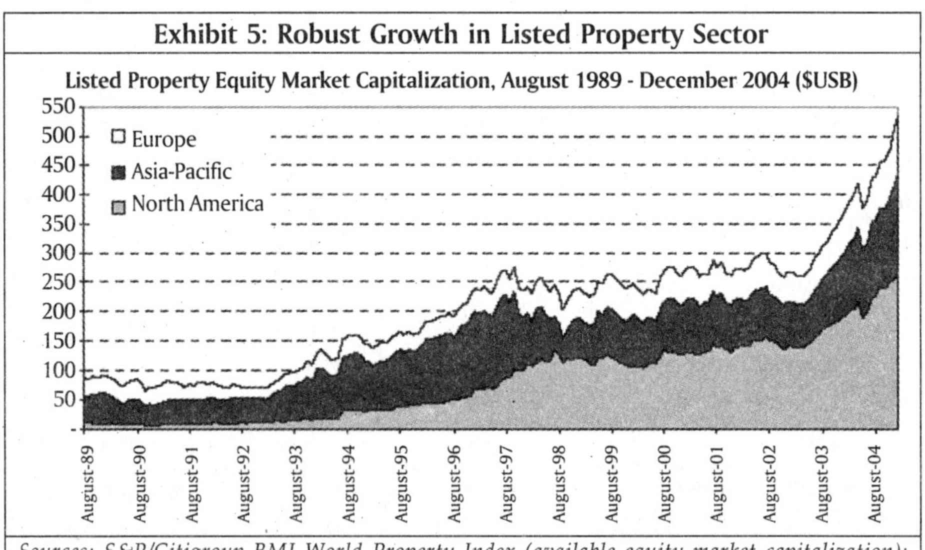

Sources: S&P/Citigroup BMI World Property Index (available equity market capitalization); Pramerica Real Estate Investors.

concentrated in the US and Australia, the two largest, most mature and transparent listed property markets. Together, the US and Australia account for about 61% of the growth in the BMI Property Index since the start of 2002.

Over the last decade, the equity market capitalization of the US and Australian listed property sectors has grown at a compound annual rate of more than 20%, much faster than the 6% annual growth rate for the rest of the listed market. Most of the recent growth has come from share price appreciation rather than a dramatic increase in the property holdings of REITs and LPTs. Over the last three years, US equity REITs have returned about 87%, or roughly 23% per year. Price appreciation over this period was nearly 55%, or a 15.7% annualized rate, with average annual dividends of about 7% accounting for the balance of the total return. LPTs have gained more than 130% in total over the last three years, a little more than 32% per year, including price gains of about 80%, or more than 21% per year.[4]

Although many factors have contributed to the robust investor demand for REIT and LPT shares, and for real estate securities generally, over the last few years, investors' thirst for yield has been and remains the biggest demand driver for REIT and LPT shares. Investor demand for secure, yield-oriented investments has driven share prices in the US and Australia higher and has caused yields to compress. Last year, yields fell nearly 190 basis points (bps) to about 4.7% in Australia and more than 80 bps, also to about 4.7%, in the US (see Exhibit 6).

While the new interest in real estate securities has made it relatively easy for REITs and LPTs to raise capital at historically low costs, increased capital flows to all types of real estate investments have made *deploying* capital in the US, and in most other markets, much more challenging in recent years. Intense competition for assets in the US private transaction market has led several REITs to pursue growth through alternative approaches—M&A, joint ventures and, increasingly, overseas investments. Currently, a handful of US REITs, mostly retail and industrial firms, are actively pursuing investments in Asia, Latin America and throughout Europe, including Central and Eastern European countries such as Poland and the Czech Republic.[5]

---

4 National Association of Real Estate Investment Trusts (NAREIT); S&P/Citigroup BMI Property Index – Australia.

5 Although current foreign holdings by most REITs and LPTs are relatively small, cross-border investment further complicates comparisons between countries' equity market capitalization and their underlying property markets.

Exhibit 6: Strong Investor Demand Causes Property Yields to Fall

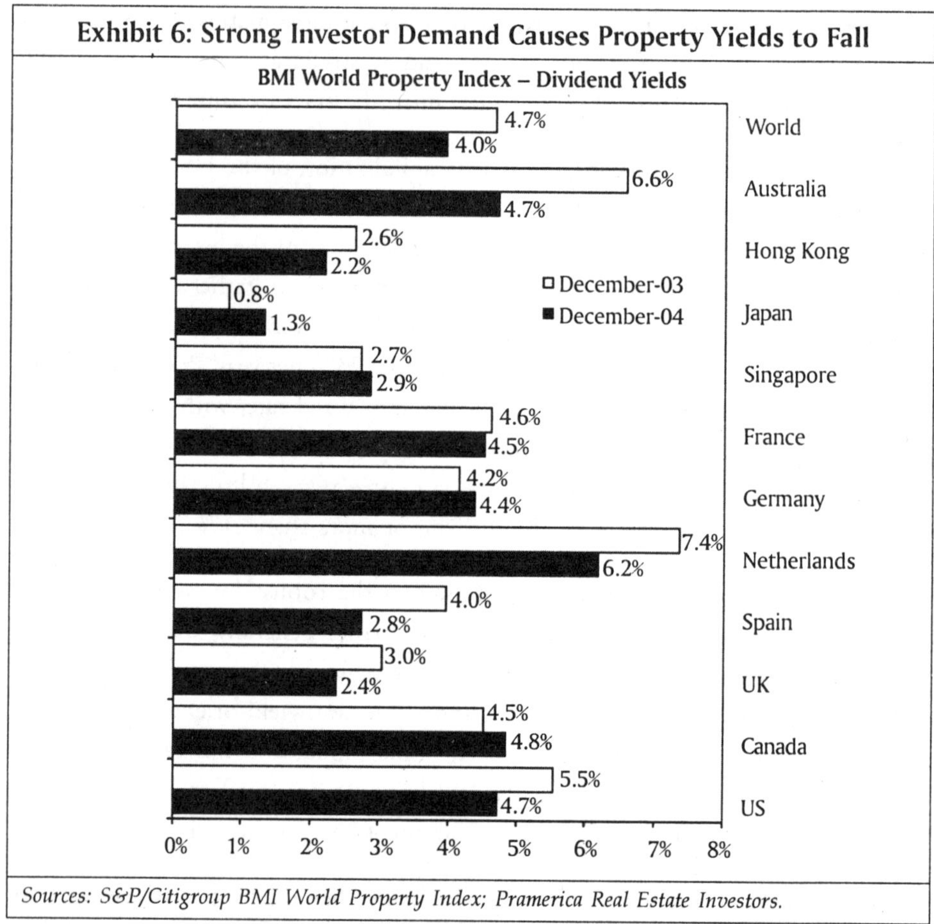

Sources: S&P/Citigroup BMI World Property Index; Pramerica Real Estate Investors.

The Australian market dynamics are similar, except that LPTs account for a much larger share of both the domestic institutional property market (between 40% and 50% by some estimates) and the Australian stock market (about 9.7% as of year-end 2004). With fewer opportunities to grow their portfolios domestically through direct property acquisitions, LPTs have little choice but to pursue growth through consolidation and, like REITs, overseas investment. M&A activity in Australia has been feverish in recent years as more trusts have taken advantage of the liquidity in the capital markets to create the scale needed to compete in the global market. In 2004, for example, Westfield merged its three listed entities into one large listed property trust, the Westfield Group. At year-end 2004, the firm had an equity market capitalization of more than $19 billion, about one-third of the Australian listed property sector, and a portfolio with over 30 million square feet of retail space in Australia, New Zealand, the US and Europe.[6]

Importantly, the current liquidity and competitive environment have also encouraged more LPTs, including the new Westfield Group, to migrate away from the externally advised, relatively passive model that historically dominated the Australian market toward self-advised real estate operating companies. This trend mirrors a similar shift in the US REIT market over the last 10 to 15 years in response to investors' more favorable view of internal management teams and the potential efficiencies and alignment of interests they offer.

REITs in the Making

The success and impressive growth of the REIT and LPT markets in the US and Australia, and in various other markets with tax-transparent vehicles, is helping to drive the proliferation of REIT-like vehicles worldwide. Government authorities

Exhibit 7: Selected REIT Regimes

	Vehicle(s)	Year Introduced		Vehicle(s)	Year Introduced
Asia-Pacific			**Europe**		
Australia	LPT	1971	Belgium	SICAFI	1995
Hong Kong	REIT	2003	France	SIIC	2003
Japan	J-REIT	2000	Germany	N/a	2006?
Korea	RETF, K-REIT, CR-REIT	2001	Italy	FII	1994
Malaysia	REIT	Late-'80s	Luxembourg	FCP, SICAV, SICAF	1988
Singapore	S-REIT	2002	Netherlands	BI	1969
Taiwan	REIT	2003	Spain	REIF, REIC	1994
			United Kingdom	N/a	2006?
Latin America			**North America**		
Brazil	FII	1993	Canada	REIT	1994
Mexico	Fibras	2004	United States	REIT	1960

Sources: EPRA/NAREIT; UBS; Bloomberg; Pramerica Real Estate Investors.

[6] Standard & Poor's Index Services, Global Index Review 2004.

in Asia, Europe and Latin America are introducing tax-transparent property investment vehicles, although the sheer scale of the REIT and LPT markets dwarfs the contribution that these new vehicles have made to the recent growth in the listed property sector. Exhibit 7 shows a summary listing of selected REIT vehicles in the major property markets and the year they were introduced or, for Germany and the UK, the year they are expected to be introduced.

The legal and tax features of the various REIT regimes vary widely by country. However, a common motivation for the new interest among government authorities has been the desire to provide investors, particularly smaller institutions and individuals, access to real estate investments and to a significant and attractive part of the broader investment universe. Hence, their essential characteristics include a relatively high, stable cash yield that (1) passes directly through the entity, exempt from corporate taxes, to the shareholders, and (2) represents all (or a substantial share) of the capital gains and income from the real estate asset(s) owned and/or managed by the company or fund. Not all vehicles offer these features—Hong Kong REITs, for example, are not tax transparent.

In theory, tax transparency provides investors access to investments with the same cash flow characteristics as owning real estate directly, but through a more liquid (and volatile) structure. In practice, while shares of US REITs, LPTs and similar tax-efficient listed vehicles generally have delivered stable yields comparable to direct property, market forces such as investor sentiment have caused their performance to diverge at times from private, direct investment in the underlying assets.[7]

European REITs

Europe has a long history of listed property companies, and a few countries (e.g., Belgium, Luxembourg and the Netherlands) already have well-established tax-transparent vehicles. However, most European listed property companies have traded at persistent discounts to the net asset value (NAV) of their property holdings, at least until recently. Although many factors affect share prices, the discounts to NAV in the European listed property market are partly – if not mostly – a product of the corporate taxes that most European property companies must pay on income and capital gains. Corporate taxes represent an embedded

[7] For more about public and private property market performance and pricing, see "Rational Differençes Between Public and Private Real Estate," Pramerica Real Estate Investors, May 2004.

tax liability for shareholders that they would not incur if they invested directly in property. As Exhibit 8 shows, within the last two years this discount has narrowed considerably. Some European property companies in countries where REITs have been introduced are even trading at premiums to NAV.

Exhibit 8: Persistent Discounts to NAV Have Narrowed Recently

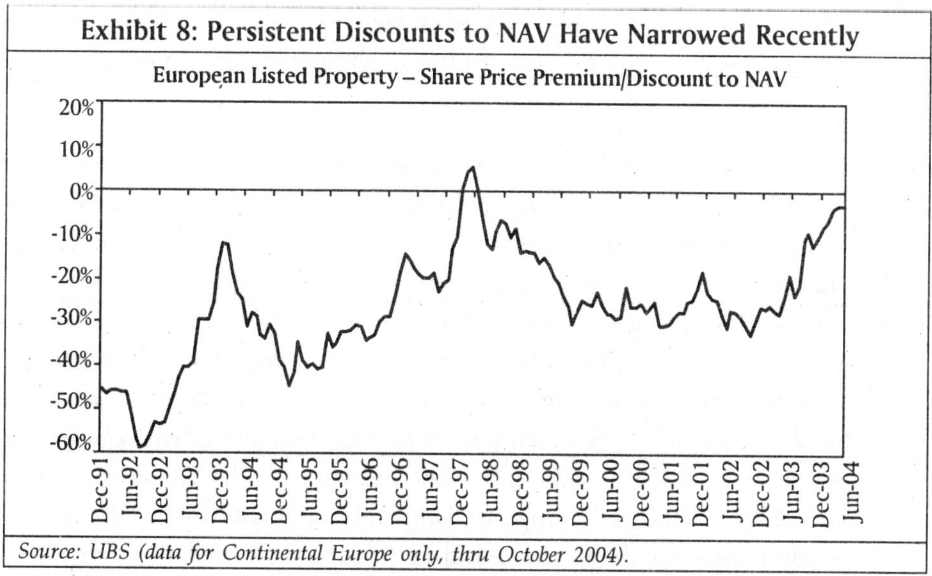

Source: UBS (data for Continental Europe only, thru October 2004).

France, which launched a REIT-like structure, SIICs (société d'investissement immobiliers cotés), in 2003, is leading the new REIT movement in Europe and, therefore, the re-pricing of European property companies. In the nearly two years since SIICs were introduced, every major French listed property company has elected SIIC status. The early adoption of the SIIC structure by existing property companies already appears to be benefiting the property sector and investors. Rising share prices for French listed property companies, whose shares began to trade higher in anticipation of the formal launch of the new structure, have rewarded investors and erased the discounts to NAV at which most companies' shares traded. According to UBS, French property companies traded at an average discount of about 25% over the last 12 years. As of November 2004, however, they were trading at nearly a 10% premium to NAV.

Although it remains to be seen how much influence SIICs will have in the real estate property and capital markets, the quick acceptance of the structure is a promising start for the newly minted and soon-to-be launched SIICs and for the

French property markets generally. As important, the success in France should serve as a catalyst for other European countries that do not already have competitive REIT-like vehicles. Most REIT structures, including SIICs, allow at least some investment in foreign assets. If tax transparency rewards firms with a lower cost of capital, they should have a competitive advantage over local investors in markets that do not have a similar structure, especially as the global capital and investment markets become more integrated.

The increased competition from SIICs and from the growing number of REITs and LPTs that are expanding globally certainly increases the pressure on the UK and Germany, which have the largest developed property markets in the world without a REIT-like vehicle.[8] Both countries are considering REIT legislation. In the spring of 2004, the UK Treasury solicited feedback from industry participants through a formal consultation process for the design of a tax-transparent vehicle, tentatively referred to as a Property Investment Fund (PIF), for the UK market. However, government officials indicated recently that the legislation will not be introduced in 2005, as many in the property industry had hoped. Nevertheless, UK property company shares rose in anticipation of the legislation, nearly halving the discount to NAV at which the shares had traditionally traded. According to UBS, UK property companies have traded at discounts to NAV of 30% to 40% in recent years but are now trading at about a 15% discount to NAV.

The idea of a REIT-like vehicle has gained momentum in Germany, however, in part because of bribery allegations at a few of the very large and influential open-end property funds. The ongoing scandal has cast a shadow over the open-end fund structure and has raised questions about its lack of transparency. But it may also have helped move German REITs closer to becoming a reality. Because the open-end funds already enjoy tax advantages over ordinary German listed property companies, fund managers, mostly German banks, have done little to promote a REIT-like structure that would compete with their fund products. Together, the calls for increased transparency and better corporate governance amid the turmoil in the open-end fund market and increasing competitive pressures could be the catalyst needed to launch a German REIT,

8 Although German investors can invest in property through relatively liquid open- and closed-end property funds, these vehicles are not listed and are not truly comparable to listed property companies such as REITs and LPTs.

possibly before a similar vehicle can be introduced in the UK. The German government is studying the tax issues associated with creating a REIT vehicle, and has expressed an interest in modeling the vehicle after US REITs and French SIICs.

Asian REITs

Most of the new REITs are from Asian countries, many of which also have long histories of public real estate ownership, usually through large conglomerates and property development companies. The potential market growth in Asia is enormous from a supply and demand perspective. On the supply side, if Asian REITs become established, the massive property holdings of the existing property companies, conglomerates and government authorities could provide a significant source of assets for the market's growth, particularly as the Asian economy gains strength and the property markets move into recovery. At the same time, the potential demand for new investment vehicles of almost any type that offer secure, attractive yields could be vast. A significant amount of investment capital – personal savings and institutional funds (i.e., national pension schemes) – is currently invested in money market and similar accounts, earning very little interest.

The current environment in many parts of Asia is similar to US conditions in the early 1990s, when the REIT market expanded rapidly. The US economy was recovering from the 1991-92 recession, and real estate market fundamentals were beginning to stabilize from the early-90s market crash. But liquidity remained constrained because traditional private capital sources were either saddled with huge portfolios of non-performing real estate or had no appetite for real estate investments. With few alternatives available, the industry turned to the public equity and debt markets to re-capitalize, which resulted in a significant shift in property ownership from the private to the public market.

A similar pattern may already be emerging in Japan. The Japanese REIT market has grown quickly since J-REITs were introduced in 2000, making Japan the largest REIT market in Asia (excluding Australia) by a wide margin. Fifteen J-REITs have gone public since 2001, and many more are reportedly in the pipeline for 2005. As of year-end 2004, the total equity market capitalization of J-REITs was more than $17 billion. To put this into perspective, the market capitalization of the US REIT market did not reach $17 billion until 1992, nearly 33 years after REITs were first introduced. The J-REIT market already has injected liquidity, directly and indirectly, into the Japanese property market. Before J-REITs were introduced, many investors were reluctant to enter the market, even though prices had fallen sharply, due to exit strategy concerns. Today, after years of stagnation, transaction activity involving J-REITs and other investors has increased significantly.

The same factors that have created demand for real estate securities in markets everywhere have fueled the J-REIT market's rapid growth. The Bank of Japan's zero interest rate policy, intended to stimulate the economy and head off deflation, has depressed bond yields and savings rates. Since the start of 2000, the yield on 10-year Japanese government bonds has averaged about 1.4%. Although property yields have compressed since the first J-REITs were introduced to about 3.5% to 4% currently, they still compare very favorably with yields from bonds and other Japanese listed property companies.

Singapore REITs (S-REITs) have also enjoyed success in the first two years since they were introduced, making Singapore Asia's second-largest REIT market. Five S-REITs, with a total equity market capitalization of more than $3 billion, have listed on the Singapore exchange since 2002. These include Fortune REIT, which owns retail assets in Hong Kong, and the recently launched Suntec City REIT. As in Japan, more IPOs are expected in 2005. However, retail (individual) investor demand is noticeably higher in Singapore than in Japan for at least two reasons. First, retail investors have relatively easy access to the S-REIT market and can even purchase S-REIT shares through automated teller machines. (Recent changes by the Japanese government to allow banks and other outlets to sell J-REIT shares directly to retail investors should improve access.) More importantly, S-REIT dividends paid to individual investors are currently tax-exempt in Singapore, which makes their yields, now about 5 to 6%, even more attractive in today's low interest rate environment.

South Korea and Hong Kong also have introduced REITs in the last few years. However, the growth and development of the REIT market in both countries has lagged Japan and Singapore, largely because of their more restrictive REIT structures. Two REIT regimes, the General REIT (K-REIT) and the Corporate Restructuring REIT (CR-REIT), were created in Korea in 2001, but numerous restrictions in the initial legislation, including limitations on leverage and minimum capitalization requirements, have limited the market's growth. Although seven CR-REITs have listed on the Korean Stock Exchange, no K-REITs have been created yet. This is largely because K-REITs, while they are somewhat more flexible than CR-REITs, do not enjoy any tax benefits that justify the numerous other restrictions that the current legislation imposes.

Recently, the Korean government amended the REIT legislation, making it easier and more attractive for property owners and investors to take advantage of the REIT structures, particularly K-REITs. The amendment, which does not take effect until April 2005, will extend tax benefits to K-REITs and will ease borrowing and initial capitalization restrictions, among other things, for both types of REITs. While this should make both regimes more attractive and perhaps even tilt the advantage in favor of K-REITs, a third tax-transparent vehicle, the Real Estate Trust Fund (RETF), was introduced in 2004 and could overshadow both types of Korean REITs. Already, nine RETFs have been launched, including two unlisted funds.

Hong Kong's first REIT, the Link REIT, almost made its debut in December 2004 with a massive IPO of a portfolio of retail properties and parking facilities owned by the Hong Kong Housing Authority. However, the offering had to be withdrawn and postponed due to a legal challenge filed by a public housing resident who feared the sale of the assets would jeopardize low-income tenants' rent subsidies. Before the IPO was withdrawn, retail demand for the shares was very strong, in part because retail investors received a slight discount on share pricing. The retail allocation was reportedly 130 times oversubscribed.

Most market observers expect the Link REIT IPO will proceed when the appeal process has been exhausted. (The challenger has until the end of February to file a third and final appeal.) Assuming the legal issues are resolved, the Link REIT will put Hong Kong's REIT market on par with Singapore's in terms of equity capitalization. The IPO is expected to raise nearly $3 billion, making it the largest REIT IPO ever. However, Hong Kong's REIT structure has several disadvantages that help explain why Fortune REIT opted for the S-REIT format rather than a Hong Kong listing. Most importantly, Hong Kong REITs receive no tax benefits and are not permitted to own assets outside Hong Kong. As long as these restrictions remain, little incentive exists for the many large listed property companies already in Hong Kong to adopt the structure.

Implications for Investors

A handful of other Asian, European and Latin American countries either have or are considering REIT-like vehicles. Although many of the markets where these new REITs are being introduced are relatively small and/or will take years to develop, the global interest in REITs, and in real estate investments generally, is important for two reasons. First, it means that real estate is finally being recognized and accepted as an asset class. This acceptance should be more enduring than cyclical since it coincides with broad recognition that the characteristics that make real estate attractive in a diversified portfolio, namely stable cash yields with modest capital growth and low correlations with other asset classes, will become increasingly important as the world population ages.

As important, the global interest in REITs means that the infrastructure needed to support a global listed property sector is not only developing, it is gaining momentum. This infrastructure includes everything – the vehicles themselves, the investment benchmarks against which performance can be measured, the analysts and rating agencies that provide the research needed to make informed decisions about opportunities and risks, the investment banks and distribution networks of brokers and financial planners, etc. Infrastructure alone is not enough to make the promise of a global REIT market self-fulfilling. But it can be self-facilitating, particularly when combined with an increased awareness of and appreciation for real estate and the investment characteristics that property traditionally has delivered.

The growth and development of a vibrant, liquid listed property sector further expands the investment universe to an asset class that, historically at least, has been very attractive in a diversified portfolio but has been relatively difficult for smaller investors to access. As Exhibit 9 shows, property shares have significantly outperformed stocks and bonds on a three- and five-year basis, and have delivered modestly higher returns over the last 10 years. Throughout this period, the broader

Exhibit 9: Attractive Absolute and Risk-Adjusted Returns

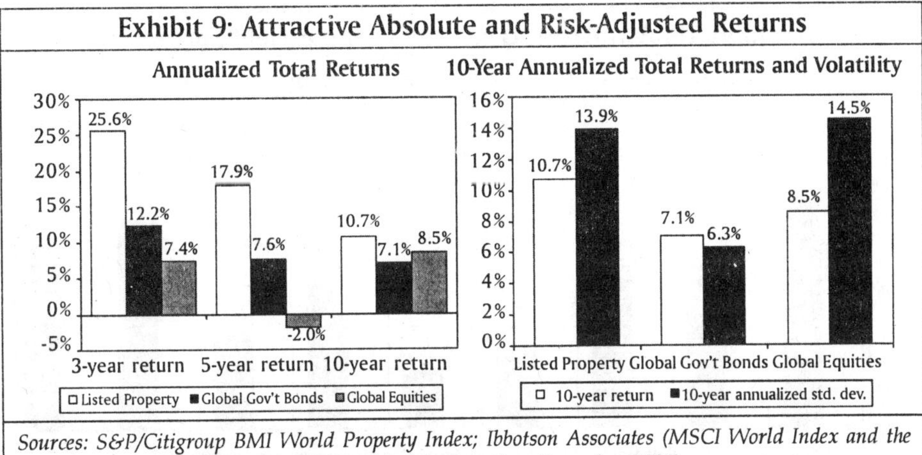

Sources: S&P/Citigroup BMI World Property Index; Ibbotson Associates (MSCI World Index and the Merrill Lynch Global Government Bond Index, data thru December 2004).

market was a little more volatile than the listed property sector, making property shares even more attractive on a risk-adjusted basis.[9]

Although price appreciation has dominated the total returns for most listed property shares in recent years, the relatively stable yields that property companies typically offer, particularly REITs, LPTs and other tax-transparent vehicles, and that are largely responsible for the increased investor interest, are attractive for several reasons. First, listed property shares typically trade at positive spreads to other relatively low-risk, income-oriented investments. Although spreads have compressed sharply this year, the average yield spread between property and government bonds in the nine countries shown in Exhibit 10 was about 41 bps at year-end 2004.

Generally, the countries with the highest listed property yields, with the exception of Germany, have well-established REIT vehicles that require companies or trusts to distribute a substantial share of their earnings to qualify for whatever tax treatment and/or other benefits the vehicle offers. Listed property yields are least attractive, on a relative basis, in the UK, where the spread between property companies and government bonds is negative by a wide margin. The yields shown in Exhibit 10 for Japan and Singapore, where ordinary (i.e., non-REIT) property companies

9 The Asia-Pacific region, which represents about 30% of the BMI Property Index, accounted for much of the volatility in the index. The region's returns were about twice as volatile as those for Europe and North America. Asia-Pacific also dragged down the listed property sector's 10-year returns with total returns of just 5.4%, compared with 15.5% for Europe and 14.8% for North America.

Exhibit 10: Attractive, Generally Positive Yield Spreads

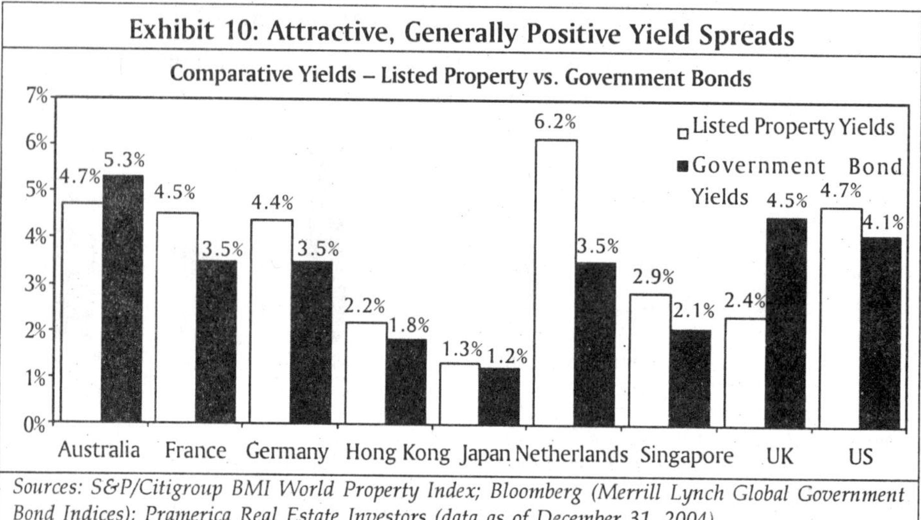

Sources: S&P/Citigroup BMI World Property Index; Bloomberg (Merrill Lynch Global Government Bond Indices); Pramerica Real Estate Investors (data as of December 31, 2004).

dominate the listed property market, significantly understate the current yields from tax-transparent property vehicles in both countries. Exhibit 11 shows the dramatic difference between the average dividend yields for the entire listed property sector in Japan and Singapore and the average yields for J-REITs and S-REITs. As long as investor demand for yield persists, the REIT markets in these and other Asian and European countries should continue to grow and capture a disproportionate share of the capital flows into listed real estate.

Exhibit 11: REIT Yields Much Higher than Property Company Yields

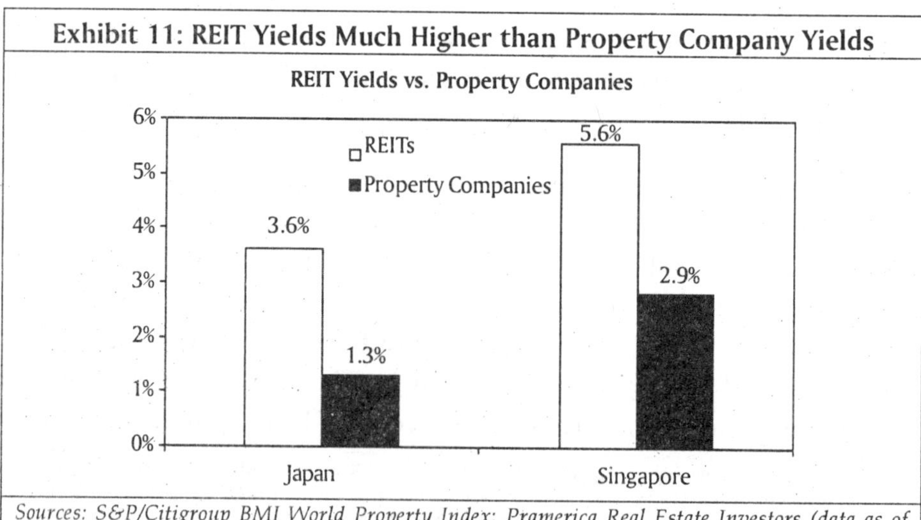

Sources: S&P/Citigroup BMI World Property Index; Pramerica Real Estate Investors (data as of December 31, 2004).

Importantly, the earnings from which these dividends are paid are also relatively transparent compared with the earnings of most corporations. The value of this attribute has appreciated significantly since the collapse of Enron and the high-profile accounting scandals at WorldCom, Tyco and other major corporations. Assuming disclosure is sufficient, REIT investors and analysts can usually get a good sense of the assets in a property portfolio, how well they are performing and their prospects for rent and value growth.

Property shares also provide an opportunity for investors to diversify their portfolios. Exhibit 12 shows the correlations between listed property shares, government bonds and equities, along with the rolling correlations between property shares and the same equity and bond indices. Between 1990 and 2004, the correlation between property shares and bonds was relatively low, about 0.35, which suggests property shares may provide an attractive yield complement to bonds in a

Exhibit 12: Low Correlations With Other Asset Classes

	Listed Property	Global Gov't Bonds	Global Stocks
Listed Property	1.00		
Global Gov't Bonds	0.35	1.00	
Global Stocks	0.69	0.23	1.00

60-Month Rolling Correlations With Global Stocks and Bonds

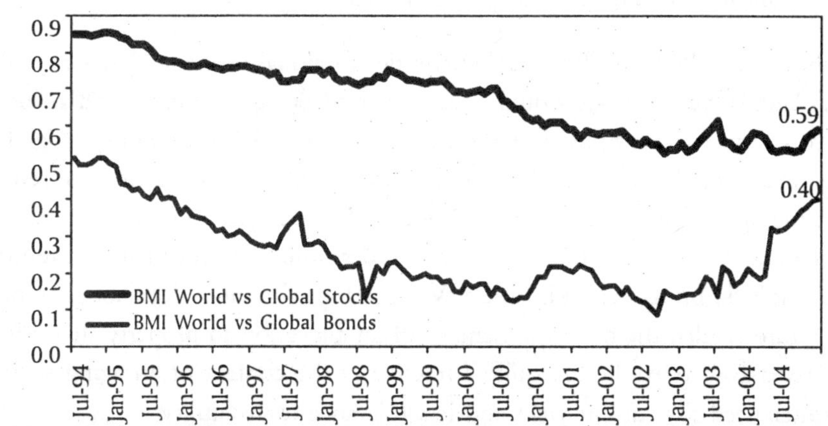

Sources: S&P/Citigroup BMI World Property Index; Ibbotson Associates (MSCI World Index and the Merrill Lynch Global Government Bond Index); Pramerica Real Estate Investors (monthly data January 1990-December 2004).

mixed-asset portfolio. While the correlation between property shares and the broader equity market was much higher over the 14-plus-year period, as one might expect since the world stock index includes property shares, the relationship between stocks and property shares has weakened steadily over the last decade or so.

Notably, although we have not shown the correlations between property share performance and direct, private real estate investment in this report, historical correlations between public and private real estate investments are surprisingly low and are even negative in certain countries. Since 1990, for example, the correlation between REITs and private, institutional real estate investments in the US, as measured by the National Council of Real Estate Investment Fiduciaries (NCREIF), has been about -0.06. Historically, therefore, REITs have been more of a complement to, rather than a substitute for, direct real estate investment in the US.

Together, these attributes – competitive returns with stable yields, moderate volatility and low correlations with other asset classes – can enhance the risk-return profile of a multi-asset portfolio. Exhibit 13 shows the risk-return effects of different allocations to global property shares (in 5% increments) over the last five- and 10-year periods. Each point on the two graphs shows the total annualized return and risk (standard deviation) for a portfolio of assets comprised of 40% global government bonds and 60% stocks and property shares. The label for each data point shows the allocation to property shares.

As shown, an allocation from global equities to global property shares over the last five- and 10-year periods would have improved portfolio returns and reduced return volatility. For example, over the last five years, a 10% allocation to global property shares would have generated an additional 193 bps per year in total return while reducing portfolio volatility by about 58 bps per year. The results are less dramatic on a 10-year basis, but still show a modest improvement in annual returns (25 bps) and a 44 bp reduction in risk.[10] While past performance does not guarantee similar future results, the historical benefits of an allocation to property shares in a global mixed-asset portfolio are quite attractive in the context of an aging society with greater need for current yield and less tolerance for volatility.

[10] For illustrative purposes, we assumed that the allocation to property shares came entirely from the global equities allocation. However, if the property share allocation is taken equally from the initial stock and bond allocations (e.g., 10% allocation to property shares, 35% bonds and 55% stocks), the total returns improve by 143 bps over the 5-year period and 31 bps over the 10-year period. However, the standard deviation is slightly higher in both the 5- year (3 bps) and 10-year (13 bps) periods.

Exhibit 13: Property Shares Improve Portfolio Efficiency

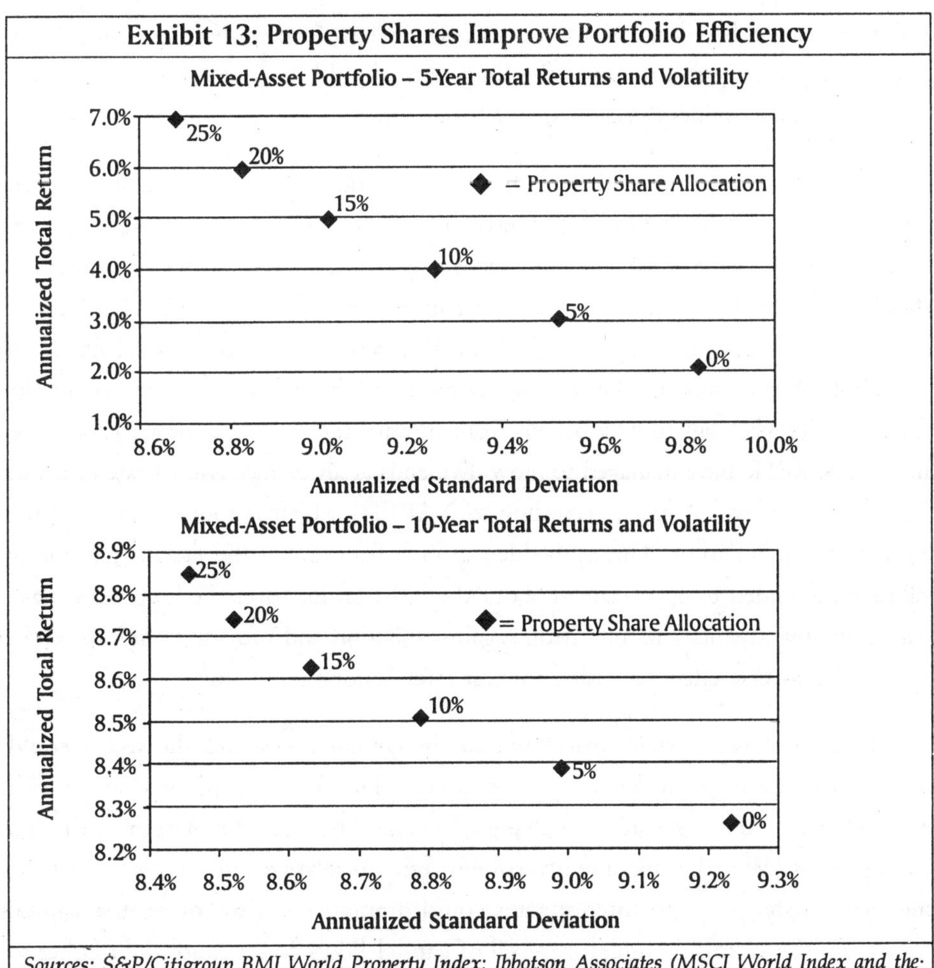

Sources: S&P/Citigroup BMI World Property Index; Ibbotson Associates (MSCI World Index and the Merrill Lynch Global Government Bond Index); Pramerica Real Estate Investors.

Caveats

A few caveats are worth noting, however. Most obviously, the sharp rise in property shares in many markets over the last 12 to 18 months means that real estate securities in these markets are probably not as attractive as they were before the current run-up. Rising share prices have depressed yields to historically low levels in some markets, which could limit share price appreciation in the near term. Over the longer term, the exceptional returns that US REITs, LPTs and other listed property vehicles have achieved in recent years are not sustainable. At some point, lower yields will create too much resistance to further share price increases, and listed property returns over the long-term should revert to something closer to their annual dividend yield, plus a little growth.

But certain factors should help ease the transition from today's capital-driven investment cycle to one in which property market fundamentals have more influence. Most obviously, as the global economy gains strength, real estate market fundamentals should improve. Higher occupancies and rising rents should mitigate the effects of higher interest rates on property values. Further, although the contractual nature of the cash flows that make up the core part of most REITs' revenues is clearly a bond-like feature, REIT earnings usually benefit from upward revisions in contract lease rates. In the US, REITs have managed to grow dividends at an average annual rate of about 5.8% over the last 10 years, according to NAREIT, which is more than twice the annual rate of inflation. This embedded growth feature and the fact that property values have tended to appreciate at about the inflation rate over the long term make real estate investments a natural hedge against inflation and provide some protection against the adverse effects of rising interest rates, among other things.

The bigger risk to share prices is that the capital flows into the sector could reverse if investor sentiment changes suddenly. The listed property sector is still relatively small and is sensitive to changes in capital flows at the margin. Although yield spreads over other income investments remain relatively attractive by historic measures, a sharp rise in interest rates could dramatically slow or reverse capital flows into the sector. A sudden reversal of capital flows could cause the market to correct quickly, similar to the sell-off in April 2004 when US REITs lost more than 20% from peak to trough in one month amid fears of rising interest rates.

Investor favor could also diminish or shift away from property due to concerns about the industry's health and/or growth potential, or as part of a broader market rotation back toward growth investments. Neither appears particularly likely at the moment, however. Most property markets are in the early stages of a recovery, with falling vacancies and very little new supply in the pipeline. And short-term economic and geopolitical uncertainties and long-term demographic forces suggest investor demand for income-oriented investments will continue.

Transparency and governance have improved, but they are not perfect. Most of the new structures have not been tested through a complete property or capital market cycle. Ultimately, the industry must still rely on market participants' discipline to keep the supply of capital and properties from getting too far out of balance. Imbalances will occur locally, sometimes regionally or nationally and, rarely, globally. When and where these imbalances occur, performance will suffer, and the results may be just as severe as in the past. But over time, as supply and demand move back toward equilibrium, markets tend to recover, and the cycle begins anew. Having dynamic public and private real estate markets provides an arbitrage mechanism that helps prevent asset pricing from getting too far out of line, at least on the downside. Over the long-term, this should reduce the risk of a severe liquidity crisis and may shorten the cycle.

Lastly, the sweeping changes that have occurred and that are taking place in the global real estate industry, particularly in the capital markets, could fundamentally alter the investment performance characteristics of the listed property sector, making historical data and trends less relevant. The US REIT and Australian LPT markets have undergone significant structural changes over the last 15 years, and the transitional nature of the last decade alone may limit the relevance of the historical data. Both vehicles could perform differently in the future, particularly if a highly dynamic, fluid global listed property market develops.

Volatility and correlations with other asset classes could both be higher (or lower) than in the past. The public markets create a much stronger link between the real estate industry and the broader capital markets that can cause liquidity to ebb and flow. Future yields could also be lower if the public markets lead to better liquidity and transparency and reduce the risk profile of the asset class as a whole. But the sources and composition of investment returns from property should not change materially, and the fundamental performance characteristics of the underlying assets – stable, attractive yields, modest asset appreciation and low correlations – should remain appealing, particularly in the context of a diversified portfolio.

Closing Thoughts

The dramatic growth in the global listed property market in recent years marks an important step in the evolution of the real estate asset class. While the increasing market capitalization of the sector is significant in and of itself, the fundamental demand and supply drivers that have facilitated its recent growth – broad acceptance of the asset class and further development of the industry infrastructure – strongly suggest the industry is starting a long-term secular growth trend. Although separating cause and effect in the investment world can be challenging, increased demand for real estate investments should continue to drive the growth of the global listed property sector, and REITs in particular.

This evolution has several important implications for the real estate industry and for investors. For the industry, the continued development of the public capital markets for real estate should improve liquidity and transparency throughout the industry, and make capital allocation more rational and efficient. At the same time, the competitive pressures that accompany the emergence of professional and increasingly global public real estate operating companies will lead to improvements in the quality of goods and services that the industry provides to space users and investors. For investors, the growth of the public markets creates more opportunities to access the attractive return characteristics of property investments, while helping to mitigate many of the risks that historically have caused investors to avoid the asset class.

(Philip Conner is Principal in the Investment Research department of Prudential Real Estate Investors. He is also a member of the Pension Real Estate Association (PREA) and the National Council of Real Estate Investment Fiduciaries (NCREIF). He can be reached at philip.conner@prudential.com

Youguo Liang is the Managing Director of Investment Research and a member of the Investment Committee and Management Committee of Prudential Real Estate Investors. Dr. Liang is a CFA charter holder, the President of the American Real Estate Society and international editor of Real Estate Finance. He can be reached at youguo.liang@prudential.com).

5

The Investor's Guide to Real Estate Investment Trusts (REITs)

Real Estate Investment Trusts deal with commercial real estate and their shares derive a great part of their value from tangible, hard assets and provide benefits of balance, diversification and greater risk/reward efficiency to a broad range of investment portfolios. The article highlights the diverse investment allocation of REIT across a broad range of specific real estate sub-sectors like industrial parks, warehouses, hotels and resorts and analyses the returns from REITs.

REIT Basics

Real estate investment trusts (REITs) are companies that own and most often actively manage income-producing commercial real estate. Some REITs originate or invest in loans and other credit obligations secured by real estate collateral. The shares of most REITs are publicly traded on major stock exchanges.

The US Congress created the legislative framework for REITs in 1960 to enable the investing public to benefit from investments in large-scale real estate enterprises.

REITs have much to offer the institutional and retail investing communities. They provide ongoing dividend income along with the potential for long-term capital gains through share price appreciation, and can also serve as a powerful tool for long-term portfolio diversification.

Research by Ibbotson Associates, a leading investment research firm specializing in asset allocation strategies, demonstrates the multi-faceted benefits of investing in REITs:

- The ownership of REIT shares has historically increased investors' total return and/or lowered the overall risk in both equity and fixed-income portfolios.
- Dividend growth rates for REIT shares have outpaced inflation over the last decade.
- The REIT business enterprise is based in large part on the value of tangible and quantifiable assets, namely large-scale commercial real estate, a defining attribute of the REIT industry.

Individual investors can choose to participate broadly in the investment opportunities available in the REIT industry by investing in one or more "pure-play" REIT mutual funds. These mutual funds are managed by portfolio managers with a high degree of expertise in the real estate industry and provide investors with an effective and cost-efficient opportunity to add to a balanced investment portfolio broad and diversified exposure to the real estate asset class.

Real Estate's Role in the Economy

The inclusion in 2001 of REITs in the Standard & Poor's 500 Stock Index, the most widely followed investment performance benchmark for US equity markets, speaks to the increasingly widespread recognition of the importance of commercial real estate in public capital markets. REITs, alongside other mainstream industries, are now widely acknowledged for the integral role they play, both in the economy and in diversified investment portfolios.

The ongoing success of REITs is a reflection of many things, from the income generating and growth potential of the REIT enterprise, to the proven portfolio diversification benefits of owning REIT shares in balanced investment portfolios; and from the benefits of active and professional management of real estate properties, to the transparency and management accountability that are essential components of REIT corporate governance.

REITs Now in the Mainstream

More than ever, REITs are vital public companies that share a multitude of similarities with other mainstream businesses:

Liquidity

Investors can purchase shares in REITs as easily as they purchase shares in any other publicly traded company. REIT shares are traded on all major stock exchanges in the US, including the New York Stock Exchange (NYSE), Nasdaq, American Stock Exchange (AMEX), as well as various after-hours markets.

Shareholder Value

Just like investors in other public companies, REIT shareholders receive value in the form of both dividend income and share price appreciation.

Active Management/Corporate Governance

Publicly-traded REITs generally are vertically integrated and professionally managed corporations. They adhere to the same corporate governance principles that apply to all major companies.

They have a senior management team that is headed by a chief executive officer (CEO) who actively manages the overall strategic vision and equity of the enterprise. The Board of Directors appoints the CEO, which in turn is elected by and accountable to the shareholders of the REIT.

Disclosure Obligation

REITs, like other public companies in the US, are required to provide regular financial disclosures to the investment community, including quarterly and yearly audited financial statements with concomitant filings to the Securities and Exchange Commission.

Limited Liability

As is the case with investments in other publicly traded companies, shareholders have no personal liability for the debts of the REITs in which they invest.

Low Leverage

One reason so many REITs (65 percent, based on equity market capitalization) are rated investment grade is their moderate financial leverage. In fact, the average REIT debt ratio has generally been below 50 percent for much of the last decade.

Returns Delivered by REITs

REITs Deliver Income and Long-term Growth

The special investment characteristics of income-producing real estate provide REIT investors with competitive long-term rates of return that complement the returns from other stocks and bonds.

High Dividend Yield

REITs are required to distribute at least 90 percent of their taxable income to shareholders annually in the form of dividends. Significantly higher than other equities on average, the industry's dividend yields generally produce a steady stream of income through all market conditions.

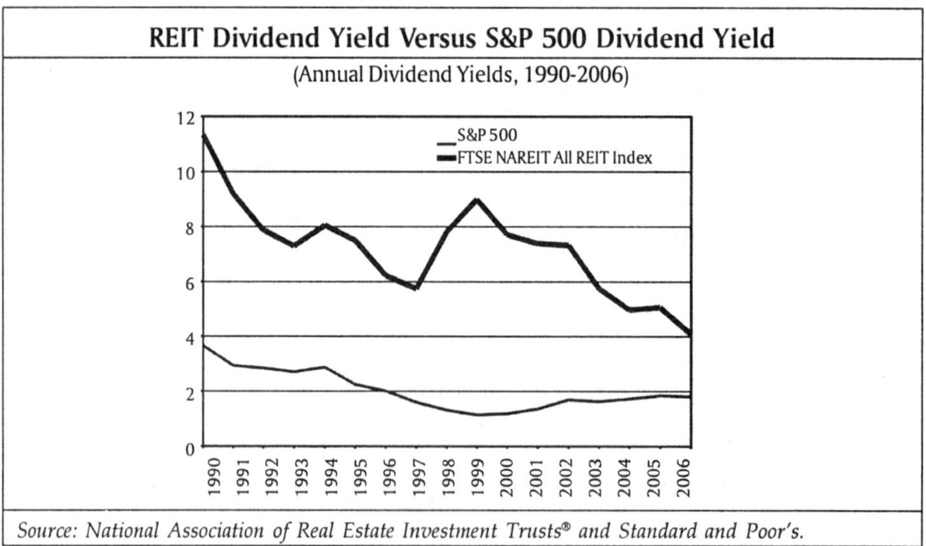

REIT Dividend Yield Versus S&P 500 Dividend Yield

(Annual Dividend Yields, 1990-2006)

Source: National Association of Real Estate Investment Trusts® and Standard and Poor's.

Share Price Appreciation

Approximately one-third of the total return from REIT stocks over the last 20 years came from moderate, long-term growth in share prices. This growth generally has matched or exceeded changes in the Consumer Price Index over the last two decades, protecting shareholders' capital from the ravages of inflation.

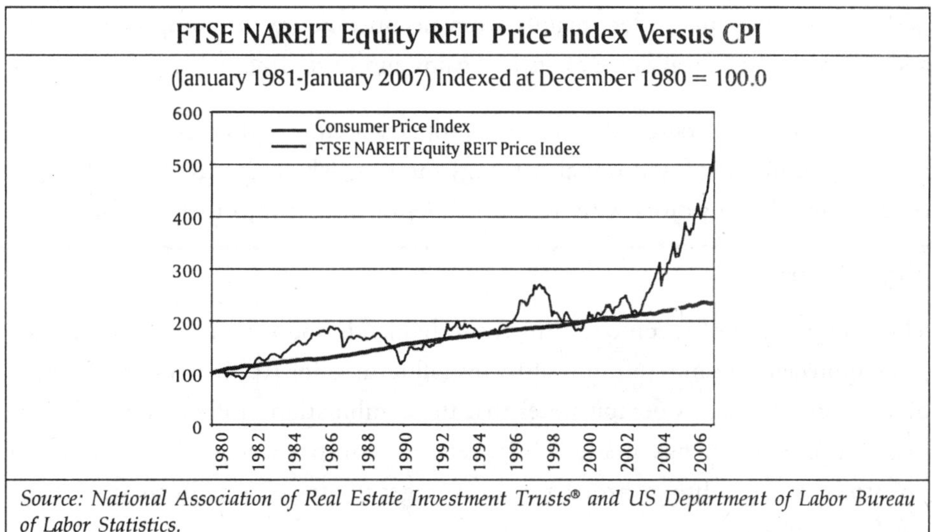

FTSE NAREIT Equity REIT Price Index Versus CPI

Source: National Association of Real Estate Investment Trusts® and US Department of Labor Bureau of Labor Statistics.

Advantages of Real Estate Investment

In addition to the investment performance and portfolio diversification benefits available from investing in REITs, REITs offer several advantages not found in companies across other industries. These benefits are part of the reason that REITs have become increasingly popular with investors over the past decade:

Predictable Revenue Stream

REITs' reliable income is derived from rents paid to the owners of commercial properties whose tenants often sign leases for long periods of time or interest payments from the financing of those properties. In addition, the companies' ownership of tangible assets with established values tends to reduce risk.

Earnings Transparency

Most REITs operate along a straightforward and easily understandable business model: By increasing property occupancy rates and rents, higher levels of income may be produced. When reporting financial results, REITs, like other public companies, must report earnings per share based on net income as defined by generally accepted accounting principles (GAAP).

Another way year-to-year financial progress can be gauged is by comparing levels of Funds From Operations (FFO). FFO, the industry's supplemental performance measure, differs mainly from net income by excluding depreciation and amortization of real estate assets and gains and losses from most property sales.

Given the broad range of real estate property sectors and business lines, there also are a number of additional earnings metrics, which are used by REITs in order to provide investors with a greater level of insight into their performance.

Total Return

The combination of income returns from dividends and capital gains from share price appreciation can result in healthy overall returns for REIT investors. Analysis by Ibbotson Associates demonstrates that the combination of dividends and share price appreciation has made REIT returns competitive with other major investments, including a broad range of largecap stocks, small-cap stocks and fixed income securities.

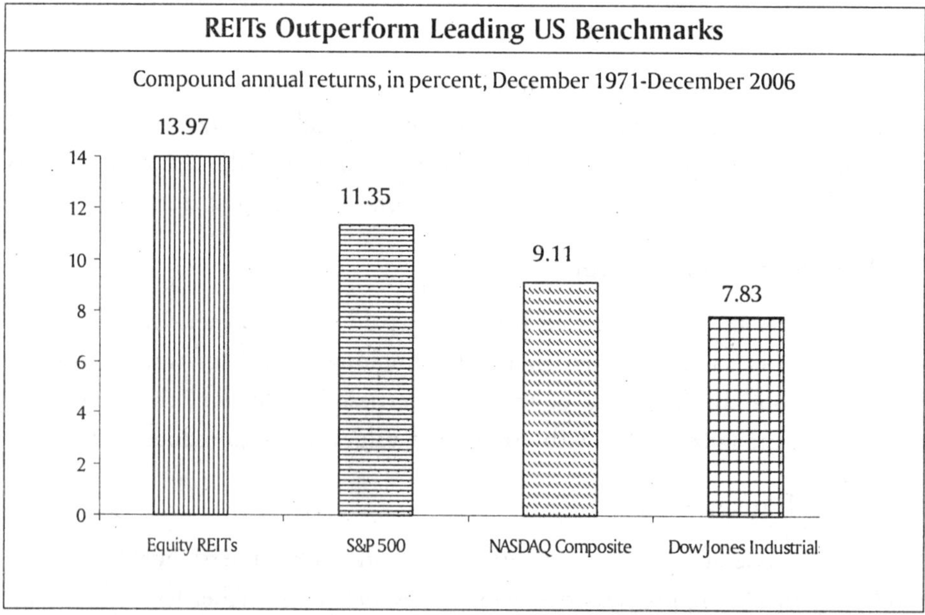

In short, REITs over time have demonstrated a historical track record providing a high level of current income combined with long-term share price appreciation, inflation protection, and prudent diversification for investors across the age and investment style spectrums.

REIT Valuation

Many factors affect the value of a REIT's share price beginning with the earnings tied to oftentimes predictable and growing streams of rental revenue and a price-earnings multiple assigned by the marketplace.

The level and growth of rents are largely determined by economic fundamentals of supply and demand in real estate markets. These fundamentals include demographic information such as population size, population growth, employment growth, construction and the level of overall economic activity. While differing from region to region, all of these factors typically have a direct impact on rents and occupancy rates, which affect projected earnings and property values.

Other factors include:

Net Asset Value Calculation

Many REIT analysts look at net asset value (NAV) as a reference point for the valuation of a company. NAV equals the estimated market value of a REIT's total assets minus the value of all liabilities. When divided by the number of common shares outstanding, the net asset value per share is viewed by some as a useful guideline for determining the appropriate level of share price. Thus, the value of a REIT's shares may be based on the value of its tangible real estate holdings.

Property Portfolio Enhancements

The value of a REIT's property portfolio frequently can be either maintained or enhanced through consistent capital expenditures. This is significant because strategic property portfolio enhancements help to maintain or increase NAVs and provide the basis for price appreciation of a REIT's shares.

Putting Portfolios in Balance with Real Estate

Given the investment strengths and historical performance of REITs, it is no surprise that REIT shares are commonly viewed as a good investment for all long-term, diversified investors.

Clearly, the inclusion of REIT shares in any investment portfolio is a prudent investment decision:

Market Variability Balance

First, the variability of market returns over time and across all economic sectors makes it clear that balance and diversification are the keys to long-term investment success. Integral toward balance and diversification is the inclusion of equities representing all sectors of the economy, including real estate.

Attractive Risk/Reward Balance

Second, REIT shares have proven to offer an attractive risk/reward balance in investment portfolios. Asset allocation analysis from Ibbotson Associates has found

Efficient Frontier with and without REITs

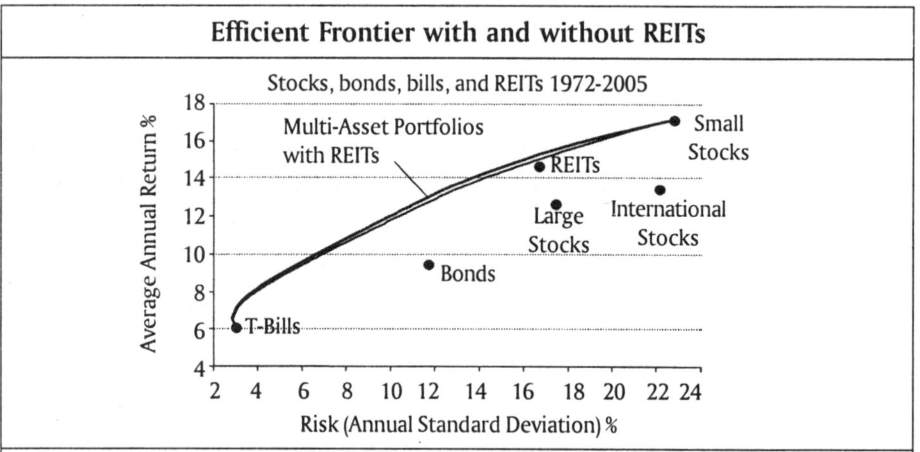

This is for illustrative purposes only and not indicative of any investment. An investment cannot be made directly in an index. Past performance is no guarantee of future results. 5/1/2006.

Source: Small Stocks – represented by the fifth capitalization quintile of stocks on the NYSE for 1926-1981 and the performance of the Dimensional Fund Advisors, Inc. (DFA) US Micro Cap Portfolio thereafter; Large Stocks – Standard & Poor's 500®, which is an unmanaged group of securities and considered to be representative of the stock market in general; Government Bonds – 20-year US Government Bond; International Stocks – Morgan Stanley Capital International Europe, Australasia, and Far East (EAFE®) Index; Treasury Bills – 30-day US Treasury Bill; REITs – FTSE NAREIT Equity REIT Index.

that investing in REIT shares historically has increased total portfolio returns or lowered overall portfolio risk for both equity and fixed income investors.

In fact, Ibbotson's research shows that, when REIT shares are added to an already diversified portfolio, the efficient frontier of the portfolio is raised. When portfolio investments are efficient, risk-averse investors can expect to realize higher portfolio returns with the low level of portfolio risk they prefer, while risk-tolerant investors can expect to realize lower risk along with the high level of returns they seek.

Ultimately, a more efficient portfolio is something that all investors – from those looking for value or income, to those who are more growth-oriented – should find attractive.

REIT Sectors

With a very diverse profile, the REIT industry offers investors many alternatives across a broad range of specific real estate property sectors, including:

- Apartment communities;
- Office properties;
- Shopping centers;
- Regional malls;
- Storage centers;
- Industrial parks and warehouses;
- Lodging facilities, including hotels and resorts;
- Health care facilities; and
- Natural resources.

REITs regularly explore new opportunities for income growth, from new acquisitions or development to providing income-producing leasing or tenant services. Regardless of specific business lines, REITs most often acquire and develop their properties primarily to actively manage and operate them as income-producing, ongoing businesses.

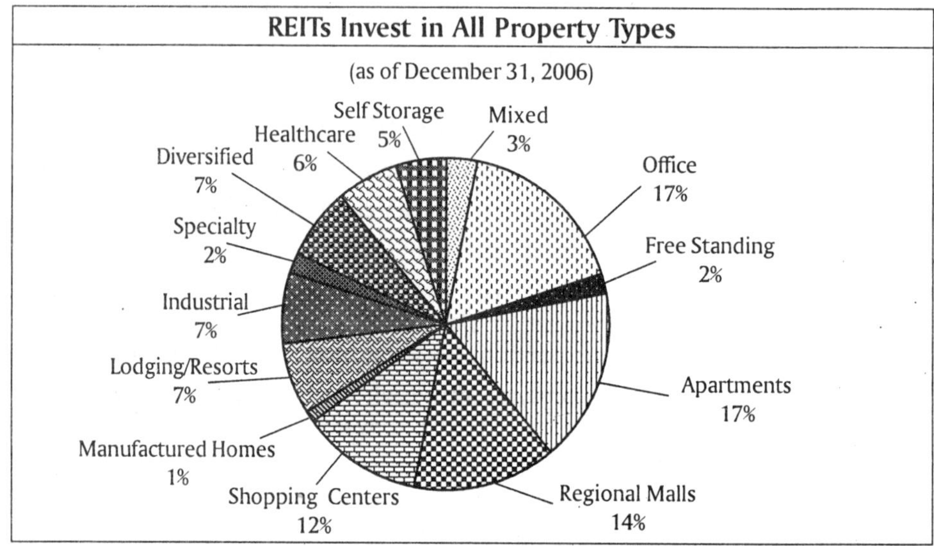

In addition, REITs that have a mortgage-focused investment strategy invest in commercial mortgages and commercial mortgage-backed securities (CMBS) or residential mortgages and mortgage-backed securities (MBS).

Real Estate Investment Benefits

REIT shares clearly can benefit most investors, whether value-driven or growth-oriented, individual or institutional. They offer the benefits of ongoing current income, with the potential for long-term capital appreciation that historically has met or exceeded inflation.

They are equities that derive a large part of their value from tangible, hard assets and the effective management of those assets.

And they have been proven to bring the benefits of balance, diversification and greater risk/reward efficiency to a broad range of investment portfolios.

6

Trends in the Real Estate Private Equity Industry

The real estate private equity fund market has matured into one of the most significant sources of equity financing for real estate transactions. Because of its yield and appreciation potential, real estate is attracting more investment capital flows and the number of funds being created has increased significantly.

Developing this Report

"The 2005 Real Estate Private Equity Market Outlook" provides a robust summary of the trends and developments in the real estate private equity fund sector. This report covers market and capital trends, fund performance and reporting, tax considerations, and infrastructure and technology trends. It is based on data collection and analysis by Ernst & Young real estate professionals dedicated to the private equity fund industry.

The research is a survey of real estate private equity fund sponsors throughout the United States. The survey included 33 questions focused on all aspects of the fund life cycle and of specific interest to the real estate fund community. The responses received were from sponsors representing 179 funds with aggregate capital of $93 billion. Not every respondent answered every survey question and, in some cases, we have supplemented the written responses with personal interviews of fund sponsors and with the general observations of the market.

The survey data in the report is based upon responses received through August 31, 2005, and performance data that are largely based on fund results through the end of 2004.

In some instances, historical data is based on current and prior survey responses, with current responses taking precedence in case of conflict.

This report consists of five parts:

- General Observations and Findings.
- Financial and Performance Reporting Issues.
- Tax Issues.
- Operations and Technology.
- Outlook.

What's Behind the Label?

The US culture is fond of labels. Americans have a deep need to see products and services correctly described and categorized. Businesses, marketers, and fund sponsors understand that if a product is appropriately labeled, it is easier to sell. Nowhere is this more evident than with the myriad labels describing today's fund universe. Core, Core Plus, Enhanced Core, Value Added, Enhanced Value, Aggressive Value, and Opportunity are a sample of the labels used today to describe and market funds. Investors frequently inquire about the definitions and distinctions among these categories.

Unfortunately, there is no bright-line test or definition that separates one category of fund from another. Broadly speaking, these categories speak to a fund's general risk profile and the investor return expectations associated with its strategy (see Figure 1). They generally range from a "core" strategy at the lowest end of the risk curve through an opportunistic strategy that has the highest risk and, potentially, the highest return. Other risk considerations include the type of real estate targeted

Figure 1

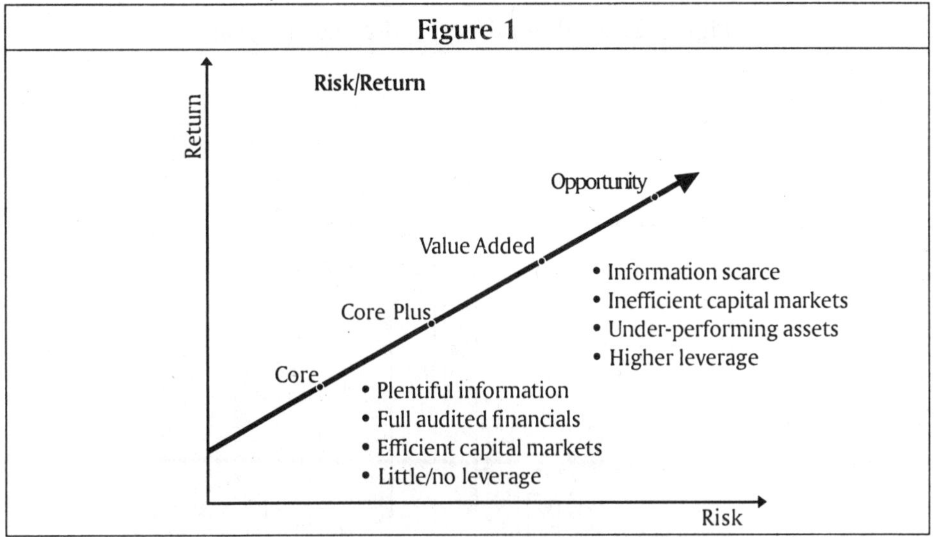

for investment, its market location and the potential volatility of its income stream, as well as the financial leverage or gearing employed in the capital structure.

The Fund-A-Mentals

At the lowest end of the risk spectrum, a Core Fund tends to focus on highly stable, well-tenanted assets that have highly predictable cash flows and are located in strong, well-diversified markets. Additionally, such funds use very little, if any, debt in their capital structures to leverage returns on equity. At the other end of the spectrum are Opportunity Funds, which are focused on "off-market" deals that have significantly higher risk profiles. These deals include distressed assets requiring significant releasing of vacant space, property repositioning or redevelopment, bankrupt real estate companies requiring complicated work-out strategies, assets in tertiary markets without deep liquidity, and international assets whose sponsors must navigate political and currency risks. At a recent Opportunity Fund industry conference, a Fund sponsor described his off-market strategy in the plainest of terms: "We acquire assets that are "broken," we fix them up, stabilize their income streams, and sell them to institutional buyers in search of yield." Opportunity Funds also are highly leveraged (typically 60-70% of a fund's capital structure) to boost equity returns.

In between these extremes is a seemingly infinite combination of profiles with varying degrees of investment and leverage risk. The ultimate risk profile will

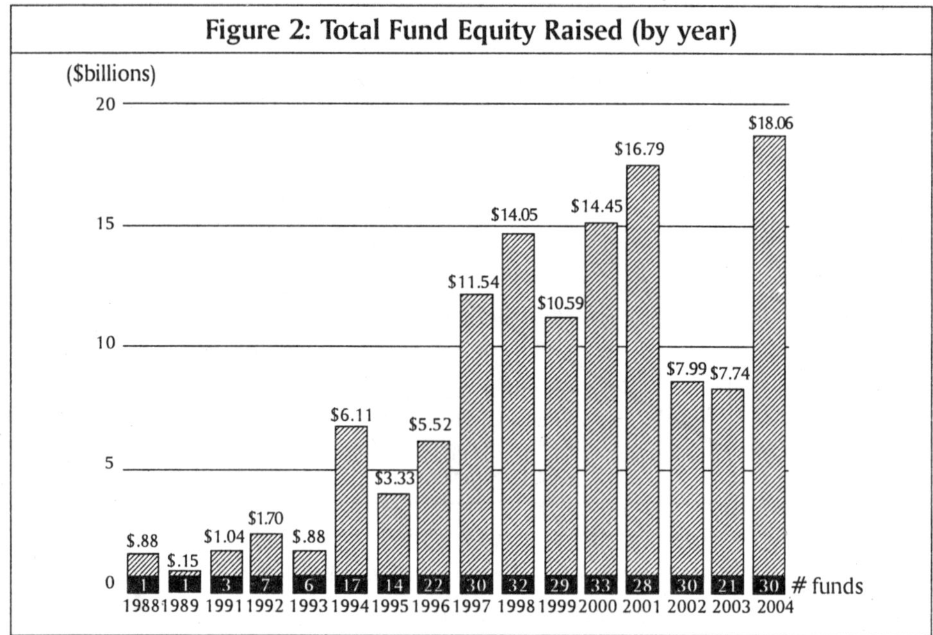

Figure 2: Total Fund Equity Raised (by year)

($billions)
20
15
10
5
0
$.88
$.15
$1.04
$1.70
$.88
$6.11
$3.33
$5.52
$11.54
$14.05
$10.59
$14.45
$16.79
$7.99
$7.74
$18.06
1 1 3 7 6 17 14 22 30 32 29 33 28 30 21 30
funds
1988 1989 1991 1992 1993 1994 1995 1996 1997 1998 1999 2000 2001 2002 2003 2004

Figure 3: Cumulative Fund Equity Raised (by year)

($billions)
150
120
90
60
30
0
$.88
$1.03
$2.07
$3.77
$4.65
$10.76
$14.09
$19.61
$31.15
$45.20
$55.79
$70.24
$87.03
$95.02
$102.76
$120.82
1 2 5 12 18 35 49 71 101 133 162 195 223 253 274 304
funds
1988 1989 1991 1992 1993 1994 1995 1996 1997 1998 1999 2000 2001 2002 2003 2004

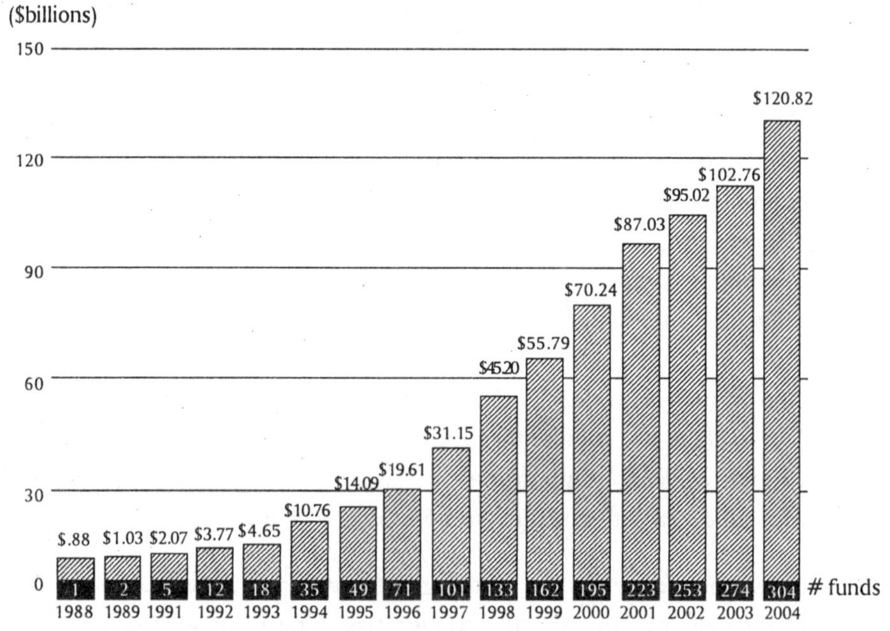

match the return expectations of the fund and marketing professionals looking for a simple moniker to describe the strategy will generally lump the fund with a relevant category. The investment continuum falls into these broad categories:

Table 1

Fund Type	Return Expectations (Gross)[1]
Core	7-10%
Core Plus	11-13%
Value Added	14-17%
Opportunity	18% +

The focus of this study and the source of our data is the portion of the fund sponsor community operating in the Value Added and Opportunity end of the spectrum.

General Observations and Findings

Capital Raising and Availability

Today, the real estate private equity fund market has matured into one of the most significant sources of equity financing for real estate transactions. The Value Added and Opportunity Funds participating in the surveys have raised approximately $120 billion since 1991. Considering that the average fund leverages this equity at 70%, this represents $400 billion of total investment capital that fund sponsors have invested or plan to invest in real estate transactions.

Today's investment markets are awash with capital seeking investments which will produce favorable returns. Investors have diligently searched for investments that meet their yield requirements, but the traditional alternatives are not compelling. Fixed-income securities have produced tepid returns, and, on a risk-adjusted basis, so has the stock market. Investors have shifted to hard assets including real estate, which they judge to have a superior risk reward ratio. Because of its yield and appreciation potential, real estate is attracting more investment capital flows. As a result, the average pension fund's allocation to real estate investment has increased. Considering the hundreds of billions of dollars controlled by pension funds domestically, this shift is clearly significant. Some would argue that the current market for raising capital for Value Added and Opportunity Funds may be the best in 15 years.

1 Before consideration of the fees and the fund sponsors' promoted/carried interest.

Figure 4: Average Fund Equity Raised (by # of funds)

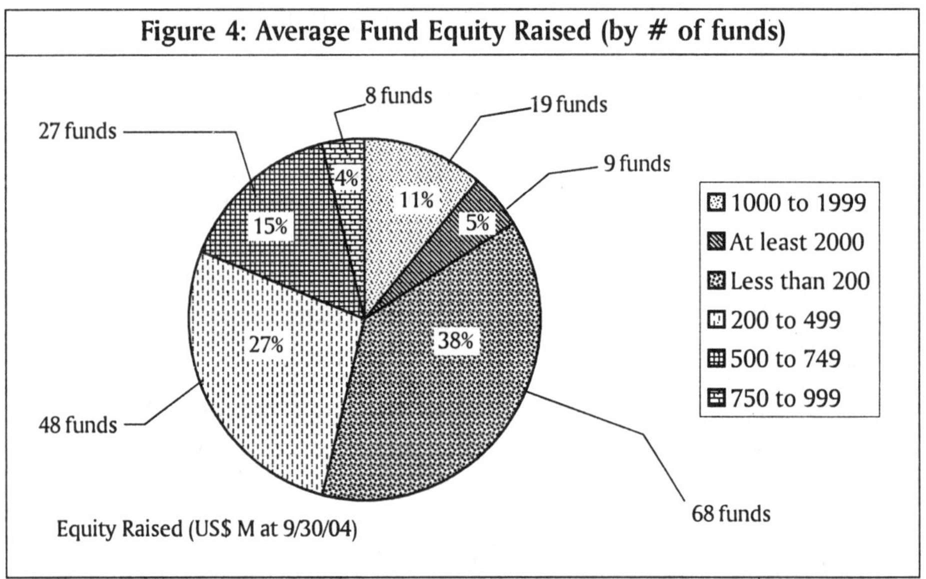

Figure 5: Sources of Fund Capital*

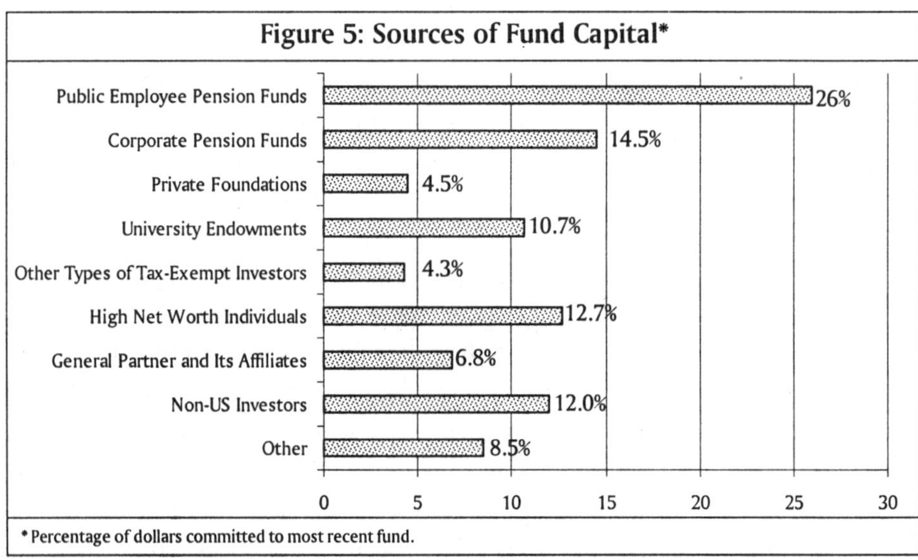

* Percentage of dollars committed to most recent fund.

With the increase in capital flows to the real estate private equity fund sector, the number of funds being created has increased significantly. In 2004, the survey identified 30 new funds representing more than $18 billion of new capital. Respondents have indicated that they had more than $17.5 billion to invest in 2005 and beyond, up from $15.9 billion, available as of 2003, as indicated in our previous survey. Additionally, 23 new funds were reported to be in the process of formation with targeted equity to be raised of $18 billion. With leverage at 70%, this represents more than $118 billion of purchasing power for new transactions. As shown in Figure 5, the majority of investment dollars is coming from public and corporate pension funds, foundations, and endowments. Most of this capital is still domestically sourced, but we have noticed an increasing portion coming from international investors.

Capital Deployment

Inevitably, more capital flowing to real estate depresses capitalization rates and increases real estate pricing. To be sure, this is ideal if a fund is in the monetization phase of its life cycle and selling off investments at near record prices. If a fund is flush with capital, however, and looking to invest, it's a whole different scenario. As fund sponsors know, competition for new investment opportunities is fierce and real estate funds must work harder and be more creative in finding acquisition targets that meet their return expectations.

The survey participants were asked what keeps them up at night. It's a broad question, for sure, but nearly three-fourths answered, "The ability to find investment opportunities that underwrite to return expectations." Also staying of late were the 41% of participants who said that "overpaying for investment opportunities" concerned them.

Interestingly, respondents indicated that their target return expectations average almost 21% on a gross basis (or 17% net of fees and fund-sponsor promote), which is fairly consistent with the prior surveys. With the risk-free rate on 10-year Treasury bonds at or below 4% for much of 2004 and 2005, this would suggest, at least for the short run, that respondents are employing an "absolute return strategy" rather than a "relative return strategy." No matter their cost of capital, these funds are looking to realize a gross return of more than 20%. To achieve this return objective, fund sponsors are moving from mainstream opportunities to "off-market" deals that draw less attention from competitors. In many cases, sponsors continue to move further out on the risk spectrum in order to meet these absolute return expectations.

It's worth noting that fund sponsors have taken full advantage of the increasingly aggressive lending practices that have developed in the marketplace.

In their efforts to put out money, lenders are participating in highly engineered debt structures that assist in leveraging a fund's return to the equity.

As for investment focus, survey respondents are still heavily focused on the US market, with 88% of fund managers indicating that they are looking to invest at least some of their capital in the United States. However, sponsors are increasing their investment allocations to other markets outside the United States, including Asia-Pacific, eastern and western Europe, and Canada. Forty percent of participating fund sponsors, and 76% of fund sponsors with aggregate capital raised in excess of $1 billion, indicated that at least a portion of their investment capital is earmarked for markets outside of the United States. By ratios of 3:1 and 3:2 respectively, respondents indicated that investors can make more than 20% returns in the Asian and European markets. Many of the largest fund sponsors have established separate funds with a focused strategy of international investment. Most respondents remain focused on traditional property types including office, retail, and multifamily, but there is significant investment activity in non-traditional property types such as lodging and leisure properties as well as homebuilders and undeveloped land.

Seventy-five percent of respondents said funds invested more capital in 2004 than in 2003, and two-thirds believed more capital would be invested in 2005 than in 2004.

Investment Monetization

Returns

In the real estate fund universe, the planets are nearly fully aligned with respect to increasing real estate values. Interest rates are at historical lows; both equity and debt capital are readily available from multiple sources. The demand for real estate investments is outstripping the supply of available transactions and the investment alternatives on a risk-adjusted basis are not particularly appealing.

Following textbook supply-and-demand theory, the capital-chasing yield has reduced capitalization rates and increased prices of most real estate. This has been a boon for real estate funds that are fully invested and looking to monetize their investments. Of the 150 funds responding to the returns part of the survey, 77% reported their returns equaled or exceeded their return expectations; 46%

said their returns exceeded expectations; and 23% reported that their returns were below expectations.

Because of the significant demand for real estate investments, funds are monetizing their investments sooner than expected. Most respondents said asset dispositions increased in 2004 and more than half expected a further increase in 2005. As a result, funds are returning capital to investors much more quickly than anticipated and investors are looking to reinvest that capital into real estate funds, starting the cycle again.

Real Estate Fund Terms

As the real estate private equity fund community has matured, the structures and terms of the funds have kept pace. Based upon the responses received from the participants of the survey, the summary of a composite of the typical fund structure is shown in the Table 2.

Table 2

Average fund size	$519 million
Percentage raised from the sponsor/general partner	8%
Original investment period	4 years
Targeted gross returns	20.9%
Target net returns	17%
Preferred return hurdle	10%
General partner promote	20%
General partner catchup percentage	50%
Total leverage limit	70%
General partner fees and reimbursements	Management fees Organization costs Due diligence costs
Permitted to have unrelated business taxable income (UBTI)	Yes, but work to avoid it

With more capital flowing into funds, their size has increased, but not as much as anticipated. A significant number of new but relatively small funds have entered the market, moderating the overall average fund size. As expected, the capital raised by funds from existing sponsors with longer track records has grown considerably, with a $2 billion fund no longer considered unusual.

Fund sponsors were asked what terms within the fund documents potential investors are looking to change or renegotiate. Approximately 28% of the respondents indicated that investors want to modify the general partner's catch-up distribution provisions and 22% indicated that investors want to change the terms of the clawback provisions for general partner promote distributions.

The general partner catch-up percentage provides for the general partner to receive a disproportionate allocation of cash after the limited partners have achieved their preferred return hurdle. The general partners typically receive this catch-up allocation (which is 50% of current distributions based on our composite) until the general partner has achieved its promote (20% of all cumulative distributions, based upon our composite). The clawback provisions provide for the general partner to return to the fund cash previously distributed to the general partner as promote in the event that the subsequent performance of the fund does not achieve the preferred return hurdle for the limited partners.

Due to investor pressure, the general partner catch-up percentage has been trending downwards and the provisions in the fund documents providing for the general partner to collateralize the clawback obligation, through a promote distribution holdback or otherwise, have been strengthening. Similarly, the terms providing for the general partners to receive a promoted distribution have been trending from an investment-by-investment basis to a promote based upon pooled investment returns.

Figure 6: Method of Financial Statement Reporting (by Equity $ Raised)

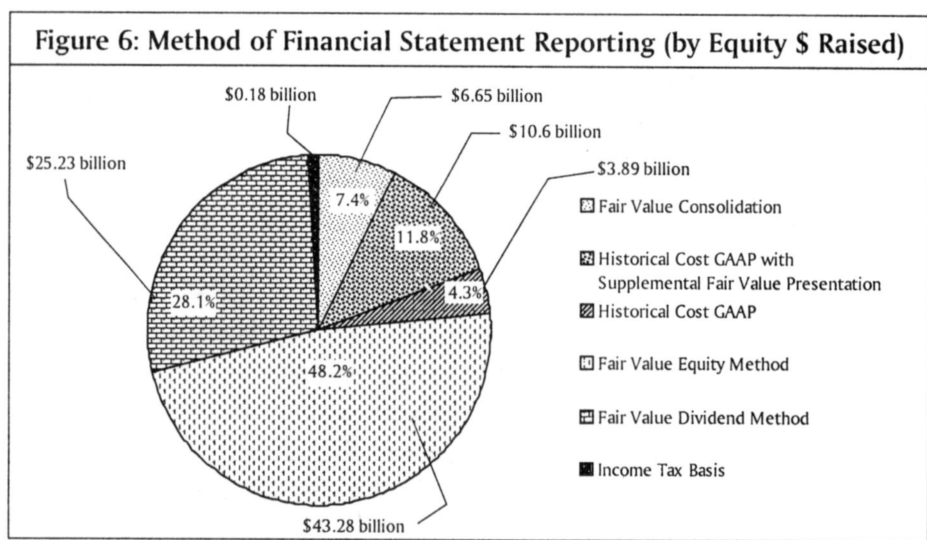

Figure 7: Method of Financial Statement Reporting (by # of Respondents)

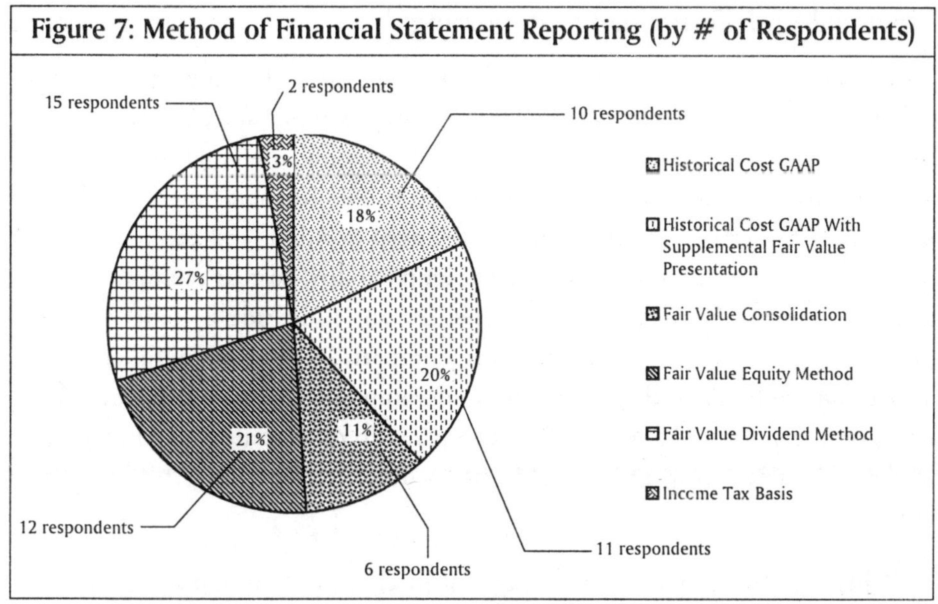

As the heated market makes it increasingly difficult to deploy capital at targeted returns, there has been a great deal of discussion about fund sponsors extending their initial investment periods. However, only 8% of respondents indicated that they would look to negotiate such an extension.

Another structure topic receiving much attention this past year has been funds investing with a joint venture partner and the resulting double promote. Given the significant capital to be deployed in a difficult market, sponsors will often look to provide capital to a local developer for a project conceived and assembled by the developer through a joint venture agreement. As a joint venture partner, the local developer is expected to play a critical role in providing extensive market knowledge and expertise. The local developer will lead the project, and the venture agreement often provides for a promote to be paid to the venture partner in the event certain preferred return hurdles are met. From the fund investor's perspective, this means two promotes may be paid on the same investment, one to the venture partner and one, assuming return thresholds are met, to the fund general partner. In a ratio of almost 2:1, survey respondents indicated that they did not see the double promote structure as a problem and would not seek to avoid it.

Financial and Performance Reporting

Two words are consistently used when the topic of financial reporting is broached: *Transparency* and *Comparability.* Transparency, simply stated, is about full disclosure. It is the reporting of financial information in enough detail that an average investor would be able to read the fund's financial report and fully understand the strategy of the fund, its financial position, and the results of its operations in carrying out its strategy. Comparability, just as it implies, is the ability to lay the financial data disclosed by one fund side by side with that provided by another fund and have the comparison be meaningful. From its earlier and wilder days, the real estate fund community has come a long way in terms of its reporting. However, when compared to other industries and segments of the real estate sector, real estate private equity fund reporting still has a long way to go.

When the survey participants were asked the simple initial question, "On what basis of accounting do you report to your investors?" the responses were highly diverse. It identified three different methods of reporting on a fair value basis, as well as two different methods of accounting (the historical cost GAAP and income tax methods) that generally ignore investment appreciation and reflect annual charges for depreciation. So hypothetically, five different funds could make a joint venture investment in one piece of real estate, and they would use five different methods in reporting to the same investor. Clearly, this is less than ideal.

Efficient markets depend on the quality, reliability, and timeliness of investment information. This data is the basis for analysis, comparison, and evaluation of performance and assists investors and analysts in predicting future returns. If investors find it exceedingly difficult to benchmark, analyze, and differentiate one fund from another, then they understandably might ascribe a higher risk premium to this asset class or, much worse, take their capital elsewhere. Consider the boost that the overall REIT marketplace received when REITs were introduced to the S&P 500. They received a heightened level of scrutiny and greater analyst coverage, which may have resulted in a few headaches for REIT sponsors, but the REIT community now, has access to a significantly broader pool of capital.

Interestingly, accounting and finance personnel at various fund sponsors generally acknowledge the inefficiency caused by the diversity of accounting practices in informal discussions. Most fund sponsors will readily admit that all funds should be on the same basis of accounting—as long as it's the one they are currently using.

All hope is not lost in this area as the AICPA is in the final stages of issuing new supplemental guidance to its *Investment Company Accounting and Audit Guide.* This will provide authoritative guidance on which types of funds qualify as an investment company and which do not. The Table 3 provides the proposed criteria for making such a determination.

Table 3: Requirements to Qualify as an Investment Company

Requirements	**Investment Company**
Expressed business purpose	A separate legal entity, investing in multiple substantive investments for current income, capital appreciation, or both, with investment plans that include exit strategies
Entity's activities, assets, and liabilities	No substantive activities, assets, or liabilities other than its investment activities
Other Factors to Consider	
Number of substantive investors	Multiple
Level of ownership interest in investees	Low
Ownership by passive investors	Substantial ownership by passive investors
Ownership by employee benefit plans	Substantial ownership by employee benefit plans
Involvement in day-to-day management of investees	Limited involvement in day-to-day management of investees
Administrative or support services	Limited administrative or support services provided by the entity or its affiliates
Guarantee arrangements	Investees do not provide financing guarantees or assets to serve as collateral for the entity
Provision of loans to investees by noninvestment company affiliates	May be inconsistent with the definition of an investment company
Compensation of management or employees of investees	Not dependent on entity's financial results
Business relationships between investees	Limited directing of integration of operations of investees

As a result of this guidance, a fund meeting the criteria of an investment company will be required to utilize the fair value accounting practices provided by the *Guide,* with no fair value accounting alternatives permitted. If a real estate fund does not fall within the definition of an investment company, then its GAAP basis accounting framework will be the historical cost method used by real estate investment trusts today. Of course, these funds will always have the option of reporting to investors on a non-GAAP basis, such as the income tax basis; however, for the sake of comparability, it is hoped to be the exception and not the rule.

Returns Reporting

Great strides have also been made to bring consistency to reporting performance returns to investors. Historically, the provisions of GAAP covering investment companies, such as the real estate private equity funds surveyed, required the reporting of a fund's "total return," which is a time-weighted return typically used by pension funds in measuring performance. This computation was largely misunderstood and roundly despised by real estate fund professionals who are largely IRR – focused The irony of the total return computation is that it generally ignores the time value of money.

To the great relief of a number of fund professionals, the GAAP guidance has been modified to allow for an "IRR since inception" computation for private funds meeting certain criteria in lieu of the total return.[2] This computation has been largely embraced by the fund community and is aiding in the fight to create greater comparability of fund returns. This computation is presented net of fees and promote to the general partner.

The Core Fund segment of the business has been greatly aided by the efforts of the National Council of Real Estate Investment Fiduciaries (NCREIF) through the population and use of the NCREIF index. Core Funds submit their property performance data (standardized) to NCREIF each quarter for compiling and publishing a composite average. The composite index is used to benchmark a fund's property portfolio performance against the average. Arguably, this index

---

2 These criteria include: 1) having a limited life; 2) not continuously raising capital and not being required to redeem investor interests upon request; 3) having, as a predominant operating strategy, the return of the proceeds from disposition of investments to investors; 4) having limited opportunities for investors to withdraw prior to termination; and 5) not routinely acquiring market-traded securities and derivatives.

has made the management of Core Fund investments a great deal more efficient. NCREIF has now developed a similar index tool for real estate private equity funds to benchmark fund level performance. However, survey respondents indicated that only 21% currently contribute data; only 10% plan to contribute in the future; and 69% have no current plans of participating. Clearly this is a good start in a positive direction but much work is yet to be done in getting the real estate private equity segment to the point where benchmarking of performance is easily accomplished.

Other Accounting Considerations

During the course of this year, GAAP-based fund sponsors are coming to grips with a new piece of authoritative guidance issued by the Accounting Standards Executive Committee of the AICPA in their Statement of Position No. 04-5. This SOP provides clarification of the guidance for general partners concerning their need to consolidate a fund (which is not a Variable Interest Entity under FIN 46) if they exercise control over the fund. A general partner would not be deemed to "control" a fund if the limited partners had participative rights in the operations and affairs of a fund or if the limited partners had substantive rights to remove the general partner. Participative rights would include approval rights on investment, sale, and financing decisions as examples. Going by the experience with real estate funds today, providing limited partners with participative rights of the kind contemplated by the SOP would be the exception rather than the rule. Substantive "kick-out" rights for the general partner are more common, however, the SOP clarified the definition of "substantive" to include the following:

- Removal of the general partner without cause.
- Removal accomplished by a simple majority of the limited partners (or the lowest possible percentage of partners that would result in an amount above a simple majority, such as 2 out of 3 or 6 out of 10).

It is noted that many fund agreements contain provisions for kick-out rights, but a good portion of them do not meet the criteria established by this SOP. Accordingly, many general partner sponsors are faced with the choice of changing their fund documents to meet the new criteria, or consolidating funds in their financial statements for the first time.

Tax Issues

In the 2005 survey and related discussions with surveyed funds showed the following key trends related to tax matters:

- Most tax-exempt investors now are willing to accept UBTI in order to provide general partners with more flexibility of investment choice to achieve the desired returns (e.g., condominiums and condo hotels). Part debt/part equity structures that meet IRS rules are being used to reduce otherwise unavoidable UBTI through interest deductions. Many general partners reported increasing amounts of time spent on fractions rule issues, including parking, asset management fee payments, and clawback structuring to avoid UBTI.
- Many general partners are foregoing future management fee payments in exchange for the right to receive an equivalent amount of cash from future sale profits. If those profits ultimately occur, this structure has the effect of converting management fee ordinary income to capital gains for the general partner.
- The use of private REITs is increasing in real estate fund structures because REIT blockers are the only way (without paying a corporate level tax) to avoid UBTI for investors who are private foundations or charities, or eliminate the Foreign Investment Real Property Tax Act (FIRPTA) withholding for foreign investors and state tax withholding for all investors.
- General partners are now generally permitted by investors to receive tax distributions for phantom income on their deferred promote, and there is increasing use of tax projections to predict the need for tax distributions and to project the need for REIT distributions to avoid tax.
- Most general partners now are adopting internal tax controls designed to spot accounting and tax allocation errors, and they are doing so early enough in the fund's life to be able to avoid any distortion in cash distributions on liquidation caused by erroneous tax capital accounts that control liquidating distributions.
- There is increased focus on meeting general partner state tax withholding obligations.

The 2005 survey discussions with general partners also showed that many had increased concern about complying with recent regulatory and legislative developments, such as:

- Proposed new rules concerning the receipt of the general partner's carried interest for services;
- New parking revenue UBTI rules; and
- The applicability of the new "Section 470" loss disallowance rules for funds having tax-exempt partners.

UBTI Obligations of the General Partner

UBTI for tax-exempt investors can result from the type of investment (e.g., condominium or home sales, direct ownership of hotels, interest computed on tenant or borrower net profits, an investment that generates operating business income, or under new IRS rules, revenues from paid parking, etc.). But it also can result merely because leverage is used in acquiring or improving an equity or debt investment (absent an exemption, profits generally are UBTI to the percentage extent of average leverage or highest leverage in the year of sale). Under a limited exception, UBTI from leveraged equity investments in real estate (but not in debt or other investments) can be avoided for pension plans and qualified educational institutions (but not by other tax-exempt investors) by complex tax allocation structuring (and following certain related business limitations including restrictions against non-pro rata preferential distributions) that satisfy the IRS's so-called "fractions rule."

Of the funds surveyed, 87% are allowed to have UBTI for pension plans and educational institutions (educational endowments); 89% may incur UBTI for private foundations and charities; and only 8% are required to reimburse the tax-exempt investors for taxes on UBTI (generally by reducing their promote unless a threshold IRR is achieved after UBTI taxes). Almost all of the funds that are allowed to have UBTI indicated that they try to avoid it, but the economics of a proposed investment almost always takes precedence over UBTI restrictions.

Fractions Rule and Other UBTI Issues

In the interviews, many general partners reported that they are spending more time and resources on fractions rule and other UBTI compliance issues, including a recent IRS position on parking revenues that treats income allocable to parking facilities as UBTI (often solved by master leasing the parking facilities to a subsidiary corporation or third-party operator in order to convert parking fees to

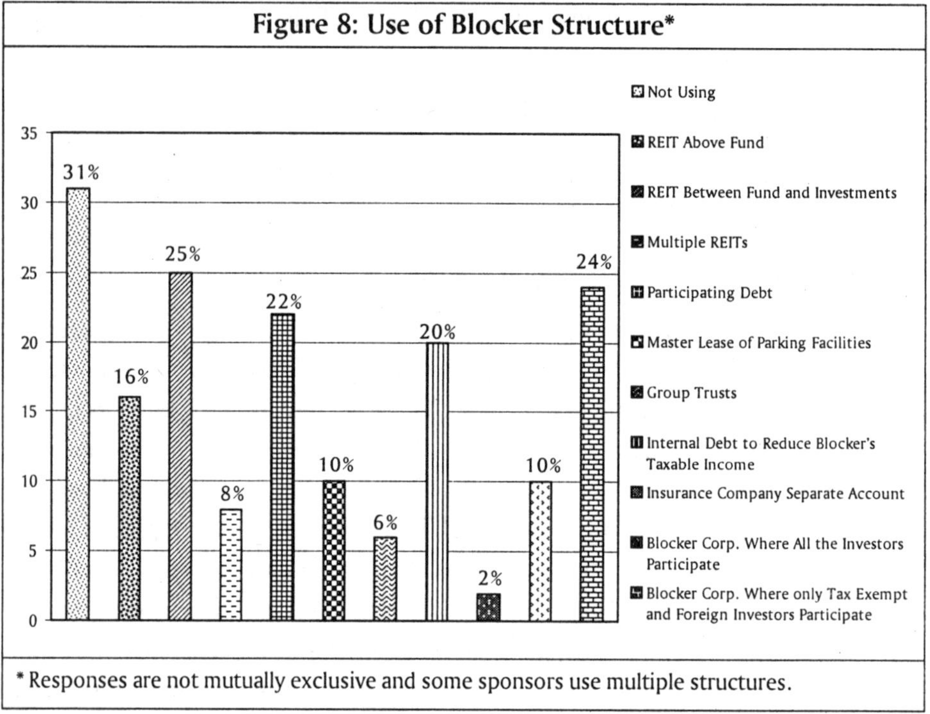

Figure 8: Use of Blocker Structure*

* Responses are not mutually exclusive and some sponsors use multiple structures.

UBTI-exempt rent). To help satisfy the fractions rule issues, surveyed funds reported that:

- More clawback arrangements are being treated as required rebates of management fees (in lieu of being treated as capital contributions that may well cause fractions rule violations if they occur and may also result in non-deductible capital losses for the principals of the general partner).
- Management fees are being paid by the individual investors instead of by the fund (particularly where some of the investors receive a discount on general partner management fees).
- They are making use of alternate default remedy elections (such as loans instead of capital contributions, and discount buyouts) that satisfy the fractions rule.
- There is more extensive UBTI/fractions rule due diligence using the fund's attorneys, tax accountants, internal resources, and UBTI checklists.

UBTI Blockers

A UBTI blocker will have to be used if a fund is required to avoid UBTI for investors such as charities and private foundations (who, by statute, never can qualify for fractions rule relief from leverage-caused UBTI). The most commonly used structure is a privately held REIT, which can be a fund subsidiary through which all of the fund's assets are held, or alternatively, an entity that is an investor in the fund (i.e., the REIT is "above" the fund) through which the UBTI-sensitive investors will invest. Sometimes a corporate blocker (called a taxable REIT subsidiary (TRS) if a REIT is the parent) is used for income that cannot be received by a REIT (e.g., condominium sales profits) or for a UBTI-generating investment owned directly by a fund that is prohibited from having UBTI (the cost is a corporate tax instead of having UBTI). If a REIT blocker is used, the fund no longer is deemed to receive UBTI tainted income – instead, it receives REIT dividends that are tax-exempt for all types of tax-exempt investors (unless the REIT shares are acquired using borrowings).[3]

The 2005 survey showed that almost 70% of surveyed funds use a blocker structure, including 25% that use one or more REITs as a subsidiary of the fund, and 22% that make investments as a participating lender.

General Partner Right to Waive Management Fees

Of the surveyed funds, more than half report that the general partner has the right to waive future management fees that have not yet been earned for tax purposes by the general partner (or by its affiliated investment manager) in exchange for an increased interest in future residual profits of the fund. If structured properly, and the management fees for a property are waived before the investment is acquired, the waiver of the fees creates income deferral for the general partner and the effective conversion of its ordinary fee income (otherwise taxed at a federal 35% rate) to capital gains (taxed at a 15% federal rate). This represents an increase in the after-tax profits of the general partner of more than 30% of the amount of the waived fees. The downside to this arrangement is that the management fee waiver carries with it the economic risk that there will be insufficient appreciation in the properties for which the fee was waived to cover the waived

[3] The sole exception is where the REIT is deemed to be "pension-held," in which case the REIT is disregarded (and the regular UBTI rules apply) for any pension plan that owns greater than a 10% interest in the fund.

fees (which would otherwise have been retained by the general partner even if the investments did not show any overall profit). Additionally, this structure requires careful tracking of the waived fees, investment elections and the related investment income allocations, which can be fairly complicated.

Tax Distributions

A general partner needs to be concerned that it has sufficient distributions from the fund to pay the taxes on its allocated income with respect to it's promote or carried interest. This is particularly true where the general partner's promote distribution from an investment either is placed in escrow to secure the general partner's clawback obligation to repay such promote distributions to the extent necessary to repay investor capital (and/or pay preferred return) on other investments, or where the general partner does not receive its promote until the investors' entire capital and return is repaid (i.e., fully pooled funds). Fund sponsors are sensitive to this "phantom income" issue and 41% of the funds surveyed allow for minimum tax distributions to be made to the general partner to the extent of the deemed tax on promote income allocated to the general partner (This is an exception to the "waterfall" priority for distributions, which require that general partner distributions be escrowed or that capital and preferred return of investors on all investments first be repaid before the general partner receives its promote). All of the funds that provide for special tax distributions require those distributions to be offset against future distributions of promote otherwise due to the general partner, and 14% of the funds surveyed require a clawback of those distributions upon liquidation to the extent there were insufficient cumulative general partner distributions of promote to fully offset the tax distributions made to the general partner. Careful quarterly tax and cash projections are essential to plan for the required distributions and estimated tax payments.

Clawback Issues

A general partner's capital account is potentially overstated whenever it is allocated taxable income attributable to promote distributions that are subject to clawback. To the extent a promote distribution is deemed repayable under IRS rules, however, the promote payment is more akin for tax purposes to a loan than a distribution when it is received, and like a loan, no income should yet be allocated to the general partner. To do otherwise might subject a general partner to having a capital loss on liquidation to the extent it repays distributions of promote that have been matched with income allocations (such a loss would be usable by an individual partner of the general partner only to the extent of $3,000 per year beyond the partner's capital gains for that year). This is a new concept for most general partners and, despite the authority under law, only 16% of the funds surveyed permit the general partner to defer current tax allocations on the promote received subject to clawback to the maximum extent allowed by IRS rules.

Error-Free Distributions/Capital Account Monitoring

General partners need to ensure that distributions are made as advertised – in the order of priorities agreed to in the waterfall distribution provisions of the fund's partnership agreement. However, in order to meet IRS safe harbors and to avoid UBTI, nearly every real estate fund is required to make its liquidating distributions in accordance with the final capital accounts of the partners. Thus, if upon liquidation there is a distortion in the partners' capital accounts caused by improperly allocated tax items (whether by mistake in structure or application, or as a result of an IRS reallocation of tax items), distributions will not be able to be made in the priority originally negotiated in the cash distribution waterfall section of the fund's partnership agreement.

It is important to identify as early as possible whether a fund has this problem. As a result, most of the funds surveyed are instituting procedures that regularly test the partners' relative capital accounts against the intended ultimate waterfall distributions (after tentatively allocating taxable income and loss each year, but before filing the returns). The 2005 survey showed that 67% of funds monitor capital accounts at least annually, with 57% doing it quarterly. Many funds are also adopting savings clauses in their partnership agreements that satisfy the IRS safe harbors for tax allocations, satisfy the UBTI fractions rule, and ensure that tax allocations will produce correct tax capital accounts that will permit the intended cash waterfall distributions on liquidation. The earlier a distortion problem is discovered, the more options are available to the general partner to cure the distortion without violating the fractions rule. General partners should have authority to perform corrective allocations not just in the year of liquidation, but during the entire life of the fund.

Figure 9: Frequency of Analysis of Capital Accounts to Match Intended Waterfall*

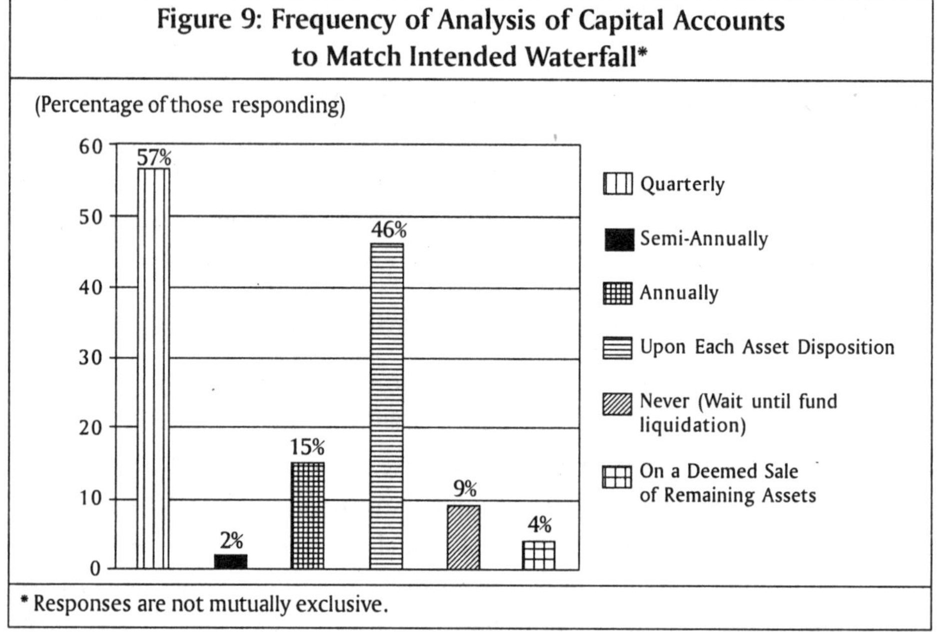

* Responses are not mutually exclusive.

Tax Projections

Tax projections that show UBTI and taxable income or loss are necessary for proper investor tax planning and management of REIT and other distributions. However, less than 20% of the funds surveyed say they prepare tax projections for all investors, and 50% of those funds do so as a partnership expense.

Tax Return and Withholding Obligations

General partners and investors alike share the common desire to receive timely and accurate Form K-1s showing income, loss, and UBTI for the year. Almost 30% of the funds surveyed report that they issue estimated K-1s and then update them later with final K-1s after April 15, and more than 70% of the funds only issue final K-1s. The K-1 process can be automated and often is tied in with the automated cash waterfall, tax allocation, and tax projection processes.

General partners have obligations under federal law to make sure the appropriate withholding is taken on the various kinds of partnership income attributable to partners who are foreign persons (including FIRPTA withholding). Most state laws now also impose an obligation on general partners to withhold

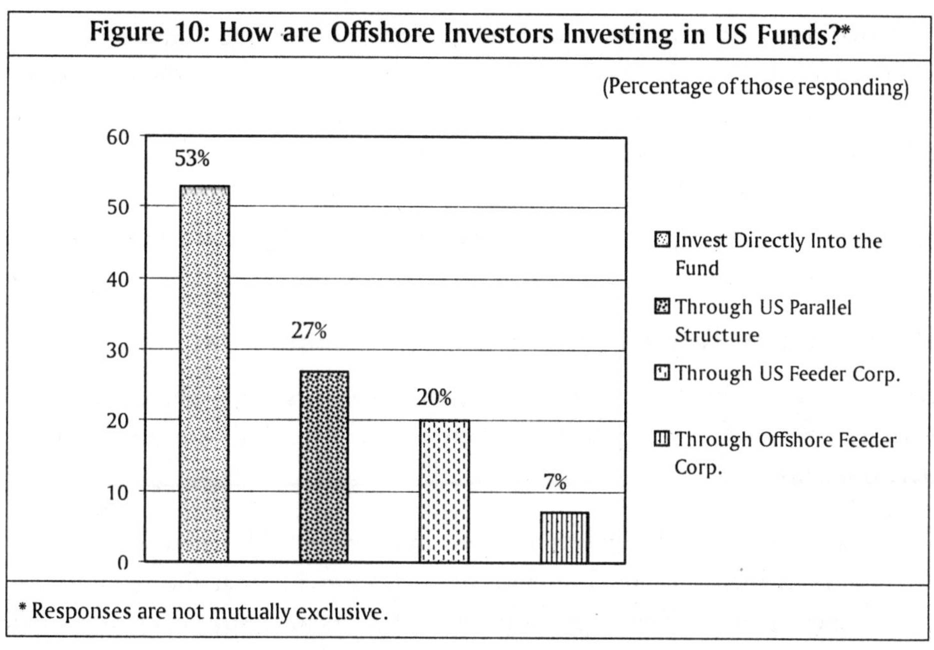

Figure 10: How are Offshore Investors Investing in US Funds?*

* Responses are not mutually exclusive.

tax on distributions to all partners (including the general partner) with respect to fund investments in those states. About half of the funds surveyed have the general partner's internal staff monitor these state withholding requirements, and almost 75% involve their outside accountants in the process. In their search for revenue, the states are beefing up their enforcement efforts. General partners should review their withholding policies each quarter to be sure they are in compliance with the constantly changing requirements of all of the jurisdictions in which their fund has invested. General partners also need to be sure that the fund treats withheld taxes as having been distributed to investors for purposes of the IRR distribution waterfall and the tax allocations.

Foreign Investors/Foreign Taxes

All of the funds surveyed that invest outside the United States indicated informally that they spend a great deal of effort, at fund expense, in structuring to minimize their foreign taxes. In most cases, the non-US structures are very complicated because offshore coinvestment vehicles must be used to joint venture with the US fund so that non-US investors will be able to participate without having any US tax reporting, withholding, or estate tax obligations.

Based on the discussions with fund general partners, the number of funds with offshore investors is increasing. Of the respondents with offshore investors, 53% have foreign investors who invest directly in the fund; 27% invest through a US parallel partnership; and 27% invest through a feeder corporation (20% use a US feeder and 7% use an offshore feeder). The country of ownership of the foreign investor and the number of foreign investors will generally determine the structure used.

Responding to Regulatory/Legislative Developments

As this research paper goes to print, the general partners surveyed are consulting with their tax advisors and return preparers as to how to deal with three new tax developments:

1. Proposed new IRS regulations issued in May 2005 (that now would apply only in their current form prospectively) provide that the receipt by a general partner of the right to receive its profits interest/promote in a fund (or the receipt by a principal of the general partner of its future profits interest in the general partner) is a taxable event. However, the proposed rules do provide for certain elections that may be made to defer income with respect to the grant of a typical profits interest.
2. The IRS parking revenue ruling discussed above leaves unanswered questions as to the extent to which parking revenues might be treated as UBTI even if there are no stated charges for parking in the tenant leases.
3. The 2004 Jobs Act Section 470 disallows the deductibility of tax losses by any fund with tax-exempt investors (to the extent of the highest income percentage of the tax-exempts) where there is "tax-exempt use property." This provision was designed to disallow tax losses of a taxable buyer of real estate from a tax-exempt entity who then leases the property back to the tax-exempt (transferring unusable losses of the tax-exempt owner to the taxable purchaser in a so-called "sale in/lease out" transaction). As drafted, however, the law arguably applies to all funds with tax-exempt investors in which the general partner has a promote. Because of the uncertainty, the IRS granted funds that had no actual leases to tax-exempt tenants an exemption from the rule for 2004 returns, but the issue still remains open for 2005 and future tax years.

Operations and Technology

The operational environment of real estate private equity funds today, driven by increasing competition and larger numbers of sophisticated investors, has become ever more challenging. Fund sponsors are struggling to keep up with the myriad of investor demands and the operations and technology solutions to meet them. Operational expenditures that have been made to date by fund sponsors are aligned first and foremost with the increasing demands of investors and secondarily with key changes and trends in the industry. However, the focus has been mainly on "front-office" functions, often at the expense of "back-office" needs.

As the real estate private equity industry has continued its maturation, the underlying technology supporting funds has matured as well, though the private real estate fund industry still has a long way to go when compared to other industries. Funds that previously focused simply on assembling the fundamental building blocks required for the baseline operations of the fund are now beginning to put their operational investment dollars toward automating manual processes and implementing new "value-added" tools. For example, 91% of fund survey respondents indicated that they have an automated general ledger in place, 89% utilize online bank interfaces or cash management systems, 85% have a website, and 72% have an asset management database.

Although comparatively slow, innovation and investment are starting to occur with respect to the external interfaces of the real estate fund community. More than a quarter of the survey respondents reported plans to implement web-based investor reporting functionality and 16% of respondents are planning to implement an investor relations database. These tools are expected to strengthen the link between investors and the funds by providing better access to more comprehensive data on a real-time basis.

Based on the survey, innovation of back-office functionality has not been a significant focus. Investment in the back office (where enhanced functionality might be transparent to investors and other parties external to the real estate fund), might include strengthening of internal controls, enhancing data security and optimizing process efficiency.

The requirements of Sarbanes-Oxley have been top of mind for many corporate leaders in the US marketplace with record levels of investment being made to improve corporate governance and internal controls. While there has been some level of discussion with investors and consultants about strengthening fund level internal controls, the movement in this area has been fairly insignificant. Supporting this notion, only 4% of respondents indicated that they plan to make improvements to their corporate/fund governance and less than 20% have plans to create an outsourced internal audit function.

Sarbanes-Oxley does not technically apply to private equity firms and as such, its impacts are only tangential. However, there are many who look to the future and see change coming. The real question that needs to be asked and answered is whether market forces will compel private equity funds to meet Sarbanes-Oxley standards, regardless of the fact that they are not required by law. Media publications abound with speculation, such as that from a CFO of a fund sponsor (reported by *Business Week),* "There is an expectation among our investors that we have an institutional approach to our accounting and reporting." *Business Week* also reported, "The move toward accounting and control for private companies is here to stay." One CEO, reported by *Financial Executives International,* was quoted as saying, "Compliance is not a matter of if, but when. Private companies have the advantage of doing it now at their own pace." *Business Week* also reported this year that New York and California were considering asking private companies to comply with Sarbanes-Oxley type regulations. Only time will tell on this particular issue, but its potential impact is such that all fund sponsors should keep their eye on it to avoid being caught off guard.

One of the back-office challenges faced by real estate funds is data security. Simply defined, data security is the means of ensuring that data is kept safe from corruption. This generally entails establishing procedures to restrict access to authorized personnel and to protect the data from unauthorized modification, destruction, or disclosure, whether accidental or intentional. At the fund level, 77% of the survey respondents indicated that appropriate security measures were in place to safeguard their financial and investment level data. Turned around, this means that one of five respondents (23%) was not confident enough to make that statement. Clearly this shows some room for improvement on a fundamental level. Furthermore, with respect to the integrity of data flowing into the fund from joint venture partners, the percentage drops considerably. Only 42% of survey respondents indicated that there were security measures in place to safe-guard joint venture partner data. Given that funds to rely on the joint venture partners' data reporting, a deficiency at the partner level may very well translate into an issue for the fund.

In the near term, it is expected to see greater focus on back-office functions and more focus on controls, especially if the influences of Sarbanes-Oxley expand into the private fund arena. As real estate market dynamics produce increased competition for investor dollars, we expect the trend toward investment in operational processes and technologies supporting investor interface to continue. Finally, as commercial vendors offer better solutions to automate functions such as waterfall modeling (and other types of modeling), we anticipate that a larger portion of funds will put their investment dollars toward such automation. Until that time, Excel spreadsheets are likely to remain the solution of choice.

Outlook

As we look to the future and attempt to predict the course of the current markets and investor sentiment, many questions come to mind: Where are interest rates headed? When will the yields on stocks, bonds, and other real estate investment alternatives improve? Will the political climate stabilize? The survey respondents were asked a number of questions about the future and responses are summarized in Table 4.

Most compelling is the sentiment that interest rates will continue to rise, but such movement in the cost of capital will not expand the availability of opportunity investments. Further, by a margin of 5:1, the survey respondents believe that investors' return expectations in this opportunity constrained environment, will trend downward over the next few years.

The performance of the real estate fund markets will be impacted by the answers to these questions. The debate about the future will continue, and the investment community will place its investment capital with those funds they feel have the best risk-adjusted return strategy. One thing seems clear – the real estate private equity market continues to mature, setting up a competitive landscape which will demand the best from each and every fund professional. As with any competitive landscape, there will be winners and there will be losers, but the real estate private equity market is here to stay.

Table 4

Question	Majority Response	Response Ratio
Do you expect interest rates to continue to rise?	Yes	19:1
Do you expect more opportunity purchase opportunities in 2005 as a result of rising interest rates?	No	50:50
Do you expect the pace of capital deployment in 2005 to be greater than 2004?	Yes	3:2
Do you expect the pace of asset dispositions in 2005 to be greater than 2004?	Yes	5:4
Will investors reduce their return expectations for opportunity investing in the next few years?	Yes	4:1
Will investors participate in a follow-on fund if the prior fund's capital is not fully committed?	Yes	3:1
Will an active secondary market for fund limited partnership interests exist in the next 12 months?	No	3:2
Will the majority of your equity be invested with local partners?	Yes	5:4

Next year it will be apparent whether real estate was on a "bubble" or just riding the established currents of supply and demand economics. We will also then bear witness to what the right fund, with the right management team, possessing the mental flexibility and business acuity to find, acquire, and reinvigorate assets in a difficult market can accomplish – and how long or well those that cannot will survive.

7

Globalization of Real Estate Capital Flows

Raj Bhandari and Tim Morris

In the international marketplace, there's a big transformation of real estate taking place. It's going from non traditional real estate owners and moving in bulk to organizations dealing with real estate funds. The ability to allocate capital to multiple markets equates to better risk adjusted returns. The article discusses about the growth of public real estate market in India and highlights the market conditions in various countries like Japan, Russia, China, Europe, Mexico and Spain.

India's Real Estate Market: On the Radar Screen at Last

Not so long ago, real estate in India failed to arouse much interest from global or domestic investors, said Raj Bhandari. Indian banks and Indian pension funds were largely not allowed to invest in real estate in India. It was almost completely financed by entrepreneurs and end users. If one wanted to buy a house or apartment a few years ago the odds were that they paid the entire purchase price in cash. Mortgages were generally too expensive. Add to that the fact that real estate in India was expensive and one of its cities (Mumbai) was ranked as one of the most expensive in the world.

Source: www.cudenver.edu © University of Colorado Health Services Center. Reprinted with permission. Permission to reprint provided by authors Raj Bhandari and J Timothy Morris and by the session facilitator, David Stanford, Executive Managing Director and Founder of Real Foundations Inc.

"As to my personal experience in India, in 1996-97, I was the only person in India representing an institutional real estate investment firm when I represented Hines' real estate fund with Morgan Stanley and TCW." After India conducted underground nuclear tests in early 1998, the Fund withdrew from the Indian market. Two years ago, Bhandari once again returned to India to explore opportunities in real estate. "People like Morgan Stanley and Hines basically said, 'Thanks, but no thanks. India is not on the radar.'" Likewise, a year-and-a-half ago, at one of the largest real estate trade shows in the world, "there was not a single desk or representative from India." Fast forward to 2005 and you find "almost every major real estate conference listing an Indian panel," said Bhandari.

"Approximately 15 firms at present including some of the largest real estate firms in the world are currently seeking to set up shops in India, including Morgan Stanley, Blackstone and Apollo." Bhandari attributes this newfound interest to a piece of Indian legislation enacted in February 2005 which relaxed government restrictions on foreign direct investment in real estate. The new FDI guidelines "opened the floodgates" of foreign investment into all sectors of India's real estate market.

But Bhandari noted, "It's still a very, very, young and emerging market, similar to what you may have seen in the US in the 1930s or 40s. India's real estate market has not matured to the level where one can get accurate and reliable numbers on market size, etc.; the information just doesn't exist. Information for a subset, which includes newer developments in larger metros, there are more reliable numbers – on rental rates, market size, cap rates, etc. But this subset is a small portion of the total market." The mortgage market is fueling real estate investment domestically.

"The mortgage market as a percent of GDP in India is one of the lowest, partly because historically the interest rates have been higher in India and tax benefits have been lagging. But that has changed," said Bhandari, pointing to the greater availability of mortgages along with a lowering of interest rates. "In 10 years the interest rates have gone from approximately 15 percent to about the current 8 percent."

10th Largest GDP

"The fact that India is the tenth largest economy by GDP can be misleading," said Bhandari. "The numbers – more than a billion people – are what make it the 10th largest economy. The average income of an Indian, meanwhile, is comparable to some of the poorest countries in the world: around $650, $700 per year." However, the average annual income doesn't tell the whole story. According to Bhandari, the purchasing power of India's middle class, which numbers 200 million, is the real driver. "Incomes of middle class Indians are growing by approximately 15 percent a year. The middle class is increasingly becoming urban and consumption oriented." As an example of how consumer patterns have changed, Bhandari offered these statistics: "In 1991, 150,000 cars were sold. The sales at present are around a million."

Reforms have stimulated growth in other areas. In 1991, there was only one airline company in India; today there are eight domestic carriers. And India has become the world's second largest market for aircraft manufacturers, a vast change in just the last 10 years.

"Organized retail outlets are also growing. One example is malls, projected to grow from 30 in 2005 to around 300 in 2008." India's highly educated, lower-cost workforce, which is drawing foreign companies to outsource various business processes to its shores, will continue to fuel growth in the country and ramp up demand for real estate, said Bhandari.

Obstacles?

"Infrastructure is a big problem. People sometimes are building Class A office buildings before there is a road to get to them. Highways are being planned and built rapidly but it's going to take time for the country to put in place an infrastructure that one expects from an economy of its size. For example, trains, the preferred form of transportation for most Indians, require large infrastructure upgrades. Three or four major airports are being privatized and Bangalore, one of the fastest growing metros and one everyone hears about as being the Silicon Valley of India, will only now have an international airport." A guest remarked, "India is still a country with enormous poverty and little infrastructure. But for what they have, they have really produced outstanding results."

Global Investing: Competition for Capital Creates Opportunities

"Morgan Stanley has been investing in real estate since 1990," said Tim Morris. "We have invested in 17 markets around the world ranging from Western Europe to Japan, China, Hong Kong, Taiwan, Singapore, Thailand and Brazil." About 50 percent of Morgan Stanley's $40 billion of real estate holdings is in the United States, 25 percent in Europe and 25 percent in Asia.

The ability to allocate capital to multiple markets equates to better risk adjusted returns. "Our total returns have been 21 percent back to investors over a 15-year period of time." Japan is Morgan Stanley's largest and best performing market, with a workforce of 120 people. "We started investing in Japan in 1997 and the return has been about 37 percent," said Morris.

"All real estate is local. So we now have 19 offices around the world including London, New York, Milan, Beijing, Shanghai, Mumbai, Tokyo and Hong Kong. The other aspect of international real estate investing is to have good local partners; you can't do it by yourself." Identifying those partners takes a lot of time, he added. Morgan Stanley has "close to 200 operating partners around the world." In China, the challenge has been to figure out who has what it takes to qualify for partner. "The prospective partners are all young, strong companies that are ambitious but they need a lot of help from us to get to the level where they can deal with international institutional investors," said Morris.

In the international marketplace, "there's a big transformation of real estate taking place," he said. "It's going from nontraditional real estate owners and moving in bulk to organizations like Morgan Stanley Real Estate Funds. We manage the properties for a couple of years, stabilize them, improve them and start to show a positive story. Then we sell them out on the retail side. That wholesale-to-retail trade has been a big market for us." Typically the buyers in these transactions are local investors.

Western-style properties have set the standard worldwide; consequently, "the architecture has become very homogeneous," said Morris. "It would be very sad if one day you wake up and can't tell whether you're in Hong Kong, Mumbai or Shanghai. But that's kind of where it's going."

Market Highlights

Morris identified what he called interesting markets and opportunities.

- "Japan's JREITs, which started about five years ago, are now a $20 billion market. We think it's probably going to $60 billion over the next five years. The dividend yield of the JREITs, many of which are portfolios of Class A office buildings, is at about 3.5 percent. It's going to make a lot of sense for a lot of capital to find its way into JREITs.
- In Russia, Moscow is a city of 12 million people and there is a huge need for housing just as there is in India. There is no lack of capital in Moscow today but clever real estate groups don't want to be associated with some of that capital because it comes with a lot of baggage.
- China is a very under-retailed market. Wal-Mart has extremely ambitious growth plans in the country. They want to have 400 stores there in 10 years. You can't own land as a private investor but you can get a 70 year lease. In other situations like Hong Kong, there are fairly well-established ways to renew that lease when it expires and investors don't seem to be deterred by this restriction.
- India's poor infrastructure is going to be one of the big challenges. Morgan Stanley is starting to look at real estate investments there. Eighteen months ago the rules were such that the only thing we could invest in was 200 acre master planned communities, which contain so much risk we would never do it.
- Mexico has a housing shortage of five million housing units; they're building about 350,000 a year. The demographics spell opportunity for investors: 700,000 new household formations a year; 60 percent of the population under the age of 30; a median age of 24.
- Turkey is a phenomenal market. Istanbul with 12 million people does not have a Western covered shopping center anywhere. The new mortgage law that went into effect November 1 is going to change the way people spend the small and precious capital they have because the first thing they'll want is a nice place to live. So you're going to see a lot of investments there.

Turkey is definitely a market that is up and coming and getting a lot of interest.

- Spain is a great call in the developed markets. It's got higher growth and the interest rates are low for what's going on in that market. So capital is going to continue to flow into Spain as long as that growth continues and interest rates are where they are. I think you're going to see it in all the European Union ascension countries.
- Europe is a very exciting place to be an investor. The various countries are still competing with each other for capital and capital competition among these governments creates opportunity. One government does something that turns out well and other governments copy it and try to do it better. The competition continues to create good investment opportunities."

A pan-European environment would be a turnoff for investors. "In Europe we want Europe-specific opportunities and country specific opportunities because the cycles in these countries differ from one another. A pan-European block would flatten everything out and make it less interesting to us as professional investors." Social issues at the local level will keep this from happening, he added.

Capital is flowing freely across borders in search of opportunities. That makes capital less of a prize. "What we say to people right now is that your competitive advantage in landing a good investment is not capital; everybody's got capital. If you've got access to deals, that's the most precious commodity in these markets today."

To illustrate this point, Morris referred to a transaction involving a publicly traded company that Morgan Stanley took private a year ago. The company was Canary Wharf, a $10 billion office estate in London. "It took us only six phone calls to raise the capital based on our ability to control the deal internationally and then go into syndication."

Billions of dollars in capital earnings are piling up in the oil producing countries. "At $60 a barrel, the oil countries are flush with cash and they have a hard time figuring out how to get that money invested. "So we are benefiting tremendously from people coming to us – as I'm sure all the international managers are –

wanting to write checks for $200 million to $400 million a pop and asking how soon we can get it invested," said Morris.

"We're seeing a lot of that capital and the deals that we're pursuing are big and complicated and must be worked out. We're not just buying an office building."

(Raj Bhandari is principal at West University Capital. He has 20 years of real estate experience in the areas of principal investment, development and management including with Hines and Bakers Trust. Bhandari is actively evaluating several investment and development opportunities in India. Bhandari has been instrumental in the formation of SUN-Apollo Indian Real Estate Fund, which is currently raising $300 million in equity. Previously, he represented Hines and its real estate fund in India. Bhandari has a BSc from the University of Bombay and an MBA from Kellogg Graduate School of Management.

J Timothy Morris is a managing director of Morgan Stanley, serves as the global chief financial officer of Morgan Stanley's real estate investing business, is the global chief investment officer of the Morgan Stanley Real Estate Special Situations Fund II and is an investment committee member of the Morgan Stanley Real Estate Funds. He previously served as the co-head of Morgan Stanley's European real estate investing business in London and spent the previous 13 years in New York and Hong Kong assisting real estate clients in accessing the international debt and equity capital markets. He received his BS in finance from Indiana University.)

World Development Indicators Database World Bank, 15 July 2005 Top 20 Countries		
	Total GDP 2004	
Ranking	Economy	(Millions of US dollars)
1	United States	11,967.515
2	Japan	4,923.398
3	Germany	2,714,418
4	United Kingdom	2,140,808
5	France	2,002.582[a]
a	Italy	1,672.302
7	China	1,649.329
8	Spain	991.442
9	Canada	979.794
10	India	691.876
11	Korea, Rep.	679.674
12	Mexico	676.467
13	Australia	631.256
14	Brazil	604.855
15	Russian Federation	582.395
10	Netherlands	577.260
17	Switzerland	359.465
18	Belgium	349.830
19	Sweden	346.404
20	Turkey	301.950

[a] Data includes the French overseas departments of French Guiana, Guadeloupe, Martinique, and Réunion.

8

Global Real Estate Securities – Where do they Fit in the Broader Market?

Fraser Hughes and Jorrit Arissen

The real estate investment market is increasingly global. It seems that a growing number of real estate operating companies and Real Estate Investment Trusts (REITs) are investing cross border. In addition, listed real estate investment managers are continuing to role out multi-region/global investment products. This globalisation trend begs the question: what is the size of the investment grade, or high quality commercial[1] global real estate market?

The Methodology

It is clear that we cannot value every individual building and combine their values to arrive at a figure for the total global real estate universe. However, we can estimate the size of individual country commercial real estate markets using a Gross Domestic Product (GDP) top down approach, and aggregate their values to arrive at a total global estimate. Of course, individual countries are in varying stages of development, therefore, we must adjust country estimates to account for the economic situation. With regard to the sample, we selected 49 countries

1 Not including residential property.

from four separate regions: Asia-Pacific, Europe, Latin America and North America. In developed countries[2] high quality commercial real estate represents approximately 45 percent of GDP. In developing countries[3] this figure is lower. We based our estimates on a formula devised by Prudential Real Estate Investors.[4]

Figure 1: The Prudential Formula

The Formula:

For developed countries: $RE_i = GDP_i \, x \, 0.45$

For developing countries $RE_i = GDP_i \times 0.45\left(\frac{GDH_i}{20{,}000}\right)^{\frac{1}{3}}$

Where:

RE_i = Country high-quality commercial real estate value

GDP_i = Country Gross Domestic Product

GDH_i = Country Gross Domestic Product per capita

We used weighted average GDP figures from the World Bank Organisation for the years 2001, 2002, 2003 and 2004. The years are weighted 10, 20, 30 & 40 percent, with the lightest weighting applied to 2001 and the heaviest to 2004. The weighted procedure dampens the effects of GDP and currency fluctuation. The latest 2004 population figures were used to calculate GDP per capita[5]. We adjusted the Hong Kong and Singapore markets by doubling, or using a factor of 100 percent to adjust for density issues and the UK market was re-valued up by 25 percent to take into account the heavy presence of the London market. The complete results can be viewed in Figure 6. It is worth noting that it does not attempt to assess the 'invested' universe. In other words, the real estate that is of suitable investment grade, and held directly by investors[6].

---

2 In this analysis, "Developed countries" are classified as those countries with GDP per capita greater than US$20,000.

3 "Developing countries" are classified as those countries with GDP per capita less than US$20,000.

4 "A Bird's Eye View of Global Real Estate Markets" – Prudential Real Estate Investors, Dr. Youguo Liang & Nancy Gordon. March 2003.

5 Liang & Gordon used weighted averages for GDP, and GDP per capita, in their March 2003 report for the years 1999 through 2002.

6 For further reading in this area see: "An Inventory of the investible market in 11 European countries", Hordijk and Ahlqvist, 2004.

Figure 2: Top 15 Real Estate Markets Globally					
Countries	**GDP ($bn)**	**GDP per capita ($bn)**	**Real Estate ($bn)**	**Weight**	**Cumulative**
United States	11,105	37,897	4,997	34.42%	34.42%
Japan	4,370	34,316	1,966	13.54%	47.96%
Germany	2,388	28,977	1,075	7.40%	55.36%
United Kingdom	1,847	30,641	1,039	7.15%	62.52%
France	1,757	29,075	791	5.45%	67.96%
Italy	1,461	25,162	657	4.53%	72.49%
Canada	879	27,046	396	2.72%	75.22%
Spain	840	20,863	378	2.60%	77.82%
Hong Kong/China	1,618	1,239	288	1.98%	79.80%
South Korea	612	12,689	237	1.63%	81.43%
Australia	516	25,937	232	1.60%	83.03%
Netherlands	508	31,122	229	1.57%	84.61%
Mexico	654	6,235	200	1.38%	85.98%
Switzerland	320	42,995	144	0.99%	86.98%
Belgium	304	29,413	137	0.94%	87.92%
Other Countries	5,596	-NA-	1,754	12.08%	100.00%
Global Total	**34,776**		**14,519**	**100.00%**	

Sources: World Bank Organisation, FTSE, EPRA.

Top 15 Real Estate Markets

Figure 2 shows that the total size of the global real estate market is estimated to be nearly US$14.5 trillion. No surprises that the United States has by far the largest real estate market in the world. The estimated size of the US market is approximately US$5 trillion, or in other terms, one third of the world's high quality commercial real estate is located in the United States. Japan ranks second with around US$2 trillion, followed by the four major European economies. The German market is approximately US$1.1 trillion, with the UK just behind at approximately US$1 trillion. France is close to US$800 billion. Italy is approximately US$660 billion. Canada comes in at just under the US$400 billion mark. The top 15 countries comprise around 88 percent of the total global real estate market. Interestingly, the top five countries hold 68 percent of the total. The next ten countries add 20 percent and the remaining 34 countries make up the final 12 percent.

Figure 3: Market Share Breakdown Under Asset Class Category

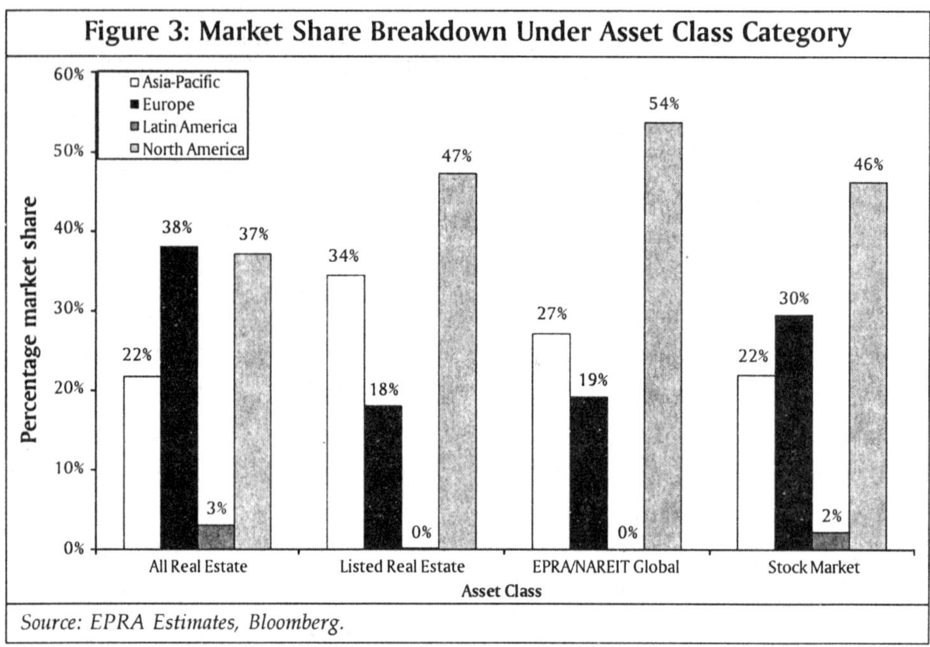

Source: EPRA Estimates, Bloomberg.

Figure 3 (reading from left to right), is split into four separate 'asset classes', or investment categories. The first category is all commercial real estate. At a regional level, total commercial European real estate, Europe is the most heavily weighted at approximately 38 percent of the total market. North America just falls behind at around 37 percent, with the Asia-Pacific region a long way off at 22 percent. Latin America makes up approximately three percent of the total. Focusing on the second section of Figure 3, the composition is very different. This section details the total listed[7] real estate markets. North America leaps head and shoulders above the three other regions. North American listed real estate comprises 47 percent of the global total. Asia-Pacific makes up 34 percent, with Europe lagging significantly behind at 18 percent. Latin America has no real listed real estate market to speak of. Section three, the FTSE EPRA/NAREIT[8] free float market capitalisation percentages, pushes the North American market still further (54 percent), at the expense of Asia-Pacific

[7] The estimated market value for the stock exchange listed real estate is based on equity market capitalisation. The figures do not include leverage, and therefore, do not include the total size of the property portfolio owned by the company. For example, in North America leverage is in the range 35-55%, Europe (including UK) 80-100%, and Asia-Pacific 40-60%.

[8] The FTSE EPRA/NAREIT Global Real Estate Index Series is widely seen as the leading benchmark for investing in real estate securities. To ensure the tradability of the index, companies must meet a number of criteria such as a minimum level of free float market capitalisation, traded volume, a minimum level of real estate related activities and provide annual accounts in English. The Ground Rules of the index are available from http://www.epra.com.

(27 percent). Europe adds one percentage point (19 percent). Adjustments for free float play an important role. In the FTSE EPRA/NAREIT Global Real Estate Index, the North American region has a weighted average free float figure of 96 percent, Europe is 82 percent and Asia-Pacific is 78 percent. In addition, the differences highlight the focus and maturity of the United States and Canadian REIT market. Asia-Pacific loses ground, mainly because of the diversity of the Hong Kong market. Many Hong Kong real estate companies are involved in other 'non-real estate related' activities, making them non-eligible for the index. We expect this to change in the future under Hong Kong REIT legislation[9]. The fourth and final category examines the global stock market breakdown.[10] North America comprises the largest portion (46 percent), followed by Europe (30 percent) and Asia-Pacific (22 percent). Latin America is 2 percent of the global total.

Figure 4: Relative Market Share Breakdown Under Asset Class Category

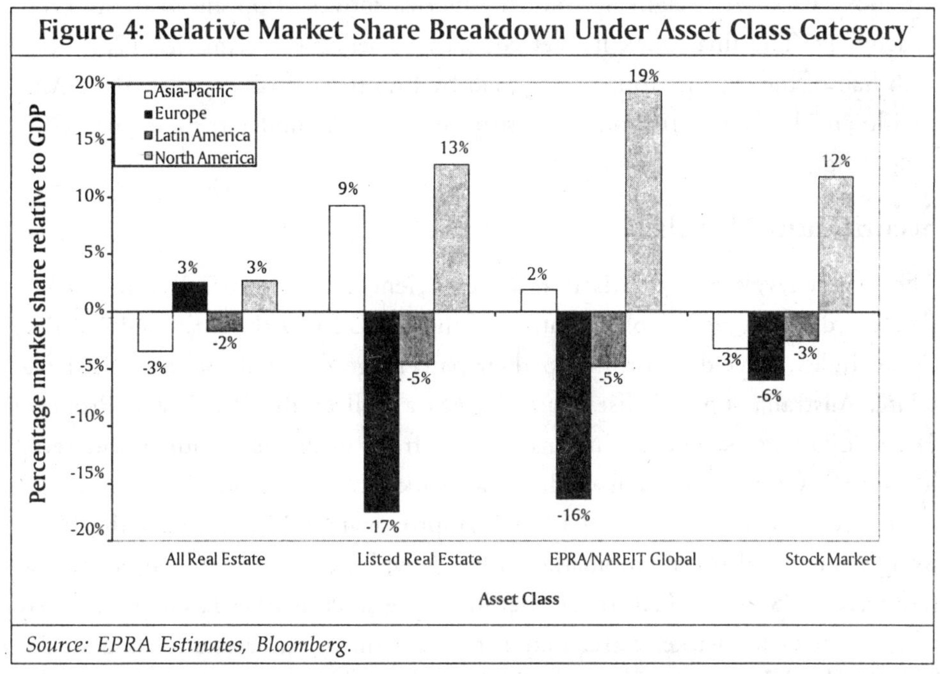

Source: EPRA Estimates, Bloomberg.

[9] REIT legislation offers conglomerates the opportunity to spin off buildings into a REIT. For example, the Hong Kong Housing Authority plans to IPO the Link REIT valued at US$2.7 billion later in 2005.

[10] Stock market capitalization estimates include the value of company real estate. Therefore, in this simple exercise we will have effectively double counted real estate. For example, in Europe's largest economy – Germany, UBS estimate that approximately 20% of the market capitalisation (€600 billion) of the DAX 30 is real estate held at book value. In addition, over two percent of global stock markets are comprised of dedicated listed real estate trust/ operators – see Figure.6.

Figure 4 attempts to highlight the differences between each regions natural GDP weighting against its weighting in each of the four asset categories. Reading from left to right again, in the first section, we see that the European and North America total commercial real estate markets are more mature than their Asia-Pacific and Latin American friends.[11] Both markets are three percentage points in excess of their GDP weightings. Moving on, section two highlights the fact, that listed real estate in Europe is significantly underweight (17 percentage points (pp)) compared against its far heavier GDP weighting. Both North America (13pp) and Asia Pacific (9pp) come in well above GDP weightings. Latin America is 5pp under. Looking at weightings in the FTSE EPRA/NAREIT Global Real Estate Index, Europe remains significantly behind. Asia-Pacific loses ground because of the free float and activities diversification issue, but still remains two pp above its GDP weighting. North America moves 19pp ahead of its GDP benchmark. The final stock market comparison sees North America 12pp head, with half of the expense (6pp) being paid by European stock markets. Both Asia-Pacific and Latin America are three percentage points under their natural GDP weighting.

Securitisation Levels

The largest levels of securitisation are experienced in the Asia-Pacific market. Figure 5 displays the eligible countries of the FTSE EPRA/NAREIT Global Real Estate Index, ranked according to their percentage of listed, or securitised real estate. Australia tops the list. Australia has a well established Listed Property Trust (LPT) market attracting investment from both institutional and retail investors[12]. Over ten percent of the total market capitalisation of the Australian stock market is in the form of LPTs[13]. Approximately 27 percent of the Hong Kong/China total real estate market is listed, with Singapore not too far behind (26 percent). Similar to Australia, the Singapore stock market has approximately ten percent of its market capitalisation in the form of real estate focused stocks. The listed market heavyweight, the United States, is just over the seven percent mark, in terms of total real estate listed, contributing approximately two and a

---

11 This outcome is, of course, the result of applying the GDP per capita adjustment factor in the formula.

12 UBS estimate the institutional/retail split to be approximately 65/35 respectively.

13 Again, it is worth noting that these figures are an under estimation, as many non-real estate specific companies will hold real estate on their balance sheet. This applies to all countries in the table.

Figure 5: Securitisation Levels of the FTSE EPRA/NAREIT Global Real Estate Index Countries

FTSE EPRA/NAREIT Countries	Real Estate % Listed	Real Estate % of Stk Mkt
Australia	30.24%	10.67%
Hong Kong/China	27.46%	5.84%
Singapore	25.98%	9.29%
Luxembourg	12.48%	5.94%
Sweden	9.90%	3.54%
Canada	7.49%	2.62%
United States	7.18%	2.32%
Netherlands	6.49%	3.36%
New Zealand	5.61%	5.21%
Austria	5.14%	4.62%
United Kingdom	4.59%	1.66%
Japan	4.23%	2.24%
France	3.47%	1.56%
Switzerland	3.07%	0.63%
Spain	2.94%	1.71%
Belgium	2.90%	1.51%
Finland	1.61%	0.61%
Norway	1.58%	0.88%
Poland	1.47%	1.34%
Denmark	1.09%	0.63%
Greece	0.96%	0.58%
Italy	0.90%	0.79%
Germany	0.49%	0.45%
South Korea	0.39%	0.18%
Hungary	0.19%	0.16%
Ireland	0.00%	0.00%
Portugal	0.00%	0.00%
Czech Republic	0.00%	0.00%
World	**5.66%**	**2.29%**

Source: EPRA.

half percent to total stock market capitalisation. Canada achieves comparable figures to the United States. In Europe, from the larger countries, approximately five percent of UK real estate is traded on the stock market, equating to around 1.7 percent of the FTSE All-Share. France's figures are just behind the UK. Interestingly, Germany looks significantly underdeveloped on the listed side, with less than half a percent of total German real estate traded on the stock market. The German listed real estate market comprises 0.45 percent of the total German stock market. The envisaged introduction of the German REIT structure in 2006 is expected to change the face of the German securitised market over the next five years.[14] Taking a simple average, on a global basis, around 6 percent of total estate is traded on global stock markets, contributing to approximately 2.5 percent of stock market capitalisation.

Developments

Faster growing developing economies such as China, India, the Eastern European countries and Latin America will achieve growing shares of the total global real estate market going forward. These countries are increasing their higher-quality commercial real estate at quicker rates than the developed economies. In addition, companies who have historically developed and invested in the mature economies are expanding out into developing regions. At the listed real estate market level, REIT legislation is set to push growth in Europe, as it has done historically for the North American market during the nineties, and is currently doing so in the Asian region. It is estimated that the market capitalisation (currently US$565 billion) of the FTSE EPRA/NAREIT will reach US$1 trillion in the next five years[15]. In the mature REIT markets such as the United States, the Netherlands and Australia, the build up of capital over the years has led to a trend for management to seek opportunities outside the borders of their domestic market. For example, Westfield, the largest global listed real estate trust, is listed on the Sydney stock exchange, but currently holds over 60 percent of its portfolio outside of Australia.

Summary

It is clear that Europe is significantly underdeveloped in terms of securitised real estate, compared against Asia-Pacific and North America. Germany is the prime

[14] UBS estimate that the German REIT will be launched in the second or third quarter of 2006, to be enacted respectively from 1 January 2006. The impact on the European sector could be significant. The IFD estimate that $70 billion of equity from tax paying companies is 60% free float weighted, and then Germany would leap from its current weighting of 3% in the FTSE EPRA/NAREIT Europe Index to approximately 30%. The effect on a global basis would be that Europe increases to approximately 25% of the global real estate market.

[15] Pan-European REIT – A long, long road. EPRA Article, August 2005.

Figure 6

Countries	GDP ($bn)	GDP per capita ($)	Real Estate ($bn)	30-Jun-05 Total Listed ($bn)	30-Jun-05 Total RE v Listed RE (%)	30-Jun-05 Stock Market ($bn)	30-Jun-05 Stk Mkt v Listed RE (%)
Japan	4,370	34,316	1,966	83.2	4.23%	3,705	2.24%
Hong Kong/China	1,618	1,239	288	79.1	27.46%	1,354	5.84%
South Korea	612	12,689	237	0.9	0.39%	529	0.18%
India	583	548	79	0.3	0.33%	450	0.06%
Australia	516	25,937	232	70.3	30.24%	659	10.67%
Taiwan	292	12,840	113	4.9	4.31%	502	0.97%
Indonesia	231	970	38	1.8	4.74%	81	2.22%
Thailand	145	2,238	31	5.7	18.18%	107	5.37%
Malaysia	106	4,509	29	8.3	28.41%	187	4.41%
Singapore	97	22,204	87	22.6	25.98%	243	9.29%
Philippines	80	923	13	4.1	32.19%	35	11.94%
New Zealand	79	19,862	36	2.0	5.61%	38	5.21%
Vietnam	40	480	5	–	0.00%	–	0.00%
Total Asia-Pacific	**8,769**	**20,758**	**3,155**	**283.1**	**8.97%**	**7,891**	**3.59%**
Germany	2,388	28,977	1,075	5.3	0.49%	1,188	0.45%
United Kingdom	1,847	30,641	1,039	47.7	4.59%	2,863	1.66%
France	1,757	29,075	791	27.4	3.47%	1,756	1.56%
Italy	1,461	25,162	657	5.9	0.90%	757	0.79%
Spain	840	20,863	378	11.1	2.94%	650	1.71%

Contd...

Contd...

Russia	462	3,162	112	0.5	0.41%	339	0.14%
Netherlands	508	31,122	229	14.8	6.49%	442	3.36%
Switzerland	320	42,995	144	4.4	3.07%	704	0.63%
Belgium	304	29,413	137	4.0	2.90%	262	1.51%
Sweden	300	33,360	135	13.3	9.90%	377	3.54%
Turkey	244	3,546	62	1.1	1.80%	104	1.06%
Austria	252	30,843	113	5.8	5.14%	126	4.62%
Norway	222	48,459	100	1.6	1.58%	178	0.88%
Denmark	211	39,010	95	1.0	1.09%	165	0.63%
Poland	216	5,604	64	0.9	1.47%	70	1.34%
Greece	173	16,227	78	0.7	0.96%	128	0.58%
Finland	162	31,012	73	1.2	1.61%	193	0.61%
Ireland	153	38,501	69	–	0.00%	100	0.00%
Portugal	146	13,893	58	–	0.00%	64	0.00%
Czech Republic	91	8,847	31	–	0.00%	38	0.00%
Hungary	83	8,248	28	0.1	0.19%	34	0.16%
Romania	59	2,635	13	–	0.00%	16	0.00%
Ukraine	53	1,094	9	–	0.00%	23	0.00%
Slovakia	33	6,137	10	–	0.00%	5	0.00%
Slovenia	28	13,844	11	–	0.00%	7	0.00%
Luxembourg	27	58,574	12	1.5	12.48%	26	5.94%
Bulgaria	20	2,662	5	–	0.00%	2	0.00%
Total Europe	**12,361**	**26,670**	**5,527**	**148.4**	**2.69%**	**10,615**	**1.40%**

Contd...

Contd...

Mexico	654	6,235	200	–	0.00%	220	0.00%
Brazil	535	2,904	126	0.5	0.41%	339	0.15%
Argentina	146	3,733	38	0.5	1.30%	58	0.84%
Venezuela	99	3,963	26	–	0.00%	7	0.00%
Colombia	86	2,041	18	–	0.00%	30	0.00%
Chile	79	5,017	23	0.3	1.26%	123	0.23%
Peru	62	2,250	13	0.0	0.28%	22	0.17%
Total Latin America	**1,662**	**4,383**	**444**	**1.3**	**0.30%**	**798**	**0.17%**
United States	11,105	37,897	4,997	358.8	7.18%	15,477	2.32%
Canada	879	27,046	396	29.6	7.49%	1,129	2.62%
Total North America	11,984	37,101	5,393	388.4	7.20%	16,606	2.34%
World	**34,776**	–	**14,519**	**821.3**	**5.66%**	**35,910**	**2.29%**

Sources: World Bank Organisation, FTSE, EPRA.

example of this underdevelopment, with only half a percent of the country's high quality commercial real estate available to investors on the stock market. However, changes in tax legislation are set to address this situation. Continuing levels of cross border investment will drive harmonisation in the industry, forcing higher levels of transparency and governance in developing countries.

Real Estate markets are highly dynamic. From developing markets such as India, China and Eastern Europe, to changes in tax legislation in developed countries. These are exciting times for companies and investors alike. As real estate continues to establish itself as an intrinsic part of a broad investment strategy, investors demand a broad range of real estate investment products. From investing directly, using non-listed real estate funds, to trading REITs/real estate operating companies on global stock markets. It is widely envisaged that global listed real estate markets will continue to grow in the future, offering a broader range of opportunities to investors. We expect the market capitalisation of the EPRA/NAREIT Global Real Estate Index is to break the US$1 trillion barrier in the next five years.

(Fraser Hughes is the Research Director at EPRA. He holds an MSc in Investment Management and a BA in Finance. He can be reached at f.Hughes@epra.com

Jorrit Arissen is a Researcher at ERPA. He graduated in 2003 with an MSc in Investment Analysis and holds a BA in Business Administration. He can be reached at j.arisen@epra.com).

Global Real Estate Investment Trends

The continued performance of real estate investment and high returns has increased the interest of all investors. This increase has also influenced the cross border investment. The global markets are matured and the investors require a diversified real estate portfolio. The cross border investment in 2006 was around US$116 billion. America's stands first in terms of cross regional investment accounting for US$28 billion. Many of the European investors concentrated on investment within Europe, and hence the cross regional investment of Europe accounted for only around US$5 billion.

In US market, of the total cross border activity, two thirds of the investment was made in office. Though the retail real estate investment has reduced, there was an increase in apartments. The composition of the cross border investment market has changed. In 2001, Germany was leading with a share of 49 percent. In 2005, Australia's share was high (39 percent) and in 2006 the Middle East share increased to 26 percent as shown in Figure 1.

Europe direct real estate investment in 2006 was US$212 billion. The cross border investment increased to US$84 billion in 2006 and UK, Germany and France were the major contributors. In case of cross regional investment, US was the major player accounting for 40 percent of the activity in 2006.

In Asia, the cross border investment was US$12 billion in 2006. The cross border investment market was dominated by Australia and US. In comparison with the investment activity in 2005, the Australian share of investment has increased in the Asian region in 2006 and decreased in US.

The increasing interest of the investors in real estate has led to strong cap rate compression. As a result of this compression the performance of real estate has increased. In US, the cap rate compression has become stable and the returns from the market were around 17 percent in 2006. In Europe the average returns were around 16.4 percent and there was cap rate compression throughout the year. Even in Asia, there was an increase in returns as a result of increase in rents and cap rate compression. The capital flow into real estate and growth in rental income spurs the income and returns from real estate. Hence majority of the real estate markets across the world will have favorable returns from real estate.

Figure 1: Share of US Cross-Border Real Estate Investment by Investor's Nationality

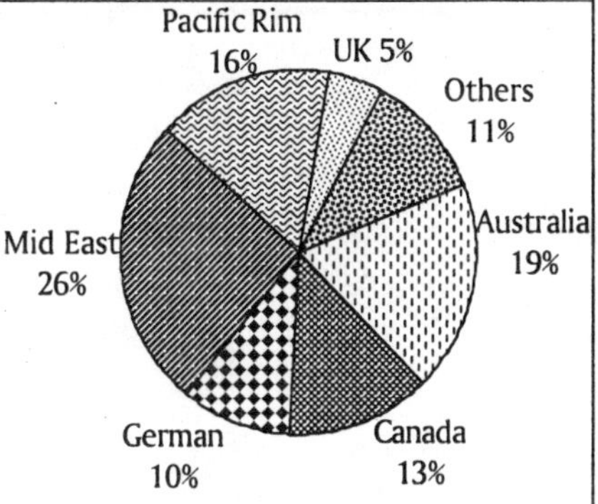

Total transactions: US $ 20 Billion

Source: RREEF Research, RCA

Compiled from www.rreef.com

Section II

Country Experiences

9

What can Europe Learn from US REITs
Lessons from the Ivory Towers

Tobias Just

REITs were introduced in the US in 1960 under the Real Estate Investment Trust Act. Since then, many countries have created similar real estate investment instruments. The article gives an overview of REIT market in US, its growth and development and how its success can be emulated by other countries.

The US REIT market has not developed evenly. Key pieces of legislation have accelerated the process. The volume of IPOs in particular expanded noticeably in the wake of new laws.

In the short-term, US REITs correlate with equities but not with direct investments in real estate. However, the correlations with capital market products especially are not stable; they exhibit strong fluctuations over time.

There is a long-term correlation between US REITs and directly held real estate, but not with equities. So, all in all, REITs are an asset class of their own. Portfolio performance can be enhanced by adding REITs.

Specialisation on a certain type of real estate is more important than a regional focus. REITs that concentrate on one class of real estate frequently generate above-average returns. A regional focus on several types of real estate is often not worthwhile, however.

US REITs are not a good hedge against inflation. This holds for the short run. Over the long-term there appears to be a weak correlation between the performance of US REITs and consumer prices.

There are optimum company sizes for REITs. REITs enjoy considerable economies of scale, but these hold primarily for smallish REITs. Very big REITs might in fact suffer from diseconomies of scale.

Limits on short-term trading strategies. While REITs do show some systematic developments in their price performance, these are in some cases not very pronounced. Consequently, trading strategies do not excel.

REIT Performance Recently Above Par

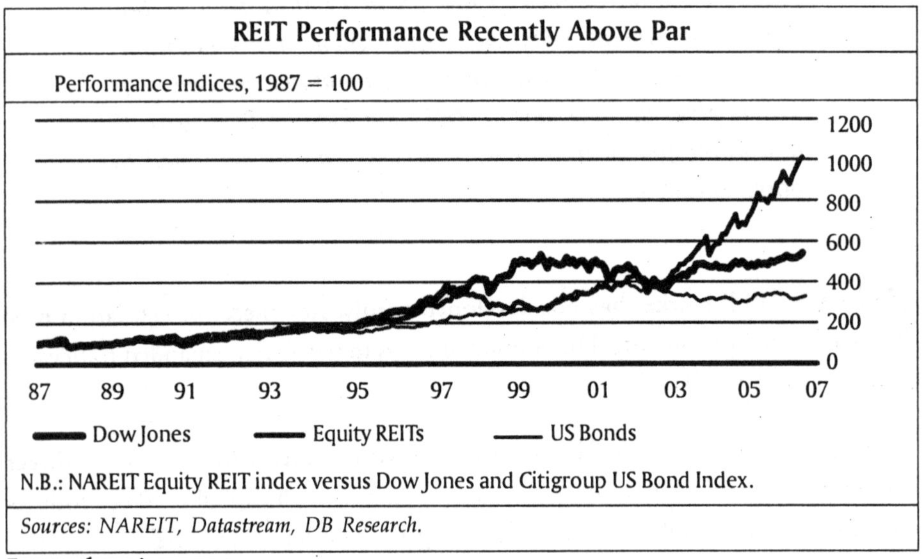

N.B.: NAREIT Equity REIT index versus Dow Jones and Citigroup US Bond Index.

Sources: NAREIT, Datastream, DB Research.

Introduction

Around the world, the integration of the real estate and capital markets is growing at an impressive pace. This is a sensible development, for it is the only way to enable fast and simple trading of comparatively illiquid investments in real estate as well as efficient structuring – and especially restructuring – of investor portfolios. Real estate stocks in particular are rightly gaining significance. More and more

Development of the Global REIT Market		
Selection		
1960	US	Real Estate Investment Trusts
1969	NL	Fiscale Beleggingsinstelling
1985	AU	Listed Property Trust
1994	CA	Mutual Fund Trusts
2000	JP	Real Estate Investment Trusts
2002	SG	Real Estate Investment Trusts
2003	FR	Sociétés d'investissement immobilier cotées
2003	HK	Real Estate Investment Trusts
2007	UK	Real Estate Investment Trusts
(?)	DE	Real Estate Investment Trusts
Sources: ZEW, EPRA, Deutsche Bank		

countries are taking the US approach and paving the way to tax-transparent real estate stock corporations, known as real estate investment trusts, or REITs for short.

REITs were introduced in the US in 1960 under the Real Estate Investment Trust Act. Since then, many countries have created similar real estate investment instruments. Since the turn of the millennium alone it has become possible to set up REIT-like vehicles in seven countries, among them Japan (2000), Hong Kong (2003) and France (2003). The United Kingdom will launch REITs at the beginning of 2007 and on November 2, 2006 the German cabinet approved draft legislation to introduce REITs, so Germany may also see the adoption of a REIT law in the coming year.

This report will give an overview of the key findings of academic research on REITs, though primarily on the US variant, in order to derive possible lessons for the countries that have been slow off the mark and are now jumping onto the REIT bandwagon.[1] Since real estate companies that are listed on the stock exchange offer data which is easy to obtain at highly frequent intervals, they are particularly well suited for empirical analysis. Zietz *et al.* (2003) published an overview article which already lists around 140 academic studies on REITs. Since 2003, researchers' interest has not ebbed in the least. Companies, analysts and the media would be well advised to pay heed to these findings, for they (probably) also apply to the budding developments in Europe.

1 Reference is made solely to articles in academic books and publications in refereed journals.

Important Milestones in US REIT Legislation		
Number corresponds to charts and graphs in the Annex		
1*	1960	Real Estate Investment Trust Act
2	1986	Tax Reform Act
3	1993	Omnibus Budget Reconciliation Act/1992 first UPREIT
4	1997	REIT Simplification Act
5	1999	REIT Modernization Act
6	2004	American Jobs Creation Act
* Not illustrated		
Sources: NAREIT, Block (2006), DB Research.		

What Can we Learn from the Development of US REITs?

Since 1960, the US REIT market has developed anything but evenly. While there were already roughly 50 REIT companies by the mid-1970s, their total market capitalisation was very small (less than USD 500 m). The breakthrough did not come until the 1990s. Today, the 143 equity REITs alone have a market cap of nearly USD370 bn (the market development is illustrated in the Annex).

Four aspects are particularly important:

- The growth of the REIT market has accelerated with every amendment of the law. Evidently, the rules for REITs were steadily improved. This suggests that the European REIT laws will also need to be amended over time. The market needs to gather experience, and this can only be done in practice.
- Amendments to REIT legislation have often gone hand in hand with peaks in related initial public offerings, so the amendments mirrored the market's demands. Intensive discussions between industry representatives and legislators are thus essential.
- The consolidation in the REIT sector continues. This is happening not only through mergers, but partly also through market delisting. Going private will always be the correcting force for the REIT market.
- Equity REITs dominate activity in the US market, accounting for more than 90% of the REIT market cap. While mortgage REITs have lost importance, they remain established vehicles. Nevertheless, it is right that Europe is keeping its sights focused on equity REITs.

American Myths about US REITs

There are serious misgivings about REITs in Germany in particular. Primarily, these preconceptions focus on fears of tax revenue shortfalls and worries about additional social hardships in the markets for rented accommodation. A look at the US shows that deep-seated prejudices are not easily overcome. Block (2006) devotes an entire chapter of his textbook to the myths about US REITs, only to identify them as prejudices in the end.

American Myths about REITs	
Myth 1	REITs are only packaging for real estate
Myth 2	Real estate is a high-risk investment
Myth 3	Real estate is primarily a hedge against inflation
Myth 4	Difficult real estate environment *per se* is bad for REITs
Myth 5	REITs are particularly well suited for trading strategies
Source: Block (2006).	

So if a standard textbook on REITs devotes a chapter to such biases some 45 years after their establishment, it follows that knowledge about them only spreads at a snail's pace. European REITs and real estate shares are likely to share the same fate. This can only be overcome with detailed information campaigns and experience.

The REIT as an Asset Class in its Own Right

Ultimately, the question of whether Europe really needs REITs is only warranted if the REIT is an asset class in its own right. It is reasonable to presume that REITs perform either like directly held real estate, equities or a mixture of both. Interestingly, a synopsis of the literature at hand would suggest that REITs are indeed a unique mixture of direct real estate investments and equity-based investments.

For example, REITs perform considerably differently than directly held real estate in the short term. On a long-term horizon, though, REITs are cointegrated with directly held real estate, i.e., there is a long-term correlation between directly held real estate and real estate shares.[2]

2 See e.g., Myer and Webb (1993), Glascock *et al.*(2000), as well as Lee and Stevenson (2005). Furthermore, US REITs seem to lead the direct real estate market, so some authors say they have forecasting value (e.g., Barkham and Geltner, 1995).

Yet for equities there is a diametrically opposed relationship: over the short-term REITs correlate with equities very noticeably in some cases, especially with shares of small and medium-sized companies.[3] This leads some analysts to say, in fact, that REITs have limited diversification potential. However, this is wide off the mark for two particular reasons. First, the correlations are by no means constant over time. Therefore, the results of studies may vary considerably depending on the period of the analysis. Some researchers claim in fact to have found indications that the correlation between the performance of REITs and equities is systematically closer in phases of downswings than in upswings.[4] However, this correlation is neither robust nor stable over time. In any event, it is not possible to derive a concrete trading strategy from it (Chiang *et al.*, 2004). It continues to hold, however, that the short-term correlation between equities and the real estate stock market fluctuates. Westerheide (2006) determines that the difference between the risk-adjusted performance (RAP) of REITs and equities has been positive since 2001; however, before this it had been slightly negative for ten years.

The second reason is that no long-term cointegration has been found between a general equity market index and REITs. This would mean that REITs offer more diversification potential for long-term investment strategies than for short-term strategies. Neither a short-term nor a long-term relationship was established with bonds (Westerheide, 2006).[5]

In a nutshell, REITs may indeed be considered an asset class of their own. However, there is a lack of studies comparing real estate stock corporations and REITs, since most countries only know the existence or dominance of one vehicle or the other.

REITs only Moderately Suitable as an Inflation Hedge

Frequently it is argued that REITs are a good hedge against inflation because of their basis in real estate. This claim requires a more detailed explanation in two respects, though. First, Block (2006) points out that the hedging qualities of real

---

[3] See among others Gyourko and Linneman (1988) and Chiang and Lee (2002).

[4] This relationship is known in the literature as the "Asymmetric REIT-Beta Puzzle" (See Goldstein and Nelling, 1999). Beta measures the relationship between a sub-(equity) market and total (equity) market.

[5] Glascock *et al.* (2000) also find a long-term correlation for the early 1990s; Clayton and MacKinnon (2003) believe, however, that this relationship has weakened since then.

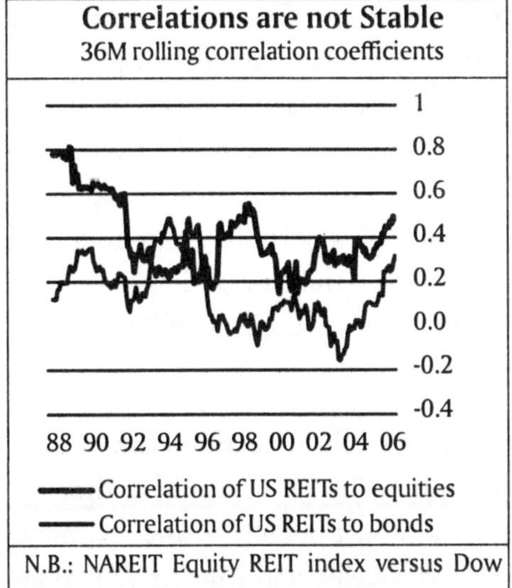

N.B.: NAREIT Equity REIT index versus Dow Jones and Citigroup US Bond Index.

Sources: NAREIT, Datastream, DB Research.

Performance of US REITs

Risk-adjusted performance spreads

	RAP bonds in %	RAP equities in %
1990-1995	-2.2	-1.4
1996-2000	0.8	-2.6
2001-2004	5.7	11.9

RAP = risk-adjusted performance

$$RAP_i = \frac{\sigma_m}{\sigma_i}(r_i - r_f) + f_f$$

with

σ_m = Standard deviation of the benchmark (here: bonds)

σ_i = Standard deviation of US REITs

r_i = Return on REITs

r_f = Return on a risk-free investment

Source: Westerheide (2006).

estate are basically limited since the general rise in inflation is only one of many factors shaping the development of real estate values.

Second, the discussion above suggests that even if direct investments in real estate were a suitable hedge against inflation and REITs were cointegrated with direct investments, REITs could only offer long-term protection against inflation at best. This is exactly what is shown by several empirical studies: in the short term REITs do not offer convincing protection against inflation; in fact, some authors find that equities offer better protection against price upcreep than REITs. All the same, there are weak indications that REIT performance and consumer prices are cointegrated. So at least there would be slight evidence of a connection in the long-term. In this case REITs could neutralise part of the inflation risk in the long run.[6]

REITs in Mixed Portfolios

At the end of the day, these findings are a preliminary step to the crucial question of whether REITs can play a meaningful role in portfolio diversification. Lee and

---

6 See Liu *et al.* (1997) for the short-term perspective and Chatrath and Liang (1998) and Westerheide (2006) for the long-term analysis.

Stevenson (2005) show for mixed capital market portfolios, i.e., portfolios consisting of bonds and equities, that performance of nearly all efficient portfolios can be improved by adding REITs. This holds in particular for portfolios with a long investment horizon and/or for portfolios at the lower end of the risk/reward spectrum. In this event, REITs would be an interesting supplement especially for old-age provision since they can raise the return on a portfolio by up to 8 basis points while the risk level remains constant. This would be a simple way for small-scale investors to add a real estate component to their portfolio without incurring the cluster risk of a direct investment.

The fact that REITs can enhance a mixed capital market portfolio comes as no surprise considering the long-term correlation with real estate held directly. Nevertheless, the question is whether this alone is attributable to the real estate bundled in the REIT. Feldman (2003) as well as Mueller and Mueller (2003) are able to prove unambiguously that portfolios which already contain direct investments in real estate can also be enhanced with REITs. In some optimised portfolios the recommended share of REITs actually exceeds the share of directly held real estate assets. This tends to apply more to institutional or extensive private portfolios.

Scale Economies of REITs

So there is a far-reaching consensus in the academic literature that REITs do constitute an asset class of their own and that they consequently also represent a sensible enhancement of the range of investment alternatives. This means the next question has to be: what constitutes an ideal REIT? How large is it? Is it diversified or specialised and which demands are to be made of the management? For the future development of the total market a key factor is whether the sector offers pronounced economies of scale, because further consolidation via mergers and market exits would then be inevitable.

Economies of scale are plausible for REITs since big companies often find it easier to attract skilled managers; there could be marketing and information benefits and above all the costs of reporting would be spread across a larger portfolio. Moreover, Below *et al.* (2000) have shown that institutional investors prefer to invest in bigger REITs. The access to capital would thus be easier for large REITs.

Glaring inefficiencies have been found in US REITs by a number of studies including Anderson *et al.* (2002). REITs were found to be too small on average and therefore, their production costs were up to 60% too high. Lewis *et al.* (2003) did establish much smaller deviations from the ideal production size, but they also concluded that the average REIT was still too small. Since here however only average values were assessed, there may well also be inefficient large REITs. There is probably an optimum size for REITs, and beyond that they deliver diminishing returns on scale.[7]

For Europe this could mean that the economies of scale will lead to a phase of consolidation. However, the end result would not be a highly concentrated sector. Since in addition the geographical concentration generates scarcely any efficiency gains – unlike focusing on one real estate segment – cross-border REITs in Europe would then be desirable as they help to exploit potential economies of scale.[8]

Management of REITs

The board of directors of a US REIT comprises the CEO, who is often also the chairman of the board, and several other individuals. In US "one-tier boards" a distinction is made between "internal" and "external" members. Externals have no executive functions within the company and are therefore considered to be more independent. Their role is more akin to that of German supervisory board members.

Several studies have found that the return of a REIT is negatively correlated with board size and positively correlated with the independence of board members. Also the REITs that tend to be more successful appear to be those where the CEO is not also the chairman and where the management owns a significant stake in the REIT.[9] These findings are plausible on the one hand and on the other they would also be interesting for valuing European REITs, but the transferability onto European systems is likely to be limited to countries where there are structures similar to one-tier boards.

---

7 See Topuz (2005) and Devaney and Weber (2005). It may be that the consolidation which has taken place over the last few years has partially tapped the economies of scale. Then the more recent study findings would be compatible with the older ones (Miller *et al.*, 2006).

8 See Ambrose (2000) regarding the cost efficiency of geographical concentration and Block (2006) regarding the benefits of concentrating on types of real estate.

9 See Ghosh and Sirmans (2003), Feng *et al.* (2005) and Block (2006).

Limited Short-Term Trading Opportunities

Active trading strategies attempt to exploit arbitrage opportunities. Larson (2005) found, for example, that after REITs suffer particularly large daily losses (of at least 5%) a correction often follows on the next two days.

In addition, Payne and Zuehlke (2006) conclude that it must be possible in principle to correctly forecast key inflection points in the price performance of a REIT. Expertise on real estate securities could then be rewarded. However, the question of how an appropriately tailored strategy might look is left unanswered by Payne and Zuehlke. Furthermore, it is possible that this market inefficiency is merely a manifestation of how new the segment still is and that this arbitrage opportunity will disappear as the market matures.

All in all, active trading opportunities are probably limited. For the fledgling European REIT markets it is however to be expected that – especially in their early stages when experience is being gathered – information asymmetries at least give the impression that arbitrage opportunities exist. It is, however, just as plausible that the high degree of integration between international capital markets will quickly correct this as the European markets benefit from the experience gathered in the US.

Concluding Remarks

Real estate stock corporations are gaining importance internationally. The success of US REITs is increasingly being copied in other countries.

It is however correct that the trend towards more real estate stock corporations/ REITs will not be a linear process, as there will always be phases when "going private" makes sense for individual companies. Here, too, the issue is not a simple either/or decision – there is likely to be a multiplicity of financing instruments in the future as well. At the end of these intermediate cycles the importance of real estate shares and of REITs will be much bigger than is the case today.

Furthermore, it is plausible that growth is occurring less and less within confined national boundaries. There will be increasingly international REITs. This trend is likely, however, to be restricted to the big REITs.

(Tobias Just is a Senior Economist at Deutsche Bank Research. In 1997 he graduated and started working on his PhD, which was awarded the university science prize in 2001. Since 2001 he has been working for Deutsche Bank, focussing on real estate and regional economics. He has been playing an active role in the working group of the Finance Initiative Germany dealing with the introduction of G-REITs. Tobias now regularly lectures on real estate issues at various German universities. He can be reached at tobias.just@db.com).

Secondary Literature

Ambrose, B.W. *et al.* (2000). "REIT Economies of Scale: Fact or Fiction?" In *Journal of Real Estate Finance and Economics* 20, pp. 211-224.

Anderson R.I. *et al.* (2002). "Technical Efficiency and Economies of Scale: A Non-Parametric Analysis of REIT Operating Efficiency". In *European Journal of Operations Research* 139, pp. 598-612.

Barkham, R. and D. Geltner (1995). "Price Discovery in American and British Property Markets" In *Real Estate Economics* 23, pp. 21-44.

Below, S.D. *et al.* (2000). "The Determinants of REIT Institutional Ownership: Test of the CAPM". In *Journal of Real Estate Finance and Economics* 21, pp. 263-278.

Block, R.L. (2006). *Investing in REITs.* Third edition, Bloomberg Press, New York.

Chiang, K. and M. Lee (2002). "REITs in the Decentralized Investment Industry". In *Journal of Real Estate Portfolio Management* 20, pp. 496-512.

Chiang K., *et al.* (2004). "Another Look at the Asymmetric REIT-Beta-Puzzle". In *Journal of Real Estate Research* 26, pp. 25-42.

Chatrath, A. and Y. Liang (1998). "REITs and Inflation: A Long-Run Perspective". In *Journal of Real Estate Research* 16, pp. 311-325.

Clayton, J.G. MacKinnon (2003). "The Relative Importance of Stock, Bond and Real Estate Factors in explaining REIT Returns". In *Journal of Real Estate Finance and Economics* 27, pp. 39-60.

Devaney, M. and W.L. Weber (2005). "Efficiency, Scale Economies, and the Risk/Return Performance of Real Estate Investment Trusts". In *The Journal of Real Estate Finance and Economics* 31, pp. 301-317.

Feldman, B.E. (2003). "Investment Policy for Securitized and Direct Real Estate". In *Journal of Portfolio Management, Special Real Estate Issue*, pp. 112-121.

Feng, Z. *et al.* (2005). "How Important is the Board of Directors to REIT Performance?" In *Journal of Real Estate Portfolio Management* 11, pp. 281-293.

Ghosh, C. and C.F. Sirmans (2003). "Board Independence, Ownership Structure and Performance: Evidence from Real Estate Investment Trusts". In *Journal of Real Estate Finance and Economics* 26. pp. 287-318.

Glascock, J.L, *et al.* (2000). "Further Evidence on the Integration of REIT, Bond and Stock Returns". In *Journal of Real Estate Finance and Economics* 20, pp. 1-9.

Goldstein, A. and E.F. Nelling (1999). "REIT Return Behaviour in Advancing and Declining Stock Markets". In *Real Estate Finance* 15, pp. 68-77.

Gyourko, J. and P. Linneman (1988). "Owner-Occupied Homes, Income-Producing Properties, and REITs as Inflation Hedges: Empirical Findings". In *Journal of Real Estate Finance and Economics* 1, pp. 347-372.

Larson, S. (2005). "Real Estate Investment Trusts and Stock Price Reversals". In *The Journal of Real Estate Finance and Economics* 20, pp. 81-88.

Lee, S. and S. Stevenson (2005). "The Case for REITs in the Mixed-Asset Portfolio in the Short and Long Run". In *Journal of Real Estate Portfolio Management* 11, pp. 55-80.

Lewis, D. *et al.* (2003). "The Cost Efficiency of Real Estate Investment Trusts: An Analysis with a Bayesian Stochastic Frontier Model". In *Journal of Real Estate Finance and Economics* 26, pp. 65-80.

Liu, C.H. *et al.* (1997). "International Evidence on Real Estate Securities as an Inflation Hedge". In *Real Estate Economics* 52, pp. 193-221.

Miller, S.M. *et al.* (2006). "Economies of Scale and Cost Efficiencies: A Panel-Data Stochastic-Frontier Analysis of Real Estate Investment Trusts". In *Manchester School of Economic Studies*, Vol. 74, pp. 483-499.

Mueller, A.G. and G.R. Mueller (2003). "Public and Private Real Estate in the Mixed-Asset Portfolio". In *Journal of Real Estate Portfolio Management* 9, pp. 193-203.

Myer, F.C. and J.R. Webb (1993). "Return Properties on Equity REITs, Common Stocks and Commercial Real Estate: A Comparison". In *Journal of Real Estate Research* 8, pp. 87-106.

Payne, J.E. and T.W. Zuehlke (2006). "Duration Dependence in Real Estate Investment Trusts". In *Applied Financial Economics* 16, pp. 416-423.

Topuz, J.C. *et al.* (2005). "Technical, Allocative and Scale Efficiencies of REITs: An Empirical Inquiry". In *Journal of Business Finance and Accounting* 32, pp. 1961-1994.

Westerheide, P. (2006). Cointegration of Real Estate Stocks and REITs with Common Stocks, Bonds and Consumer Price Inflation – an International Comparison, ZEW Discussion Paper 06-057, Mannheim.

Zietz, E.N. *et al.* (2003). "The environment and performance of Real Estate Investment Trusts". In *Journal of Real Estate Portfolio Management* 9, pp. 127-165.

Annexure

Important Milestones in US REIT Legislation

Number corresponds to charts and graphs

1*	1960	Real Estate Investment Trust Act
2	1986	Tax Reform Act
3	1993	Omnibus Budget Reconciliation Act/1992 first UPREIT
4	1997	REIT Simplification Act
5	1999	REIT Modernization Act
6	2004	American Jobs Creation Act

* Not illustrated

Sources: NAREIT, Block (2006), DB Research.

REIT Market has Boomed Since the Early 1990s

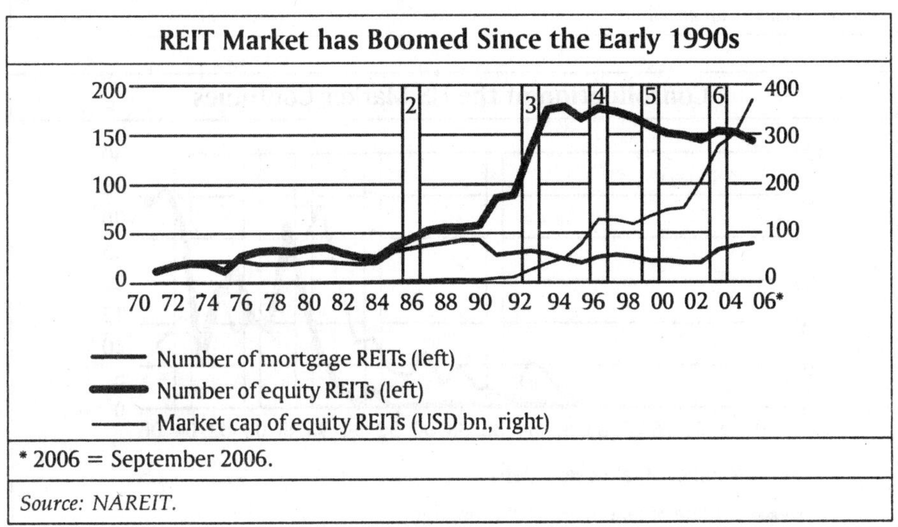

* 2006 = September 2006.

Source: NAREIT.

Contd...

Contd...

Four Waves of REIT IPOs

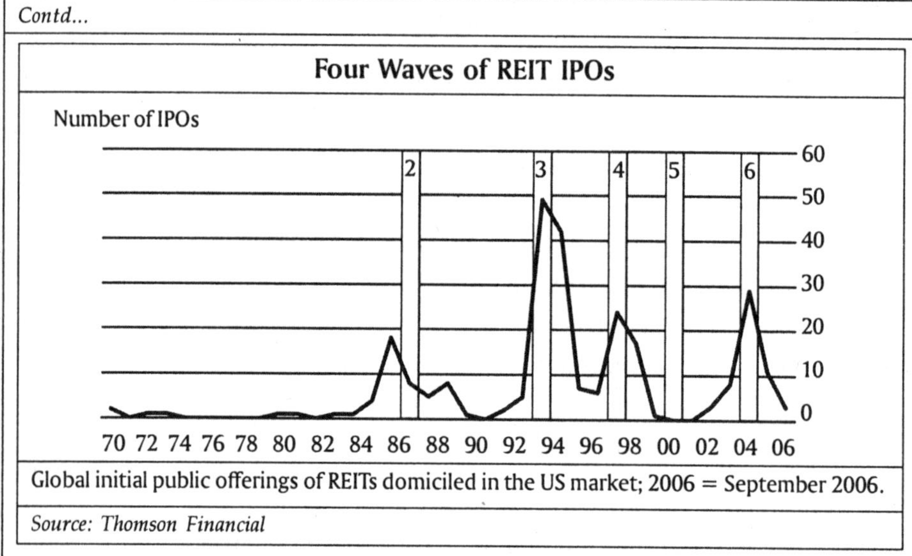

Global initial public offerings of REITs domiciled in the US market; 2006 = September 2006.

Source: Thomson Financial

Consolidation of the US Market Continues

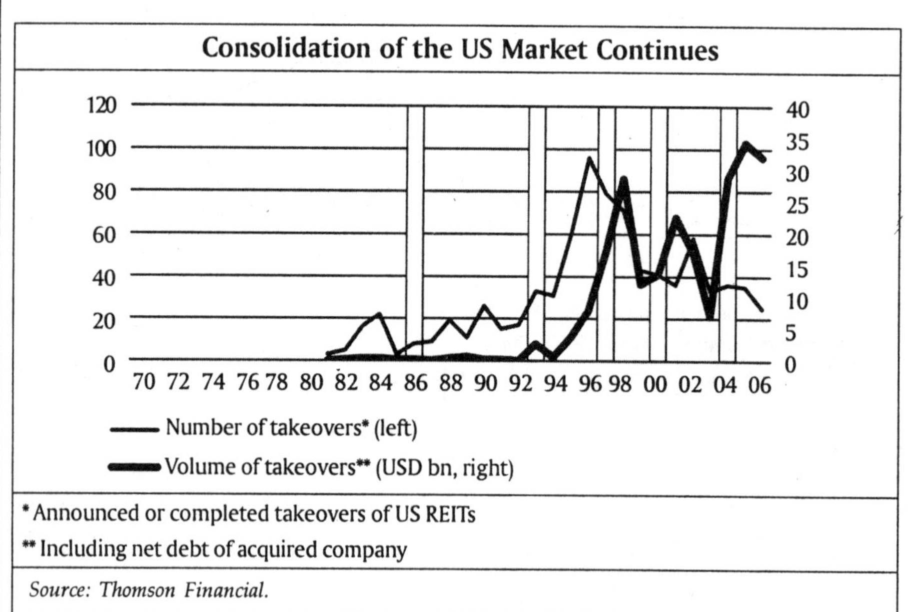

* Announced or completed takeovers of US REITs

** Including net debt of acquired company

Source: Thomson Financial.

10

The Introduction of Real Estate Investment Trusts (REITs) in Germany*

Constantin M Lachner and Rafael von Heppe

The introduction of the Real Estate Investment Trust (REIT) is an important issue at present for many real estate companies, investors in real estate, as well as for companies with significant real estate holdings in Germany. The German Real Estate Investment Trust or, G-REIT is in the centre of interest in Germany these days and is expected to be introduced in Germany in the beginning of 2007. A swift introduction of G-REITs is expected to fill a national gap in the international range of real estate investments, to vitalize the business location Germany, and to professionalize the German real estate economy. The article discusses about G-REIT legislation, corporate structure and requirements of G-REITs. It further discusses about taxation of G-REITs.

A. Introduction

The German Real Estate Investment Trust – or, G-REIT – is in the centre of interest in Germany these days and is expected to be introduced in Germany in

* An earlier version of this paper was presented at the Conference of the Canadian-German Lawyers Association in Toronto, Canada, 11 May 2006.

Source: www.germanlawjournal.com © German Law Journal GbR. Reprinted with permission. This article was first published in 8 German Law Journal 133-142 (2007) and is reprinted with permission by the German Law Journal.

the beginning of 2007. After a preparation phase initiated in 2003 by a lobbying group ("IFD")[1] under the former[2] German government, the new government has most recently drafted a bill with respect to the introduction of G-REITs ("bill").[3] This bill remains to be subject to parliamentary discussion and is likely to be partially modified before its final adoption: in addition to its passage in the *Bundestag* (Federal Parliament), it requires the approval of the *Bundesrat* (German Federal Council). Following its first reading it will be committed to the Financial Committee, which will conduct hearings. However, the legislator intends to pass the bill in the first quarter of 2007 to take retroactive effect as of 1 January 2007.[4] This essay intends to outline fundamental corporate, capital market, and tax related G-REIT parameters provided for by the G-REIT Act in its present form.

B. Background of the G-REIT Legislation

By introducing REITs, Germany follows various international paradigms.[5] Yet, the present bill testifies to a considerable number of specific variations 'made in Germany'. The bill is the outcome of political discussions between the *Bundesfinanzministerium* (Federal Ministry of Finance – BMF), the political parties, the IFD as most involved lobbying group, and other interest groups[6] about considerable tax issues raised by the planned Act. The taxation-related linchpin of the REIT legislation is the idea of tax exempting the REIT company, binding it to distribute most of its profits to its shareholders, and collecting taxes on shareholder level, a concept conceived as supporting above all tax transparency.

---

1 "Initiative Finanzstandort Deutschland" (*www.finanzstandort.de*).

2 German general elections took place in September 2006, resulting in a change of government.

3 Entwurf eines Gesetzes zur Schaffung deutscher Immobilien-Aktiengesellschaften mit börsennotierten Anteilen (Draft of an Act introducing German Real Estate Stock Corporations with listed shares), dated 2 November 2006, available online at: *http://www.bundesfinanzministerium.de/lang_de/nn_82/nsc_true/DE/Aktuelles/Aktuelle__Gesetze/Gesetzentwuerfe__Arbeitsfassungen/007,templateId=rend erPrint.html* (last visited 22 December 2006)

4 Art. 7 of the bill. The G-REIT Act will be published in the Bundesgesetzblatt (German Federal Law Gazette).

5 E.g. US-"REITs" (since 1960), Dutch "Fiscale Beleggingsinstelling" ("FBI", since 1969), Australian "Listed Property Trusts" (since 1971), Canadian "REITs" (since 1994), Belgian "Société d'Investissement à Capital fixe en Immobilière" (SICAFI, since1995), Japanese "J-REITs" (since 2001), South Korean "KREITs" (since 2001), Singaporean "S-REITs" (since 2002), French "Sociétés d'Investissement Immobiliers Cotées" ("SIIC", since 2003), Hong Kong "H-REITs" (since 2003), British "Property Investment Funds" ("PIF", starting 2007).

6 E.g. the "Deutscher Mieterbund" (German umbrella organization of tenants – DMB, *www.mieterbund.de*).

The first aspect, the tax exemption, has been highly controversially disputed, as it privileges the REIT company towards other company forms. The BMF considers the REIT necessary to preserve Germany's competitiveness on international financial markets and to maintain jobs for highly skilled employees. Furthermore, the introduction of REITs is expected to have strong positive fiscal and economic impacts:[7] Germany has by far the largest real estate reservoir in Europe, which at this time remains, for the most part, not yet institutionally invested, but owner-occupied or held by private owners.[8] Channelling these assets to REITs would make bound resources more fungible, release current owners from the complex everyday management of real estate, opening up substantial efficiency gains. As highly regarded investment vehicles, REITs are expected to be more attractive to foreign investors. Different from traditional real estate investments, a REIT investment is independent of the individual financial capacity of the investor.

As a consequence of the tax exemption, REIT legislation has to take into account specific taxation issues on the shareholder level, especially with respect to the taxation of foreign investors, which in many cases may fall under double taxation agreements. Central here is the problem of tax equity applied when taxation on shareholder level only affects German investors, whereas foreign investors enjoy tax reduction or even tax exemption.

C. The G-REIT

I. Corporate Structure of a G-REIT

According to Section 1 para. 1,[9] a G-REIT is a stock corporation whose business purpose is limited to:[10]

---

7 See the purpose of a G-REIT Act under A. I. of the bill's explanatory statements.

8 There is a total estimated real estate reservoir of about 7,200 billion €. So far, only a very small fraction of it – valued approximately 400 billion € – is held by institutional investors. The value of real estate held by other companies is estimated to be 1,500 billion €. About 73% thereof is owner-occupied commercial real estate, e.g. production sights, office buildings etc. In comparison, British companies occupy only 54% of their real estate assets, and in the US the respective figure is only 25%. By far, the lion's share of German real estate is owned by private individuals (approx. 5,300 billion €), see A. I. of the bill's explanatory statements.

9 If not stated otherwise, quotations within this essay refer to the regulations of the bill.

10 Specifically, the G-REIT may not engage in trading real estate; the bill considers as trade if the G-REIT has, within five years, gross revenues from the sale of real estate which exceed 50% of the value of the average holdings of real estate within the same period, Section 14.

(a) Acquiring, holding, managing by renting out and leasing, including essential property-related ancillary business, and selling of real property[11] or rights of use of real property, except for apartments built before 1 January 2007[12], and

(b) Acquiring, holding, managing, and selling shares in real estate business partnerships.[13]

and whose shares are listed on an organized market within the European Economic Area ("EEA"), not necessarily in Germany.[14] Therefore, the *Aktiengesetz* (German Stock Corporation Act – AktG) and the *Handelsgesetzbuch* (German Commercial Code – HGB) apply to G-REITs as long as the G-REIT Act does not provide otherwise.[15] Moreover, due to the requirement of listing the codes of conduct with respect to listed stock corporations of the *Wertpapierhandelsgesetz* (Securities Trading Act – WpHG) are observed.[16]

The G-REIT has to have its official residence[17] and its management[18] in Germany. It requires a share capital of at least 15 million Euro,[19] which has to be fully paid up; each share must grant the same rights.[20] The company name has to include the words "*REIT-Aktiengesellschaft*" or "REIT-AG" which are

---

11 Real property may be located in or outside Germany.

12 The exception of apartments built before 1 January 2007, so called "*Bestandsmietwohnungen*", has been most recently included into the bill as concession to opponents of the G-REIT Act who fear that profit maximizing G-REITs will raise rents and reduce tenant protection to a minimum; however, this exception and its argumentation is highly disputable and may be questioned again.

13 Specifically, the G-REIT may not hold shares in limited liability companies that in turn own real estate.

14 The listing shall assure that G-REITs do not compete with, but rather complement existing real éstate investment vehicles such as Open Property Funds. If listed in Germany, G-REITs may be listed on the organized market in terms of Section 2 para. 5 of the Securities Trading Act, i.e., on the so called official market in terms of Sections 30 et seq. of the *Börsengesetz* (Stock Exchange Act – BörsG) ("*amtlicher Markt*") or the organized market in terms of Sections 49 et seq. of the Stock Exchange Act ("geregelter Markt"), but not on the inofficial market in terms of Sections 57 of the Stock Exchange Act ("*Freiverkehr*"); see the bill's explanatory statements under B. Article 1 Section 10.

15 Section 1 para. 3.

16 E.g. insider rules according to Sections 12 et seq. of the Securities Trading Act, etc.

17 Section 1 para. 2.

18 Section 9. The bill does not exclude consulting external investment advisors, such as asset managers; this might be recommendable, however, calling external advisors may smoothly blend to turning away from the AG's corporate structure if the board of directors only controls the advisors.

19 Section 4; the legislator considers this amount as usual minimum capitalisation for listing; see the bill's explanatory statements under B. Article 1 Section 4. However, experience shows that by far higher capitalisation is recommendable for listing.

20 Section 5.

exclusively reserved to *GREITs*.[21] As such it is to be registered with the Commercial Register.[22]

Before becoming a *G-REIT*, the stock corporation passes the stadium of a pre-REIT.[23] This is a stock corporation resident in Germany,

(a) Having the same limited business purpose as a G-REIT;

(b) Complying with the G-REIT requirements regarding its asset structure;[24] and

(c) Being registered as pre-REIT with the *Bundeszentralamt für Steuern* (German Federal Central Tax Authority – BZSt).[25]

The pre-REIT already enjoys certain tax privileges[26] as long as it applies for listing on an organized market within three years[27] after its application for registration with the BZSt.[28]

II. G-REIT Requirements

To enjoy G-REIT tax privileges[29] on an ongoing basis and to prevent being sanctioned by the imposition of penalty fees[30], the G-REIT has to meet a number of legal requirements ruled in the second chapter of the bill, Sections 8 to 15, and set forth as follows.

The G-REIT requires a free float of at least 15% of the shares or, in the moment of listing on the organized market, of at least 25%, in order to allow small investors to participate in fungible real estate investments.[31] The free float is defined as the sum of all shares held by shareholders, who each individually

---

[21] Sections 6 and 7.

[22] Section 8.

[23] Section 2.

[24] Section 12.

[25] The stock corporation is registered as pre-REIT if in the application it asserts, and if necessary proves, that it complies with the other pre-REIT requirements.

[26] With respect to the Exit Tax, Article 2 of the bill.

[27] This term may only be extended under certain external conditions for another year, Section 10 para. 2.

[28] Section 10.

[29] See *infra*.

[30] See in each case the footnotes of a requirement.

[31] See the bill's explanatory statements under B. Article 1 Section 11.

have less than 3% of the G-REIT's total voting rights.[32] The G-REIT has to annually notify the *Bundesanstalt für Finanzdienstleistungsaufsicht* (German Federal Financial Supervisory Authority – "BAFin") of the free float quota, who in turn notifies the BZSt, if the free float quota falls below 15%.

No shareholder may directly hold 10% or more of the shares. Shares held for third party account are deemed to be held by the third party.[33] Holding 10% or more of the shares in the short-term[34] does not affect the G-REIT's tax exemption, nor does the respective shareholder lose his dividend or voting right;[35] however, he may not take advantage of the violation.[36]

After dividend distribution and allocation to reserves, at least 75% of the G-REIT's total assets have to consist of real estate.[37] At least 75% of the gross yields have to arise from renting out, leasing, and selling of real estate.[38] The G-REIT may raise credits only to the maximum of 60% of its total assets, on marketable conditions, and if provided for in the Articles of Association.[39]

The G-REIT may provide additional services to third parties such as real estate management only by a REIT service company. These service company's assets may not exceed 20% of the G-REIT's total assets after dividends and reserves, and its gross yields may not exceed 20% of the G-REIT's total gross yields.[40]

At least 90% of the G-REIT's distributable profits (according to the annual accounts) have to be distributed to the shareholders within the following business year.[41]

---

32 Section 11.

33 Section 11 para. 4.

34 If the 10% limit set forth in Section 11 para. 4 is ignored for three consecutive years, the G-REIT loses its tax exemption, Section 18 para. 3.

35 Section 16 para. 2.

36 E.g. as regards the withholding tax rate according to an applicable double taxation agreement, see the bill's explanatory statements under B. Article 1 Section 16.

37 As a first sanction of non-complying with this requirement in the end of the business year, the Tax Authority in charge determines a penalty fee dependent on the extent of non-compliance, Section 16 para. 3.

38 Section 12. Assets are evaluated at their market values. Non-compliance with this requirement is sanctioned by the Tax Authority in charge by means of a penalty fee dependent on the extent of noncompliance, Section 16 para. 4.

39 Section 15. The bill only provides for bank financing; it is to be hoped that the G-REIT Act will provide for financing on capital markets by floating bond issues or participating certificates, too.

40 Section 12. Assets are evaluated at their market values.

41 Section 13. Non-compliance with this requirement is sanctioned by the Tax Authority in charge by means of a penalty fee dependent on the extent of non-compliance, Section 16 para. 5.

D. Taxation with Respect to G-REITs

I. Tax Exemption on G-REIT Level

According to Section 16 para. 1 of the bill, a G-REIT complying with the requirements according to Sections 8 to 15 is exempted from trade tax. Furthermore it is exempted from corporate tax, if it is (i) in principle subject to corporate tax and (ii) not deemed to be resident in another state according to any double taxation agreement.[42]

Tax exemption is for the first time applicable with respect to the business year in which the G-REIT as such is registered with the Commercial Register.[43] Tax exemption is limited to the G-REIT itself and does not apply for its subsidiaries. Tax exemption ends if:

(a) The G-REIT loses its listing on an organized market within the EEA, effective as of the end of the business year preceding the loss;[44]

(b) The G-REIT engages in trading real estate, effective as of the beginning of that business year;[45]

(c) Within three consecutive business years less than 15% of the shares are in free float, effective as of the end of the third year;[46] or within three consecutive business years the 10% maximum shareholding limit set forth in Section 11 para. 4 is ignored, effective as of the end of the third year;[47]

(d) Within three consecutive business years raised credits exceed the maximum of 60% of the G-REIT's total assets, effective as of the end of the third year;[48]

---

42 Different from the REIT legislation in the U.S., Great Britain, and France, the G-REIT's tax exemption is fully granted; especially, it is not limited with respect to distributed profits or profits generated by characteristic REIT business. Thereby, the legislator intended to assure the inapplicability of the EU Parent Subsidiary Directive, see the bill's explanatory statements under B. Article 1 Section 16. In international comparison, quite a substantial part of the G-REIT's income is privileged.

43 Section 17.

44 Section 18 para. 1.

45 Section 18 para. 2; for definition of trade see footnote no. 10.

46 Section 18 para. 3.

47 Section 18 para. 3.

48 Section 18 para. 4.

(e) Within three consecutive business years the G-REIT qualifies for being sanctioned by imposition of a penalty fee, each year according to the same Section 16 para. 3, 4, or 5, effective as of the end of the third year;[49] and

(f) Within five consecutive business years the G-REIT qualifies for being sanctioned by imposition of a penalty fee, each year according to any of the Sections 16 para. 3, 4, or 5, effective as of the end of the fifth year.[50]

II. Exit Tax

Under specific circumstances and limited in time, a so called "Exit Tax" grants tax reduction to those who contribute real estate to a G-REIT. Generally, the initial transfer of real estate to a pre-REIT or G-REIT discloses hidden reserves in real estate. This disclosure of hidden reserves leads to an increase in value, which in turn leads to a realisation of profits. According to applicable German tax law, these profits are subject to full taxation. By the Exit Tax, the legislator intends to give the necessary incentives, since the G-REIT is reliant on substantial contributions of real estate to establish itself on financial markets.[51]

According to Article 2 of the bill, only 50% of the profits realised by the disclosure of hidden reserves are subject to income tax, if the real estate to be transferred belonged to the contributor's assets for more than 10 years and the contribution sale is effectively agreed upon after 31 December 2006 and before 1 January 2010.[52] Sale and lease-back is permitted.

However, the acquiring pre-REIT or G-REIT has to own the contributed real estate for at least four years. Otherwise, or if the pre-REIT does not become a REIT within that period, the Exit Tax exemption is retroactively inapplicable and the acquirer is liable to pay residual taxes.

III. Real Estate Transfer Tax

The above mentioned Exit Tax does not affect the provisions regarding real estate transfer tax. Therefore, the transfer of real estate triggers the ordinary

---

49 Section 18 para. 5.

50 Section 18 para. 5.

51 Furthermore, the financial administration expects an increase in tax earnings due to the disclosure of hidden reserves.

52 The Exit Tax is also applicable to transfers of real estate to pre-REITs and German real estate special assets in terms of Section 66 of the *Investmentgesetz* (German Investment Act).

transfer tax.[53] In this respect, the legislator expects substantial increase in tax earnings.

IV. Taxation on Shareholder Level

The main taxation is intended to occur on the shareholder level. Distributed profits and all other benefits granted to the shareholders are income from capital and therefore subject to corporation tax, if the shareholder is a corporation, or income tax, if the shareholder is an individual. This shall also apply for profits gained outside Germany which will then be subject to double taxation. In case of income from a shareholding in a G-REIT, general reductions of the taxable income, as provided for under German Tax Law, such as the exemption of 95% of the dividends distributed to corporate shareholders or the exemption of 50% of the dividends distributed to individuals ("*Halbeinkünfteverfahren*"), do not apply.[54]

As far as profits by the sale of shares are concerned, they are subject to general taxation rules; however, again, the *Halbeinkünfteverfahren* does not apply. Accordingly, gains from the sale of shares held privately are tax exempted if a participation of less than 1% of the shares of the G-REIT was held for more than a year. Dependent on the applicability of double taxation agreements, foreign investors may be tax exempted in Germany. Otherwise, capital gains from the sale of shares are fully taxable.[55]

In any case, the G-REIT's profit distributions are subject to withholding tax at a rate of 25%.[56] When setting up the bill, this taxation at source led to a highly discussed issue in Germany: the risk of a substantial loss in tax revenues, from the Tax Authorities' point of view, to the advantage of foreign shareholders who may refer to applicable double taxation agreements and reduce their tax

53 So far, the transfer tax rate is 3.5% in Germany; however, in consequence of the reform of federalism in Germany, each state ("*Bundesland*") may determine its own tax rate. The communal estate of Berlin, for example, plans to invent a transfer tax rate of 4,5%.

54 Section 19 para. 1. This applies also to income from foreign REITs, Section 19 para. 2 and 6.

55 Section 19 para. 5. This leads to double taxation of income from G-REIT service companies and foreign subsidiaries holding real estate. The legislator has realized this double taxation; it is to be hoped that ways of exemption will be opened.

56 Section 20 para. 1 and 2. This guarantees that, in principle, every investor is subject to tax in a first step and may – under certain circumstances – apply for repayment or set-off of tax paid. In comparison to taxation of other stock corporations' distributions, the higher tax rate of 25% is justified for tax transparency reasons.

rates.[57] Therefore, Section 11 para. 4 of the bill provides for a 10% maximum shareholding.[58]

E. Perspectives

There are great expectations placed in the G-REIT: accordingly, a swift introduction of G-REITs is expected to fill a national gap in the international range of real estate investments, to vitalize the business location Germany, and to professionalize the German real estate economy. By planning to enforce the G-REIT Act retroactively as of 1 January 2007, the German legislator proves to strive for competitiveness of the German financial business to other European locations.

(Constantin M Lachner is partner of the law firm, LACHNER GRAF von WESTPHALEN SPAMER, Frankfurt, Germany (www.lws-law.com); Rafael von, Heppe is employed as associate in the same firm. The authors can be reached at lachner@lws-law.com and heppe@lws-law.com, respectively.)

---

57 According to the "OECD Model Convention with Respect to Taxes on Income and on Capital" from 2003 (OECD-MC), income from dividends may be subject to taxation under the regulations of the investor's home country. Then, taxation in Germany is generally limited to 15% according to Article 10 para. 2 of the OECD-MC.

58 Instead, G-REIT income could have been classified as "income from immovable property" according to Article 6 OECD-MC, with the consequence of full taxation in the country where the property is situated. According to Article 6 para. 2 OECD-MC, the term "immovable property" shall have the meaning which it has under the law of the country in which the property is situated.

11

Swiss Issues Real Estate: Real Estate Market 2007 – Facts and Trends

Real Estate an Investment*

Ulrich Braun, Fredy Hasenmaile, Martin Neff, Thomas Rieder and Yves-Denis Schönenberger

Real estate funds remain attractive to medium-and long-term investors as rising interest rates and strong economic activity would increase the rental income from residential and office buildings. The real estate funds licensed for distribution in Switzerland often differ greatly in terms of size, mix of property types and geographical focus. Apart from the waiver of tax at company level, Swiss-law real estate funds and real estate investment companies are very similar to American REITs.

Yields on Indirect Real Estate Investments 2006

In last year's edition of this study we said that the valuation gap between real estate investment funds and real estate investment companies would continue to narrow. And this is exactly what has happened. While the agio on real estate

* This is an excerpt from the article "Swiss Issues Real Estate: Real Estate Market 2007 – Facts and Trends". The complete paper can be accessed at *www.credit-suisse.com*. For further information contact *immobilien.economicresearch@credit-suisse.com*

investment funds has fallen from 22.2 to 18.3% in an environment of slightly rising interest rates, the premium on real estate investment companies has risen to 19.4% (from 14.4% in December 2005). This trend is reflected in overall returns since the start of the year. On December 31, 2006 the SWX Immobilienfonds Index – including distributions – was 3.2 % higher than at the start of 2006. Swiss real estate shares, meanwhile, had risen by 24.4%, beating the performance of Swiss shares in general as measured by the Swiss Performance Index (20.7%).

Real Estate Investment Funds

The four largest real estate investment funds quoted on the SWX trended sideways throughout 2006 (Figure 1). Taken together these four funds represent a market

Figure 1: Performance of Swiss Real Estate Investment Funds 2006

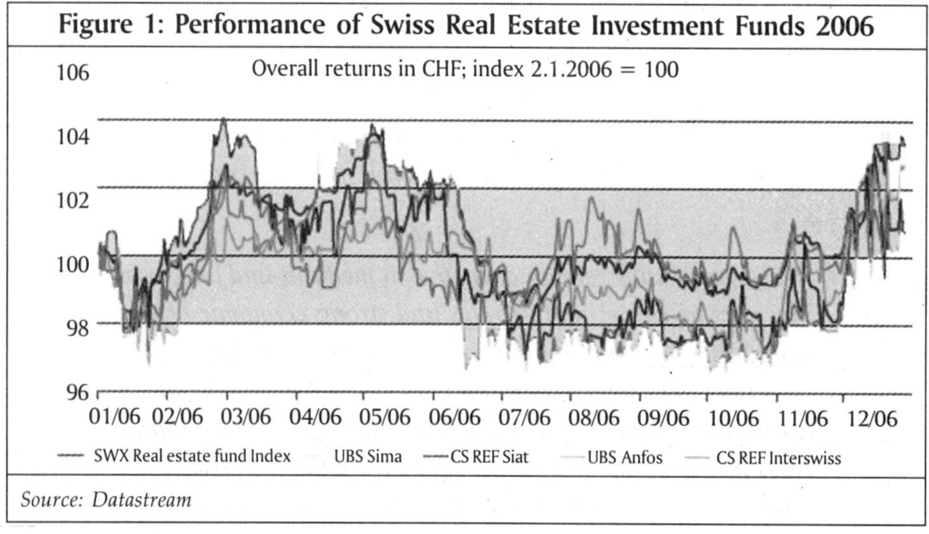

Source: Datastream

capitalization of almost CHF 8.2 billion and 58% of the funds included in the SWX Immobilienfonds Index.

Unlike with equity funds, a new price cannot be set every day for the property in a real estate investment fund – property portfolios tend to be valued annually. Usually, the price paid for a fund unit on the stock exchange will not be the same as the underlying property value per unit (NAV – net asset value). Where the stock market price exceeds the NAV, we call this extra amount the agio. There has been an agio on Swiss real estate funds since the middle of the 1990s, averaging around 10% over the long-term. It is currently at about 18%, with a wide variety of agios on different funds (Figure 2).

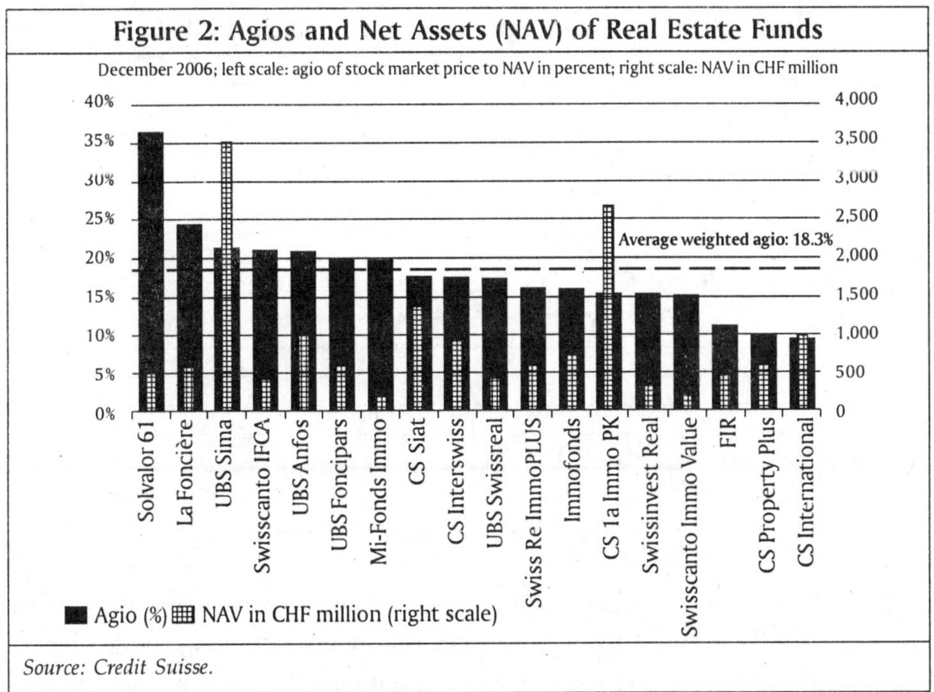

Figure 2: Agios and Net Assets (NAV) of Real Estate Funds

Source: Credit Suisse.

Many investors will ask themselves why they have to pay CHF 118.3 to buy property worth CHF 100. But there are some very good reasons for the existence of this premium on real estate investments. The Swiss version of real estate investment funds transforms a very illiquid asset into a liquid form of investment. A liquidity premium over the price of direct property ownership is, therefore, certainly justified. The greater diversification opportunities and debt financing – real estate funds currently tend to use an average of 20% debt finance – are further reasons for an agio. This does not explain, however, why the agio can fluctuate so much over time.

The significant changes in the size of the premium can be explained by investor behavior. Real estate funds are viewed by investors as a very safe investment. In addition, distributions from these funds are very steady over time – comparable to a bond's. Like bonds, real estate funds react to changes in the general level of interest rates on the capital markets, with prices changing accordingly. If interest rates rise, agios fall, and vice versa. Agios on real estate funds in Switzerland are, therefore, closely tied to interest rate movements (Figure 3). The outlook for real

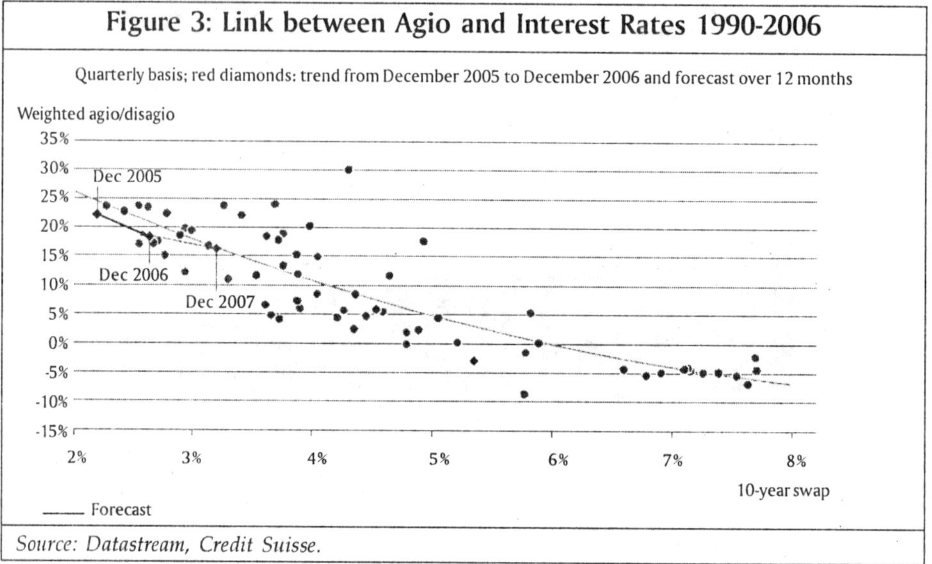

Figure 3: Link between Agio and Interest Rates 1990-2006

Source: Datastream, Credit Suisse.

estate funds thus depends a great deal on interest rate movements over the coming months. We believe that 10-year swap rates will be 0.6 percentage points higher in 12 months than they are today. Our simple model thus tells us that the agio will be about 16% in 12 months.

Real Estate Investment Companies

Real estate investment companies in Switzerland can look back on another successful year. They recorded an overall performance of 24.4% in 2006, thus beating Swiss shares as reflected in the Swiss Performance Index (SPI). Since 2003 the SWX Real Estate Index has produced an average performance of 18.3% a year. The four largest Swiss real estate investment companies performed very similarly in 2006 (Figure 4). Together they make up more than 84% of the SWX Real Estate Index. The two largest companies PSP and SPS were also the best performing at 27%, with SPS benefiting from a rally at the end of the year. Meanwhile, Mobimo produced an overall return of just under 15%.

By far the largest part of the good performance put in by real estate investment companies over recent years is due to the premium/discount trend – i.e., the premium or discount to net asset value implied by the share price. At the start of 2003, the Swiss companies were trading at an average discount of 16.3% to

Figure 4: Performance of Swiss Real Estate Investment Companies 2006

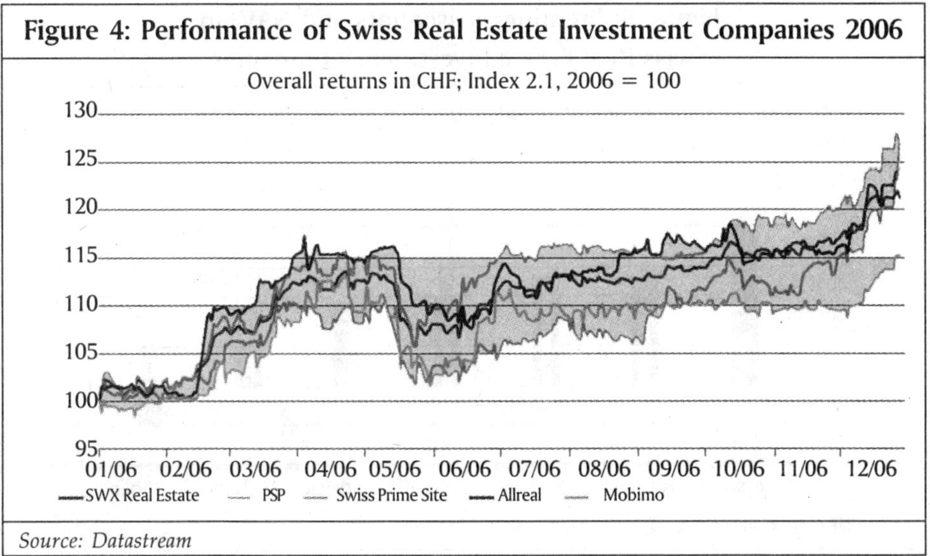

Source: Datastream

NAV; in December 2006 the average weighted premium was 22.2%. In recent years real estate investment companies have undergone a revaluation, partly because the companies provide a valuable alternative to fixed-income securities, thanks to their attractive distributions, and partly because the declining net yields "yield compression" are leading the market to anticipate further increases in property prices.

The valuation gap between real estate funds and real estate investment companies has, therefore, closed over the last year. Intershop has the highest premium at 39.7%, followed by Allreal at 27.1%. By contrast, Züblin, the only firm that is invested mainly outside Switzerland, still trades at a discount (Figure 5).

Indirect investment in property has established itself so well in recent years, especially with institutional investors, that people are already talking about "investment pressure". In other words, it is suggested, there are not enough profitable properties on the market to absorb the huge amount of capital waiting to be invested in real estate. This is mainly because of the historically low level of interest rates. Over recent years, investments in real estate have performed much better than bonds, even though the risk is comparable. As a result, investors are looking more and more outside Switzerland, a fact that is reflected in the almost

Figure 5: Premiums/Discounts and NAV on Swiss Real Estate Investment Companies

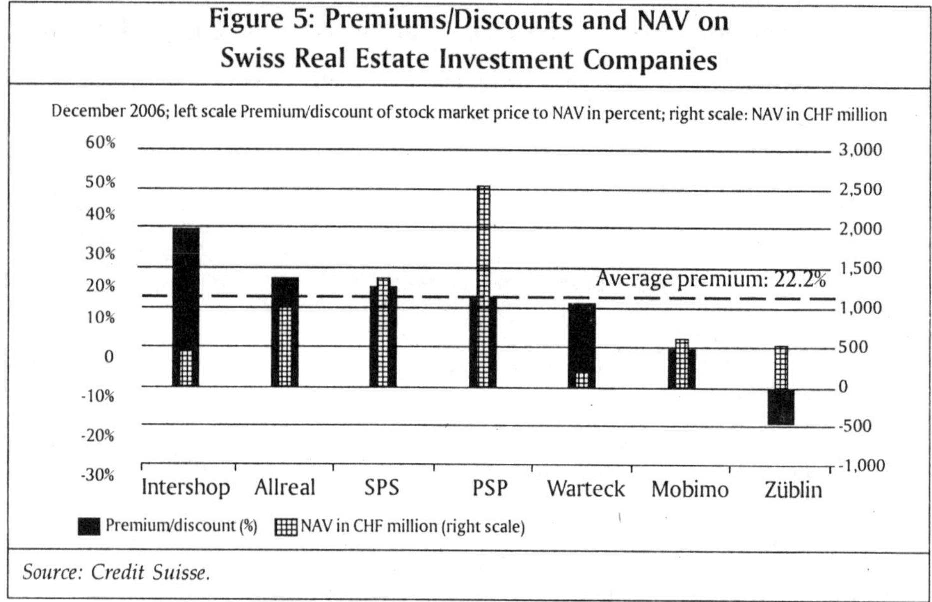

Source: Credit Suisse.

weekly appearance of new international real estate investment funds and funds of funds that include property.

This activity has been driven by the oft-discussed diversification offered by such investments, but also by the excellent performance of international indirect

Figure 6: International Performance of Indirect Real Estate Investment

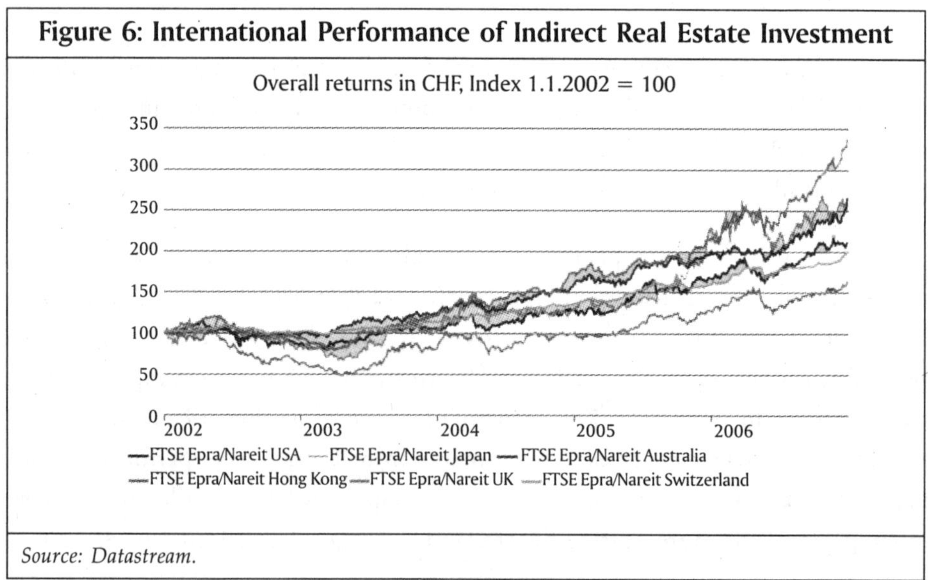

Source: Datastream.

property investments in recent years. A look at overall returns on the five markets with the largest market capitalization of real estate shares (Figure 6) reveals an extremely attractive performance.

The most attractive markets of all are Japan and the UK, with total average annual returns of 20.5% and 26.3% respectively. Many markets in which real estate investment trusts (REITs, comparable to Swiss real estate funds, but without the double taxation) have either been introduced in recent years – such as Japan and France – or are being introduced in the near future – like Germany, Italy and the UK – have done particularly well.

Real Estate in Pension Fund Portfolios

Various aspects of old age pensions have increasingly been the subject of public debate in recent years. The discussion has centered on demographics, but also on the funding structure of pension schemes. It is a very important debate: in Switzerland around CHF 494 billion is managed by more than 3,000 pension funds.

The breakdown of portfolios into individual asset classes, and thus the returns made by individual pension funds, varies enormously. According to a performance comparison made by the Swiss Association of Pension Funds in 2005, overall portfolio yields range between 9.3% and 21.6%. The average is 13.0%. We will now take a more detailed look at the investment structure of Swiss pension funds, particularly with regard to property investments. We also use a historic simulation of an optimized portfolio for the years between 1992 and 2006 to draw some conclusions about the importance of real estate in pension fund portfolios.

The rules for investing pension fund money are set out in the Occupational Pensions Act (BVG) and its implementary ordinance (BVV 2). The legal parameters for investment are relatively wide, leaving pension funds with a fair amount of scope for defining their own investment policies.

The following main investments are permitted:

- Cash (bank account balances and fixed-term deposits in CHF or foreign currencies).

- Bonds, loans (in CHF and foreign currencies; including convertible bonds, bonds with warrants etc.).
- Mortgages.
- Shares (of Swiss and foreign companies).
- Real estate (in Switzerland and abroad).

The changes to BVV2 that came into effect in April 2000 brought more flexible investment options. This greater flexibility included the addition of alternative investments to the permitted forms. These "alternative investments" include such asset classes as private equity, hedge funds and commodities investments.

Pension schemes must observe the principle of adequate risk diversification; in particular the assets must be distributed across different investment categories, regions and economic sectors. Maximum limits are defined for each asset class in the BVV2 ordinance (Figure 7). For real estate, this means that a maximum of 50% of the pension fund's assets may be invested in property in Switzerland. In addition to this, a maximum of 5% is allowed for direct or indirect property investments abroad. Altogether, material assets such as equities and property may not account for more than 70% of total assets.

Figure 7: Statutory Upper Limits for Individual Asset Classes for Pension Funds

FC = Foreign currency

Asset class	Minimum	Maximum	Limits		
Cash, money market	0%	100%			
Swiss bonds, CHF	0%	100%			
Mortgages, Pfandbriefe	0%	75%			
Foreign bonds, CHF	0%	30%	Max. 30%		
Foreign bonds, FC	0%	20%	Max. 30%	Max. 30%	
Foreign equities	0%	25%	Max. 50%	Max. 30%	Max. 70%
Swiss equities	0%	30%	Max. 50%		Max. 70%
Swiss real estate	0%	50%			Max. 70%
Foreign real estate	0%	5%			Max. 70%

Source: Ordinance of April 18, 1984 on Occupational Retirement, Survivors' and Disability Pension Plans. (BVV 2), Art 53 et. seq.

There are no statutory limits for alternative investments. However, investments in private equity, hedge funds or commodities must be properly justified and approved by the regulatory authorities.

So what does the diversification of Swiss pension fund investments look like in reality? The pension fund statistics prepared by the Swiss Federal Statistics Office give us the information we need. The survey, which is conducted every two years, reveals how pension fund assets are divided into different classes of investment. Figure 8 shows the breakdown of Swiss pension fund assets between 1994 and 2004. When compared with the long-term average values, the following main trends have become evident in recent years:

- The proportion of other assets has increased sharply. This is due mainly to the decline in investments with the employer (claims, participations and equities).

Figure 8: Investments by Swiss Pension Funds 1994-2004

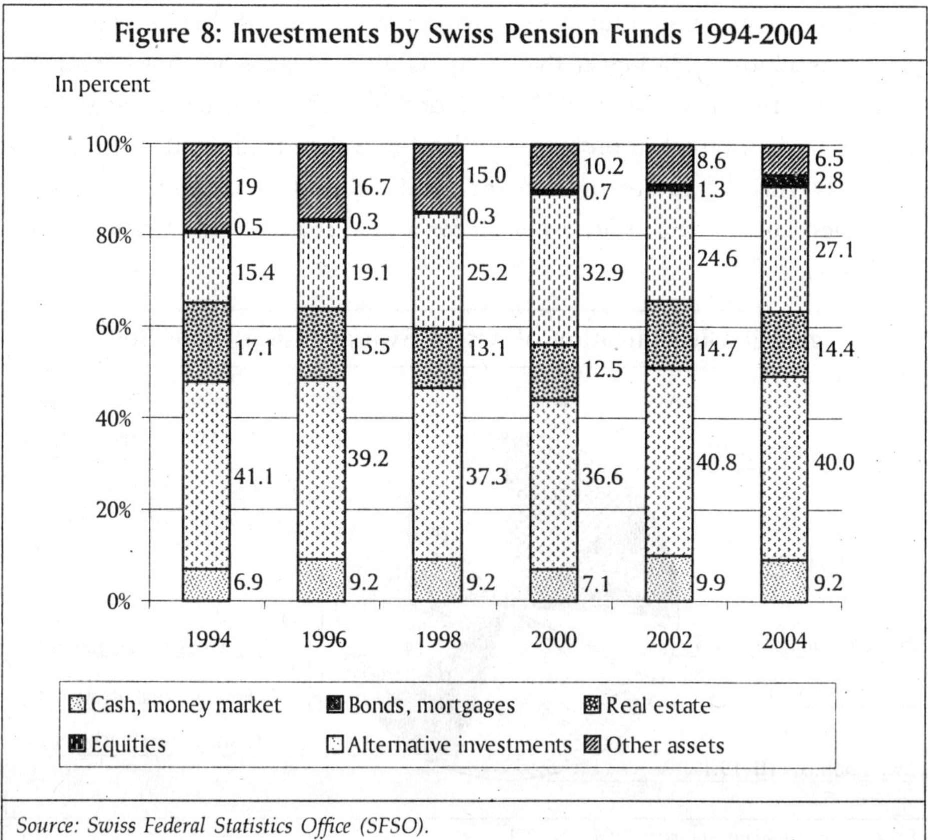

Source: Swiss Federal Statistics Office (SFSO).

- The proportion of equities has risen over the last decade. Investments in foreign shares in particular have increased.
- Alternative investments are also increasingly popular: This is hardly surprising given that this form of investment was only formally recognized in Swiss legislation in 2000. Prior to 2000, alternative investments consisted primarily of precious metals investments.

These pension fund statistics show that pension fund investment behavior is pro-cyclical. For example, the proportion of shares included in pension fund portfolios rose from 15.4 to 32.9% during the long economic upswing between 1994 and 2000. The correction that came in 2001 then led to a reduction back to 24.6%.

In 2004, Swiss pension funds were managing assets worth CHF 484.2 billion – which is almost 10% higher than Swiss GDP. As Figure 50 shows, property accounts for 14.4%, or CHF 69.7 billion of this. And by far the largest share of this amount is invested in property and land in Switzerland – either directly or indirectly via real estate investment funds, foundations and investment companies. Foreign real estate accounts for a total share of only 0.4% or CHF 2.1 billion.

Figure 9: Diversification of Assets, Swiss Pension Funds 2004

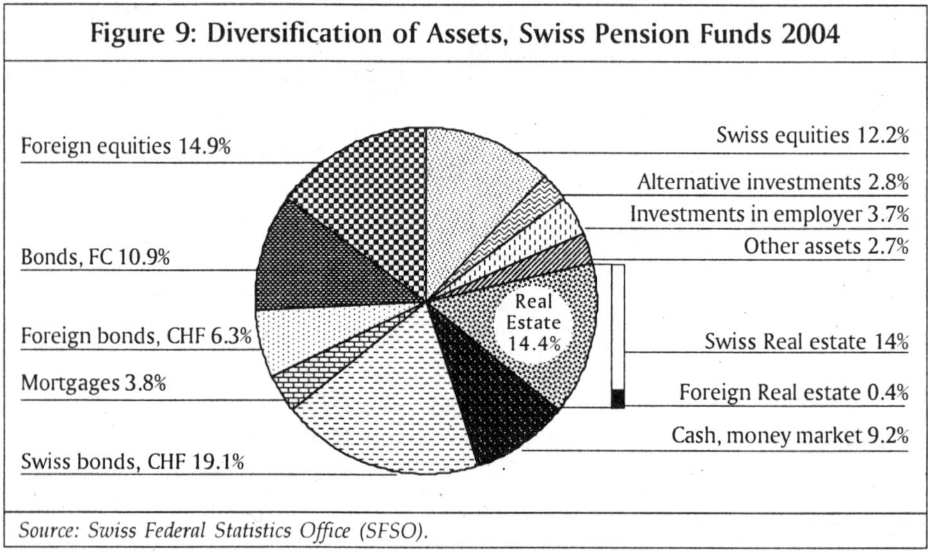

Source: Swiss Federal Statistics Office (SFSO).

So what is the optimum percentage of real estate investments for a Swiss pension fund? To answer this question of portfolio optimization we have examined the overall returns produced by different asset classes between 1990 and 2006.

We looked at the following indices:

- Money Market: JPM Switzerland Cash.
- Bonds: Index of 10-year Swiss benchmark federal bonds (CH), JPM Global Bond Index Broad (Global).
- Equities: MSCI Switzerland, MSCI Europe ex. CH, MSCI USA, MSCI Far East, MSCI Emerging Markets.
- Real estate: Rüd Blass Real Estate Fund Index (Switzerland, capital-weighted), EPRA/NAREIT Europe, EPRA/NAREIT North America, EPRA/NAREIT Asia.

We focus on the monthly data series from 1990. It is impossible to cover any longer period because data from the EPRA/NAREIT indices are only available from 1990. There are no indices for direct real estate investments in Switzerland or abroad that offer the necessary length of time or frequency. The lack of

Figure 10: Average Returns and Risks of Asset Classes in CHF

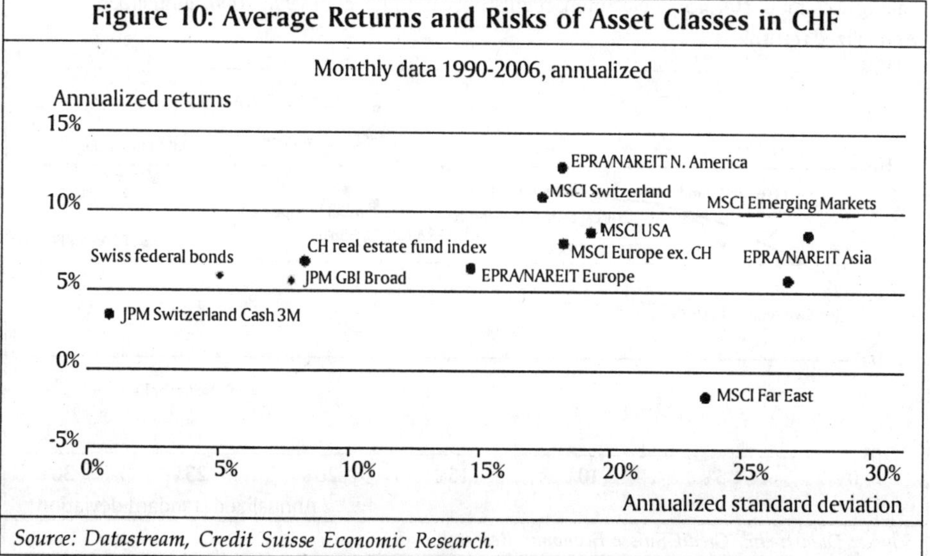

Source: Datastream, Credit Suisse Economic Research.

sufficiently long indices also means that alternative investments such as private equity, hedge funds etc. cannot be included.

The risk/return diagram shown in Figure 10 was produced from an initial analysis of the data. With an average annualized return in CHF of 12.9% and a standard deviation of 18.2%, North American real estate shares stand out from the crowd. The dominant players here are US real estate investment trusts (REITs). By contrast, the risk/return ratio on Asian shares (MSCI Far East) and Asian real estate shares (EPRA/NAREIT Asia) is relatively poor. We do not believe, however, that the historical risk/return profile for Asia is a particularly good indicator of the future prospects for this region. Many factors have had a negative influence on Asia's performance over the period we are looking at, including Japan's lengthy time in the economic doldrums, the Asia Crisis and the outbreak of SARS.

The portfolio has also been optimized over the whole period of 16 years using the portfolio theory developed by Harry Markowitz. For every risk, past data is examined to identify what weighting of individual asset classes would maximize the return. The assumption is that an investment's risk can be expressed by the standard deviation of returns around the average. Account is also taken of the

Figure 11: Efficient Margin of Pension Fund Investments in Switzerland

Taking account of statutory investment regulations, monthly data 1990-2006, annualized

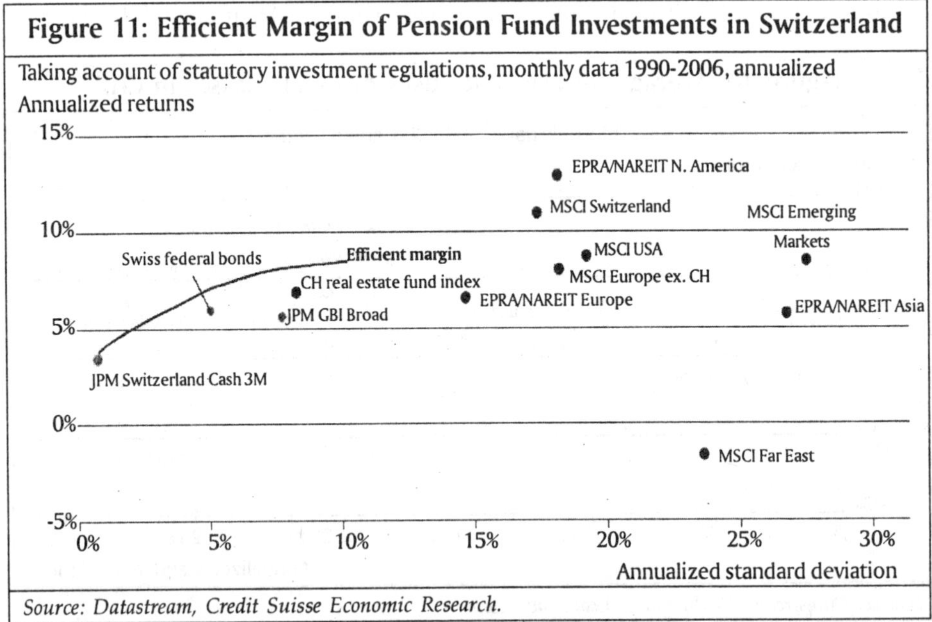

Source: Datastream, Credit Suisse Economic Research.

statutory regulations as shown in Figure 7. This means, for example, that Swiss real estate can never account for more than 50% of the whole portfolio, and not more than 5% can be invested in foreign property. In addition to these investment rules, a minimum of 8.5% is reserved for cash (money market investments). The results of this optimization are shown in Figure 11. All maximum returns that can be achieved by a combination of different investments at a given level of risk are shown by the efficient margin. The risk/return ratios for each asset class are also shown. It is clear that the statutory limits reduce the investment risks, but also reduce the returns that can be achieved.

So how are the individual portfolios made up? The optimum mix of asset classes obviously varies according to the risk assumed (Figure 12). Unsurprisingly, money market investments dominate when risk is at its lowest. As the standard deviation rises, bonds take over, and then equity investments.

Portfolios already hit the maximum 5% limit for international real estate shares at an annualized standard deviation of 1.7%. In all portfolios along the efficient margin, the proportion of international real estate investment companies is larger than in the actual pension fund portfolios we have analyzed. As well as foreign

Figure 12: Optimum Portfolio Weightings for Pension Fund Investments

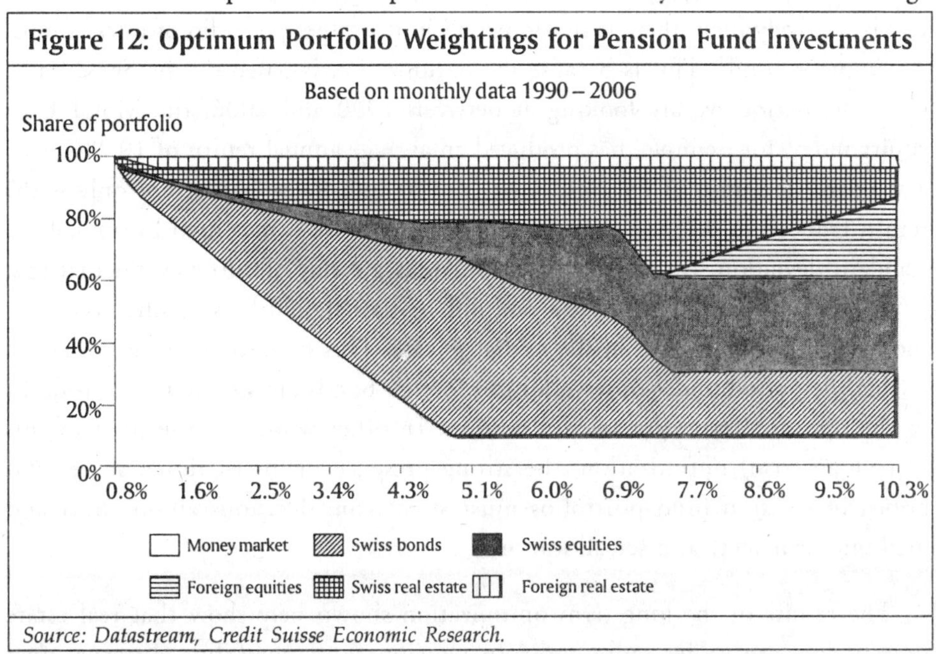

Source: Datastream, Credit Suisse Economic Research.

property investments, we have the percentage devoted to Swiss real estate: in a balanced portfolio, the optimum percentage of funds investing in Swiss property lies between 15% and 30% – depending on the investor's attitude to risk. Here too, then, the long-term percentage of a portfolio devoted to this asset class should be larger than it actually is.

So how can these findings help a pension fund? It is worth repeating that the breakdown of investments shown in Figure 12 constitutes a strategic asset allocation. It shows how pension funds should invest assets in normal situations. This strategic asset allocation serves as a long-term guideline for investment policy. It is driven primarily by the historical performance of the financial markets and is relatively independent of short-term tactical considerations. When setting the strategic asset allocation, therefore, the question is not whether equity markets are likely to rise or fall in the next few months, or whether the USA will perform better than Switzerland, for example. Such mostly temporary over- and under-weightings of individual markets and asset classes are a matter for tactical asset allocation.

At first glance the results might appear surprising, especially with regard to foreign bonds and equities. While foreign equities are only considered when the risk is relatively high, there is no sign at all in the target portfolio of international government bonds. This is because the optimization is based on the Swiss franc. Over the period we are looking at between 1990 and 2006, the MSCI USA equity index, for example, has produced an average annual return of 10.2% (with a standard deviation of 14.1%). If we convert into Swiss francs, not only is the return reduced to 8.7%, but at the same time the risk – measured by annualized standard deviation, is pushed up to 19.2% as a result of currency fluctuations. With government bonds, interest rate differentials should be smoothed out over the long-term by changes in the exchange rate. This is precisely what happened during the period under observation, so foreign bonds are simply not considered in the optimum strategic asset allocation. In other words, in the light of this (very long-term) optimization, the strong presence of international shares and bonds in pension fund portfolios must stem from decisions about short and medium-term tactical asset allocation.

The results of the long-term optimization shown here show that real estate investments are under-represented in pension fund portfolios. International property investments should account for about 5% of the portfolio – i.e., close to the statutory maximum – in all profiles. For investments in Swiss property, meanwhile, allocations of between 15% and 30%, depending on the risk/return profile, are perfectly justified according to our optimization.

The outlook for property investments is rather subdued compared with previous years. This is less to do with the fact that property has become a riskier investment, and more with the fact that high demand for property products has led to relatively high valuations in recent years. The experiences of the past show that Swiss real estate investment funds do not perform particularly well in an environment of rising interest rates because of the falling agios. Swiss real estate investment companies are also saddled with hefty valuations. However, with NAV-based products such as real estate investment foundations and open-ended German property funds, it is still possible to find property investments with barely any links to stock market performance even in the current environment. The advantages to pension funds of real estate investments remain: as well as a high level of distributions, property investments show a low correlation with other investment categories and thus deserve a larger share within Swiss pension fund portfolios.

Prospects for Real Estate Investments in 2007

As we say every year, property is under represented in the portfolios of both private and institutional investors. Owing to its diversification qualities and risk/return structure, it would be quite appropriate to maintain a property allocation of 20 to 30 over the long-term, regardless of the general economic performance. Alongside Swiss investment vehicles, pension funds should also look at international products, since international diversification works much better with property investments than for example equities or bonds. The often significant underweighting of property investments in many private and institutional portfolios continues to suggest that there is considerable potential for growth in this asset class.

But things have changed since 2002: the overall performance of Swiss real estate investment funds over the past five years is 42%, while Swiss real estate investment companies have posted a performance of 92%. The agio on real estate investment funds has risen from 5.8% in 2002 to 18%, while the 13% discount on real estate investment companies has been transformed over the same period into a 20% premium. For short-term investors, Swiss property investment vehicles are certainly "expensively" valued at the moment, and we can not expect a repeat of the excellent performance of the last five years. For long-term investors who regularly invest in directly in property, however, today's valuations represent a yield discount that will continue to fall. In addition, unlisted property investments, e.g., newly launched Swiss real estate investment funds, real estate investment foundations and open-ended German property funds, provide the opportunity to acquire indirect real estate investments with no, or only a small premium/agio.

(Ulrich Braun is responsible for Real Estate Strategy in the Asset Management Division of Credit Suisse. He can be reached at ulrich.braun@credit-suisse.com.

Thomas Rieder can be reached at thomas.rieder@credit-suisse.com

Martin Neff, Head Swiss Economy Research, Credit Suisse. He can be reached at martin.neff@credit-suisse.com

Yves-Denis Schönenberger, MA Student.)

12

Regulatory Impact Assessment for Real Estate Investment Trusts (UK-REITs)

The article discusses about UK-REITs, their requirements and costs incurred by the companies elected to join UK-REITs. The property investment market is the principal market that would be affected by the measure, though there might be some associated impacts on development activity. The article concludes with the effect of a breach of a regime condition. The effect will depend on the size of the breach, the nature of the condition and the number of times that a breach has occurred.

Purpose and Intended Effects of the Measure

The Policy Objectives

This regulatory impact assessment considers a new measure to reform the tax treatment of property investment to:

- Improve the quality and quantity of finance for investment in property;
- Expand access to a wider range of savings products on a stable and well regulated basis;

- Ensure that a fair level of taxation continues to be paid by the property sector; and
- Support structural change in the property market.

Background

The 2003 Pre-Budget Report announced that in line with the interim recommendations of the Barker Review, the Government had concluded that reform to the tax treatment of property investment would improve liquidity, transparency and scrutiny of the property market, provide access to property for long-term savings, and could complement expansion of the private rented sector.

The Government published a consultation document at Budget 2004, 'Promoting more flexible investment in property: a consultation'[1], which included a partial regulatory impact assessment.

Based on the responses received to this consultation, the Government published a further discussion document at Budget 2005, 'UK Real Estate Investment Trusts: a Discussion Paper'[2], which addressed some outstanding technical issues and contained a summary of the responses to the 2004 consultation document.

Draft legislation to establish Real Estate Investment Trusts was published by HM Revenue and Customs on 14 December 2005, together with an updated partial Regulatory Impact Assessment and a summary of responses to the Budget 2005 Discussion Paper[3]. Further draft legislation setting out how the UK-REIT regime would apply to groups of companies was published on 27 January 2006, with a further updated partial Regulatory Impact Assessment[4]. A summary of consultation responses to both sets of legislation will be published by HM Revenue and Customs in due course.

It remains the opinion of the Government that introducing a bespoke property investment vehicle will bring economic benefits to the UK property investment market and the wider economy.

---

1 *http://www.hm-treasury.gov.uk/budget/budget_04/associated_documents/bud_bud04_adproperty.cfm*

2 *http://www.hm-treasury.gov.uk/budget/budget_05/other_documents/bud_bud05_odreits.cfm*

3 *http://www.hmrc.gov.uk/drafts/estate-investment.htm*

4 *http://customs.hmrc.gov.uk/channelsPortalWebApp/channelsPortalWebApp.portal?_nfpb=true&_pageLabel=pageExcise_ShowContent&propertyType=document&columns=1&id=HMCE_PROD1_025090*

Rationale for Government Intervention

The Government believes that there are a number of features of the property market that are resulting in it operating inefficiently, thereby reducing the full potential for productivity growth for the UK economy. These can be summarised as:

- **Lack of choice for small investors** – who, if they want to access property returns, tend to do so in ways which involve a large relatively illiquid investment, such as buy-to-let investments or direct ownership. Access to this market is therefore restricted and the size of individual investments are such that investors cannot easily diversify their portfolio to reduce risk;
- **Poor Liquidity** – which is a reflection of the nature of property itself as an asset. The commercial property market is dominated by large investors and pricing and investment decisions are often determined by individual transactions among a small number of players;
- **Potential for more efficient use of commercial property** – a high proportion of commercial property in the UK is owner occupied and this tends to be used less intensively than property in the investment market. More indirect investment would promote increased efficiency in the use of commercial property stock through economies of scale;
- **Variable standards of provision in the private rented sector** – with wide variations in management efficiency. Improvements to this sector could enhance efficiency and flexibility in the housing market;
- **High levels of debt financing** – which increase the sector's sensitivity to interest rate changes and may lead to instability in the wider economy; and
- **Tax distortions** – as investors are taxed differently, depending on how they invest in property, it is not easy to compare performance of different investment choices. This may result in investors undertaking more risky, less stable investments than if it were possible to make a simple and direct comparison.

The Government believes that the proposed vehicle addresses all of the above points by introducing more choice for small investors, allowing more liquidity in the market, giving potential for more efficiently and professionally managed property, reducing dependency on debt for financing and removing tax distortions. The Government remains committed to ensuring that any reform is introduced at no overall cost to the Exchequer.

Following responses received to the 2004 consultation, the Government will bring forward legislation to repeal sections 508A and 508B of the Income and Corporation Taxes Act 1988 which deal with Housing Investment Trusts.

Options

Do Nothing

Doing nothing would mean that the property market would continue to operate in a sub-optimal way. Similar vehicles have been established in at least 11 developed economies, showing that there is widespread recognition of the benefits of such a regime.

Alternative Solution

The Government is considering in parallel the tax treatment of alternative vehicles that might be seen as close substitutes for investing in property, such as openended collective investment schemes. The Government has also considered whether private vehicles should also be permitted to participate in the UK-REIT regime and has concluded that this would not deliver against the objective of encouraging wider investment from small investors.

Real Estate Investment Trusts

The Government is publishing legislation in Finance Bill 2006. The proposed vehicle, known as a Real Estate Investment Trust (UK-REIT), would be:

- A closed-ended company, resident in the UK, that is publicly listed on a Recognised Stock Exchange[5];
- Required to separate out its income between taxable and non-taxable portions, referred to as 'ring fenced' (non-taxable) and 'non-ring fenced' (fully taxable); and

[5] As defined in section 841 of Income and Corporation Taxes Act 1988 (ICTA).

- Also required to distribute at least 90% of its ringfenced profits to investors and to withhold basic rate tax on these distributions.

The ring fenced part of the UK-REIT would represent at least 75% of the vehicle's activity by income and assets.

UK-REITs would be subject to an interest cover test on the ring fenced part of their business. Failure of this test will result in an additional tax charge rather than loss of eligibility for the regime.

The UK-REIT would be required to meet existing regulations on close companies[6], and no shareholder who had beneficial entitlement to dividends would be allowed to control (either directly or indirectly) 10% or more of the UK-REIT's share capital or voting rights. Where this rule were breached, a tax penalty would apply as set out below.

Where a UK-REIT acquired a property to develop or refurbish for its own investment purposes and subsequently sold that property within three years of the completion of such works, the proceeds of that sale would not be tax-exempt if the costs of development or refurbishment exceeded 30% of the fair value of the asset at the point at which it was brought into the UK-REIT regime.

The legislation provides for groups of companies to elect to join the UK-REIT regime.

The income and asset tests, which require that 75% of the UK-REIT's income derives from property rental and that 75% of assets are used in that business, would be applied to the group as a whole.

The parent company would be required to distribute 90% of the property rental income of its UK resident subsidiaries and rents derived from UK property owned by foreign subsidiaries.

All tax-exempt property income forms part of the distribution paid out by the group under deduction of withholding tax, or, where income is not tax-exempt, it is paid out as a normal dividend.

---

6 Within the meaning of section 414 of ICTA.

Where the UK-REIT holds property through foreign subsidiaries (which are not subject to UK taxation on overseas property), the income paid up by this subsidiary company to the UK parent company would be treated as a dividend from an overseas company, as it is now, and taxed accordingly. A foreign subsidiary holding UK property would be exempt from UK tax on the rents earned from that property.

On election, joint venture entities would have an exempt ring fence to the extent of ownership by the UK-REIT providing that a 75% subsidiary of the parent company owns at least a 40% interest in the entity.

Costs and Benefits

The Government has stated as one if its key objectives that any reform to the property investment market should be introduced at no overall cost to the Exchequer (see Budget 2004 Consultation and Budget 2005 discussion papers). It is the Government's view that the proposed model published today would lead to some overall reduction in Exchequer receipts. In order to offset this, the Government set out at Budget 2004 its intention to levy a charge for companies joining the UK-REIT regime.

The Government is committed to meeting the above objective and details of the charge applying to companies joining the regime have been announced at Budget 2006. Companies wishing to join the regime will be required to pay a sum equal to 2% of the gross value of the assets, which they intend to include in the tax-exempt ring fence. This will ensure revenue neutrality for the long-term public finances. Other costs and benefits relating to the administrative implications of introducing UK-REIT legislation are considered below.

Sectors and Groups Affected

The main business sectors that would be affected by this measure are the property investment industry and the investment and fund management industry. There are potential wider economic benefits for UK businesses and individuals from more efficient management of property as a productive factor and as a financial asset.

The property sector makes a significant contribution to the UK economy. The 2005 National Accounts 'Blue Book'[7] published by the Office for National Statistics shows that a combination of residential buildings and commercial, industrial and other buildings represented around two-thirds of non-financial assets on the national balance sheet in 2004. The value of residential buildings was £3427 billion and the value of commercial property £624 billion.

To determine what proportion of the companies likely to be directly affected by the legislation are small and medium-sized enterprises (SMEs), a sample of companies from the property investment industry was examined, which included the largest listed and private property investment companies, but possibly did not include all of the smaller companies. From this sample we found that around 80% are large companies, around 17% medium-sized companies, and the remainder small companies, according to the criteria set by the Small Business Service[8].

Benefits

This measure would have the following potential benefits:

- Small investors (retail and smaller institutions) would have greater access to property through a diversified savings portfolio, without being subject to the potential risks, large capital outlays or tax inefficiency, which they currently face when choosing to invest in property;

- Information obtained from an Investment Management Association survey[9] on the asset allocation of retail investors (as well as pension and insurance funds) found that in 2004 investment in property accounted for 2.4% of the portfolio of retail investors, compared with 4.5% for pension funds and 9.7% for insurance funds. Assuming that larger institutions have a greater proportion of their investments in property because it is more accessible to them, we might assume that the proportion for retail investors could increase to similar levels once they have access to shares in UK-REITs;

---

7 *http://www.statistics.gov.uk/StatBase/Product.asp?vlnk=1143*

8 *http://www.sbs.gov.uk/sbsgov/action/layer?r.s=sl&topicId=7000000237*

9 *http://www.investmentuk.org/news/surveys/default.asp*

- Business would be expected to benefit from an improved supply of good quality, well maintained, competitively priced accommodation, as a more efficient utilisation of financing sources allows for greater investment. Owner occupying businesses might find that the opportunity of releasing property assets to professional building managers would allow them efficiency gains from specialisation in their core business;

- The UK economy would be expected to benefit through greater efficiency in the allocation of investment resources and a rebalancing of debt and equity in the financing of property companies. The privatisation of 12 listed companies, perhaps partly driven by tax regulations, caused the listed sector to decrease by as much as 25% between 1999 and 2003 – we would expect this trend towards delisting to be halted under a UK-REIT regime, with companies' behaviour being driven by economic fundamentals and not tax regulations; and

- The private rented sector would be expected to benefit from improved management through the involvement of large institutions in the form of UK-REITs, and developers would be expected to bring forward more housing supply to the private rented sector with UK-REITs there to act as willing purchasers.

Costs

In order to illustrate the direct costs to a property company of electing to join the UK-REIT regime and then complying with it on an ongoing basis, some simple case studies were included in the partial Regulatory Impact Assessment published in December 2005. These are included at Annexure 2.

From consultation responses received from industry and others, it has not been possible to quantify the costs in detail, but these will relate primarily to the costs of monitoring the income and assets of the company and the composition of the company's shareholders, to ensure ongoing compliance with the requirements of the regime. The Implementation and Delivery Plan at Annexure 1 contains more detail.

The costs to HM Revenue and Customs in implementing the regime fall into three main areas:

- Changes to Corporation Tax Self Assessment (CTSA) forms;
- Changes to the systems for the transfer of electronic data; and
- The introduction of a new certification form that UK-REITs would complete alongside their annual CTSA return.

This new form would demonstrate how UK-REITs had met the obligations of the regime. Guidance material, including internal guidance manuals, would need to be prepared and training carried out before the introduction of the regime. Apart from issuing guidance, no impact on the income tax self-assessment return for investors is anticipated. Ongoing costs for HM Revenue and Customs will arise from the need to monitor compliance with UK-REIT obligations within the self-assessment regime. These costs are not expected to be large.

It is not anticipated that there would be any significant negative impacts on the costs of goods, services or technologies or on levels of investment.

Nor is it anticipated that there would be any additional impacts on devolved regions, human rights, the environment, rural areas or crime.

Small Firms Impact Test

From responses received to the consultation, and further discussions with the authors of these responses, the Small Business Service, and other interested parties, the Government has concluded that it is unlikely that there would be an adverse effect on small and medium sized enterprises as a result of the introduction of the UK-REIT regime. As noted above, businesses in general should benefit from a more efficient property market, since property is an important factor of production.

Competition Assessment

The impact of the proposed UK-REIT regime was assessed by applying the competition filter to the property investment market. It was found that an in-depth competition assessment is not warranted.

The property investment market is the principal market that would be affected by the measure, though there might be some associated impacts on development activity. This sector is characterised by relatively high market intensity with less than a dozen firms accounting for a majority of the whole UK listed market in terms of net asset value, employees and turnover. It is anticipated that the concentration of the UK-REIT market would largely reflect this concentration. Responses received to the consultation largely supported this view.

Enforcement, Sanctions and Monitoring

A UK-REIT would be required to meet the tests for the balance of ring fenced and non-ringfenced business, on asset and income bases at the end of each accounting period. It would be subject to the penalties and provisions of the Corporation Tax Self Assessment regime and would self assess that it has met the relevant conditions to qualify as a UK-REIT in its tax return. In the case of a Group UK-REIT, the principal company would make this declaration on behalf of the members of the group. HM Revenue and Customs would have the normal powers to enquire into the accuracy of the return. Additionally, the UK-REIT would need, without unreasonable delay, to inform HM Revenue and Customs if it had breached a condition. Failure to make this notification would result in penalties arising.

The effect of a breach of a regime condition will depend on the size of the breach, the nature of the condition and the number of times that a breach has occurred.

Breach of certain conditions will always result in the company being removed from the regime with effect from the end of the accounting period prior to the breach. The conditions falling in this category are UK tax residence, nature of share capital and debt, listing and not being an Open Ended Investment Company (OEIC) or close company.

Breaches of other conditions will not normally result in removal from the regime unless the failure is very significant or occurs on a number of occasions – a major breach.

Minor breaches of these conditions are dealt with as follows:

- Minor breaches of the distribution requirement will result in additional tax being payable to ensure no loss to the Exchequer.

- Conditions in respect of the nature and value of the properties held and the balance of business will not result in a tax penalty. However, a company may suffer removal from the regime if any one breach is very significant or if breaches occur repeatedly over a ten-year period.

Breaches of the 10% shareholding requirement will result in an additional tax charge arising unless the UK-REIT has undertaken reasonable steps to ensure that the condition is not breached. Courses of action that HM Revenue and Customs consider to be reasonable steps for this purpose will be set out in guidance in due course.

If a UK-REIT is involved in tax avoidance, HM Revenue and Customs will have the power to require that the tax, which the company sought to avoid is charged and then that an additional tax charge is assessed, which is broadly equal to the tax that the company sought to avoid. If such avoidance is entered into a second time, HM Revenue and Customs may remove the company from the regime.

Post-Implementation Review and Evaluation

Ongoing monitoring and evaluation of the impact of the UK-REIT regime will focus on the areas identified above:

- The participation by small investors in indirect investment in property;
- The degree of liquidity in the commercial property market;
- The proportion of commercial property which is owner-occupied;
- The levels of debt in the commercial property sector;
- The degree to which the introduction of the UK-REIT regime has halted the trend for UK property to be owned by unlisted or offshore vehicles;
- The degree to which removing tax distortions has aided investment choices; and
- The setting up of residential UK-REITs in the private rented sector.

Since the effects of the regime on these areas will only become apparent over a relatively extended period of time, it is unlikely that any review or evaluation will be useful until at least three years after the first companies join the regime. The costs of compliance and administration may be reviewed at an earlier date.

Annexure 1: Implementation and Delivery Plan

This plan sets out the activities a company would need to undergo in order to qualify to join the UK-REIT regime, and continue to qualify on an ongoing basis. The Government requested information from industry on the likely costs of these activities, but received no response. An assessment of the costs in Standard Cost Methodology terms will be undertaken as and when further information becomes available.

Company Activities for Qualification to Join the UK-REIT Regime

	Activity
Set Up	Set up computer and administrative systems to monitor the required splits in assets and activities.
Registration	Register the UK-REIT with HM Revenue and Customs providing the evidence requested and pay the conversion charge as assessed.
Complete the Annual Return	Ongoing monitoring using the systems outlined above Identification of dividend streams to ensure that the 90% distribution test is met and that the correct withholding procedures are applied Monitoring the size of investors' holdings, and compliance with the 10% holding restriction Provide details of non-ring fence profits in the normal CTSA form. Provide details of ring fence profits in new CTSA equivalent form. Provide details of consolidated income and assets for a Group UK-REIT.
Compliance Regime	Dealing with any compliance regime associated with the regime, for example in providing HMRC with any additional information requested.

Annexure 2: Case Studies

Case Study One: XYZ PLC

XYZ PLC is an existing property company, resident in the UK and listed on the London Stock Exchange. In order to join the UK-REIT regime, it might have to do some or all of the following, depending on the current structure of the company.

- Restructure the company, and possibly any group or subsidiary structures, so as to ensure that at least 75% of its assets and income are eligible for ring fencing;
- Pay any costs arising from this restructuring;

Contd...

Contd...

- Set up computer and administrative systems to monitor the split between ring fenced and non-ring fenced assets and income;
- Establish procedures to apportion expenditure between ring fenced and non-ring fenced activities;
- Put in place arrangements to monitor the origins of dividends derived from group companies (i.e., whether derived from property rental, capital disposals or other income), monitor foreign tax credits attaching to non-ring fenced income, and to calculate the average minority shareholding for the purposes of tax calculation;
- Apply the grouping tests; and
- Incur internal management, legal or consultancy costs associated with the above.

Once in the regime XYZ PLC would face ongoing costs to cover the following:

- Ongoing monitoring using the systems outlined above;
- Identification of dividend streams to ensure that the 95% distribution test is met and that the correct withholding procedures are applied; and
- Monitoring the size of investors' holdings, and compliance with the 10% holding restriction.

Case Study Two: LMN Property

LMN Property is an unlisted property company, resident in the UK. The costs it might face would be broadly similar to those in Case One above, with the addition of any costs associated with listing on a Recognised Stock Exchange and managing its relationship with its shareholders.

13

Asian REITs: A New Dimension for Investors*

Philip Conner and Marc Halle

REITs promise to improve transparency, liquidity and the industry's access to capital, while creating a more dynamic and competitive property market that should encourage more professionalism and best practices throughout the industry. The evolution of the new REIT vehicles in Asia is likely to mirror the development of the Australian and US markets in many respects and is expected to expand at a healthy pace over the next two years, with very strong growth in China and India.

The recent introduction of tax-transparent property investment vehicles, or real estate investment trusts (REITs), in Japan, Singapore and several other Asian countries is both an opportunity for investors and an important milestone in the development of the global real estate securities market. Listed property companies have existed in Asia for decades, as they have in most countries with developed real estate markets. However, the new REIT vehicles, because of their structural features and mandatory high dividend payout ratios in particular, add a dimension to the property investment and capital markets in Asia that has benefited both investors and the industry in countries with well-established REIT

* This report originally appeared in the Summer 2006 issue of *Real Estate Finance Journal.*

markets. This report examines the growth and development of the Asian REIT market, the economic and demographic forces that should create demand throughout Asia, not only for real estate but also for yield-oriented investment products like REITs, and the potential implications of the new vehicles in the context of a global real estate securities portfolio.

Brief History of the Asian REIT Market

Asia has a long history of listed property companies and commands a large share of the global listed property market. According to the S&P/Citigroup BMI Property Index, the Asia Pacific region, which includes Australia and New Zealand, accounted for about 35% of the global listed property sector's available equity market capitalization at the start of 2006.[1] As Exhibit 1 makes very clear, however, the region's global share has fallen dramatically since the mid-1990s, when Asia represented more than 60% of the global listed property market.

Exhibit 1: Asia Commands Large Share of Listed Property Market

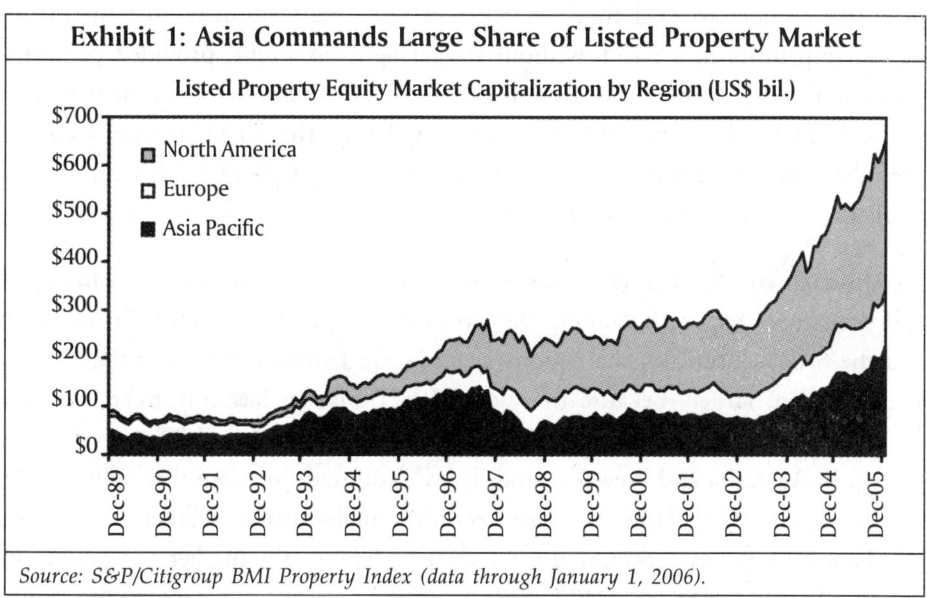

Source: S&P/Citigroup BMI Property Index (data through January 1, 2006).

The relative decline coincides with the Asian financial market crisis in 1997-98 and with the rapid growth phase of the US REIT market in the early to mid-1990s. After peaking at more than $141 billion[2] in August 1997, the equity

[1] Companies must meet certain size and trading volume criteria to be included in the BMI Property Index. Thus some Asian countries, such as Malaysia, South Korea and Thailand, are not included in the listed property universe.

[2] Unless otherwise noted, all figures are in US$.

market capitalization of the Asian listed property market declined sharply as the crisis spread throughout the region, devastating financial and real asset values. By September 1998, the Asian listed property sector's equity market capitalization had fallen to about $44 billion, or less than 22% of the total global listed property market. Hong Kong's listed property market alone suffered a 75% decline, plunging from more than $80 billion before the crisis to less than $20 billion.

The rapid expansion of the US REIT market compounded the effects of the Asian crisis on the region's share of the global listed property market. US REITs were first introduced in the early 1960s. However, they remained a relatively small and insignificant part of the US real estate investment and capital markets until the real estate market crashed in the early 1990s. The liquidity crisis in the private real estate capital markets that accompanied the severe downturn and the introduction of the Umbrella Partnership REIT (UPREIT) in 1992, which allowed property owners to exchange their direct real estate holdings for operating partnership units in a REIT without triggering a tax event, provided powerful catalysts for the tremendous growth of the REIT market over the next several years. Between January 1992 and January 1998, the REIT market's equity capitalization soared from $8.7 billion, or about 11% of the global listed property market, to $105.2 billion, or roughly 44% of the listed property market.

Although the Asian listed property market has fully recovered from the crisis and subsequent shocks (including the global equity market downturn in 2000-01 and the SARS outbreak), the region's share is still considerably lower than it was a decade ago, largely because the global REIT market has continued to grow rapidly. Since January 2002, REITs and listed property trusts (LPTs), as they are known in Australia and New Zealand, have accounted for more than 68% of the increase in the global listed property sector's available equity market cap.[3] While REITs and LPTs have accounted for a smaller share of the market cap growth in the Asia Pacific region, the REIT segment of the market has been growing nearly twice as fast as the non-REIT segment. Since 2002, the equity market cap of the Asia Pacific REIT market has grown at a compound annual rate of nearly 50%, or by more than $75 billion, while the non-REIT segment has increased roughly 29% per year, or by about $70 billion in four years (see Exhibit 2).

[3] All figures are based on available equity market capitalization of the BMI Property Index and BMI REIT Index.

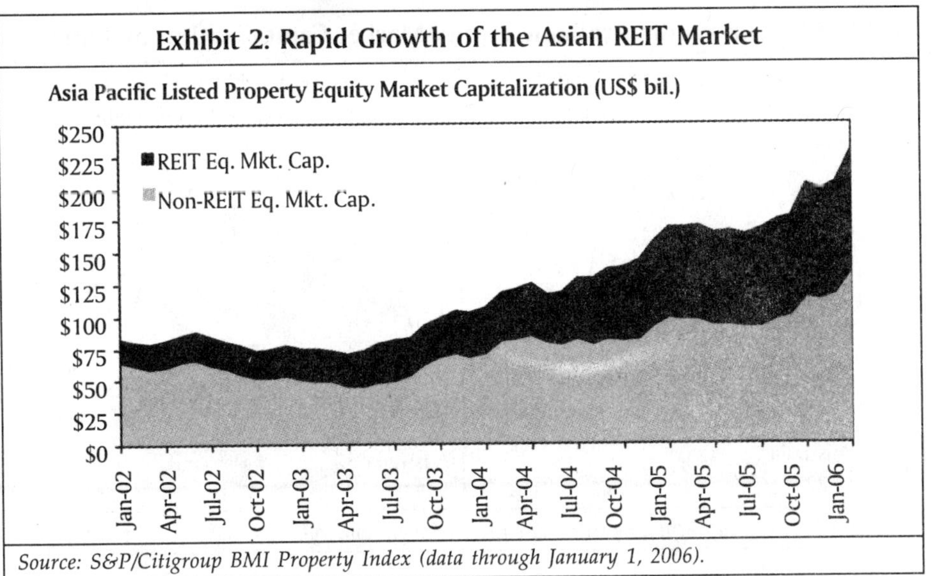

Exhibit 2: Rapid Growth of the Asian REIT Market

Source: S&P/Citigroup BMI Property Index (data through January 1, 2006).

Within the Asia Pacific region, only Australia has a long history of tax-transparent vehicles and a large, liquid and mature market.[4] LPTs were introduced in Australia in the early 1970s. However, like US REITs, they experienced relatively little growth until the property market downturn in the early 1990s. The collapse of the unlisted property trust sector in the early 1990s and the compulsory savings required under the Superannuation Guarantee introduced in 1992 fueled the LPT market's growth throughout the 1990s. As demand for investments offering secure cash yields surged, particularly in the wake of the Asian crisis and global equity market downturn in 2000-01, the equity market cap of the LPT market climbed from about $10 billion in September 1998 to more than $67 billion at year-end 2005 (see Exhibit 3).[5]

A few features of the Australian market are striking when compared with most other developed REIT markets, particularly the US. First, the LPT market is highly concentrated. The five largest LPTs account for more than 65% of the equity market cap of the BMI REIT Index for Australia, and the largest firm, Westfield Group, accounts for more than one-third. LPTs also control a much

4 LPTs were introduced in New Zealand in 1992. At year-end 2005, the BMI REIT Index included five LPTs from New Zealand, with a total available equity market cap of less than $1.4 billion.

5 Based on available equity market capitalization of the 31 LPTs in the BMI REIT Index for Australia.

Exhibit 3: Asia Pacific Available Equity Market Capitalization by Country

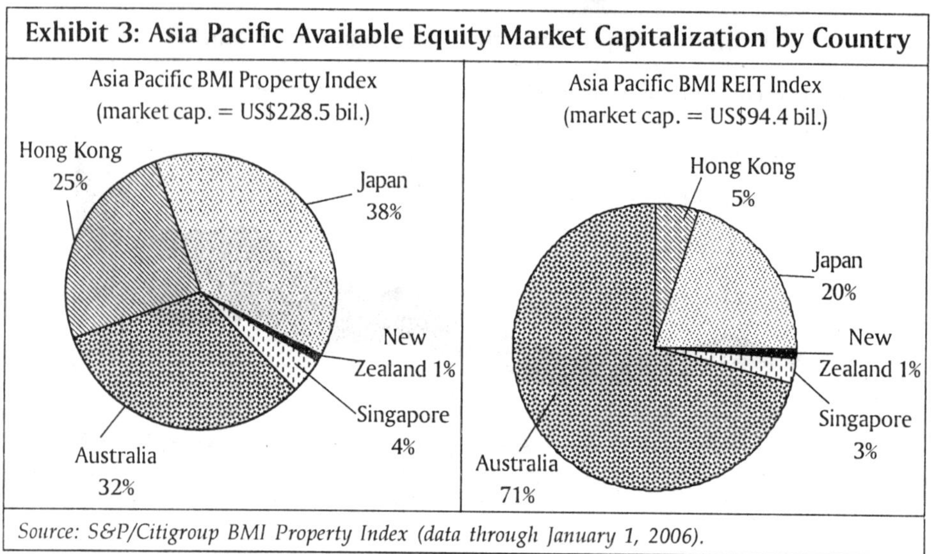

Source: S&P/Citigroup BMI Property Index (data through January 1, 2006).

larger share of the investable universe than is typical in other countries. According to UBS, LPTs own about 28% of all institutional-grade commercial property in Australia and as much as 60% of all institutional-grade property held for investment purposes. This compares with an ownership share of about 12% of all institutional-grade property for US REITs. One consequence of the relatively high penetration rate has been the growing need for LPTs to look outside Australia for growth opportunities. For example, at year-end 2005, US assets accounted for more than 25% of LPT holdings.[6]

While Australia will continue to overshadow the other countries in the emerging Asian REIT market because of its size, the most dynamic growth, at least in the near term, will occur in the newly created REIT markets in Japan, Singapore, Hong Kong and elsewhere. Japan boasts the second-largest REIT market in the region after Australia. J-REITs first appeared in 2001 with two listings and an equity market cap of about $1 billion. Last year, 13 J-REITs tapped the public equity markets with initial public offerings (IPOs), bringing the total number of J-REITs to 28 and the sector's total equity market cap to more than $30 billion.[7] The J-REIT market should continue to grow as the

6 UBS Global Real Estate Analyser, December 2005.

7 Total market cap is based on the GPR General Index as of Dec. 31, 2005. At year-end 2005, the BMI REIT Index included 22 J-REITs, with an available equity market cap of $18.7 billion.

Japanese economy and property markets finally begin to recover and J-REIT yields continue to offer an attractive premium (about 200 bps) over government bonds. Already this year, Japan Hotel and Resort, the first hotel J-REIT, debuted in February, and another three IPOs are expected before the end of the first quarter.

The nascent Hong Kong REIT market recently overtook Singapore as the third-largest REIT market in the Asia Pacific region following the much-anticipated IPO of the Hong Kong Housing Authority's Link REIT. Despite being delayed for nearly a year, the Link REIT IPO raised HK$18.9 billion (about US$2.6 billion) in November 2005 and helped catapult Hong Kong ahead of Singapore in the BMI REIT Index with a 5% regional share.[8] Although legislation for a Hong Kong REIT had been in place since 2003, flaws in the initial structure discouraged most sponsors from using the new vehicle until the regulations were substantially revised last year. Two private sector offerings, including the first REIT with assets in mainland China, followed the Link IPO in December, setting the stage for more offerings in 2006.

Despite the relative decline in its market share recently, Singapore's S-REIT market has been an important pioneer in establishing and promoting tax-transparent listed property vehicles in Asia. As in Hong Kong, flaws in the initial S-REIT legislation of 1999 delayed the launch of the S-REIT market until the regulations were revised to make the vehicle less cumbersome and more competitive with "ordinary" listed property firms. The S-REIT structure has since evolved into one of the most progressive and attractive, to both sponsors and investors, of today's REIT regimes. With two IPOs in 2005, a total of seven S-REITs have now gone public since 2002, including one company, Fortune REIT, whose entire portfolio consists of Hong Kong assets.[9]

The recent success of LPTs and REITs in Australia, Hong Kong, Japan and Singapore has encouraged industry participants and government authorities elsewhere in Asia to introduce REIT-like vehicles or to refine existing structures to reinvigorate their local property markets and to improve investor access to

---

8 Hong Kong's available equity market capitalization also includes Fortune REIT, a Singapore REIT, whose holdings include Hong Kong assets only.

9 At year-end 2005, the BMI REIT Index for Singapore included four S-REITs with an available equity market cap of $2.7 billion.

property investments. New offerings appeared in 2005 in Thailand, Taiwan and Malaysia, with more listings expected in 2006 as the structures continue to evolve and investor awareness grows. While the REIT movement in Asia has clearly gained momentum over the last year or two, not all vehicles have been as well received as J-REITs and S-REITs, at least not yet. South Korea continues to lag countries in the region due to its overly complex and restrictive REIT regulations. A few finite-lived Corporate Restructuring REITs (CR-REITs) were listed to help companies restructure after the Asian financial crisis. But the Korean REIT legislation so far has failed to promote the development of a viable listed Korean REIT market.

Cyclical and Long-Term Growth Drivers

The potential for further growth in the Asian REIT market is significant. Although REITs are not the "value" plays of a few years ago, before capital began flowing freely into the asset class, they should continue to benefit from powerful cyclical and long-term trends that should drive future growth. In most major Asian markets, as well as in Europe and North America, the property market cycle is either in the recovery or expansion phase, with rents growing (or about to grow) and occupancies improving. Economies are recovering and are poised for long-term growth, and demographic trends point to expanding demand for real estate and yield-oriented investments such as REITs.

Although space market conditions vary from market to market and by property type, the property market cycle should have a positive effect on asset values generally over the next few years. Property markets throughout Asia suffered through the global economic slowdown in 2000-01 but have since started to rebound. Major Asian office markets posted significant gains in occupancies and rents in 2005. Prime office rents jumped more than 25% in Singapore last year compared with 2004, while rents in Tokyo and Hong Kong soared 43.8% and 78%, respectively.[10] This was enough to boost yields despite the healthy capital value gains. The improving employment outlook that drove the office market recovery also helped boost retail sales and confidence among retailers, while helping support the housing market.

---

10 Jones Lang LaSalle, 4Q05 REIS.

The strength and breadth of the Asian property market recovery should help ease concerns about the impact of rising interest rates on property values and listed property share prices. Rising short-term interest rates in major economies worldwide have put upward pressure on yields, but property values should continue to benefit from increasing economic activity. Even Japan is showing hopeful signs that the country's prolonged real estate slump may be ending. In July 2005, Japan's National Tax Agency reported the first year-over-year rise in commercial and residential land prices in Tokyo's 23 wards since 1990, which the Agency attributes at least in part to increasing transaction activity involving domestic and offshore investors.[11]

Asian economies are expected to continue expanding at a healthy pace over the next two years, with very strong growth in China and India (see Exhibit 4). For real estate investors, the diversity of growth in the region is probably as important as its magnitude. The effects of economic growth in Singapore and Japan on local property markets and the opportunities for investors, for example, will differ dramatically from the opportunities that arise from growth in China

Exhibit 4: Economic Growth should Drive Demand for All Types of Real Estate

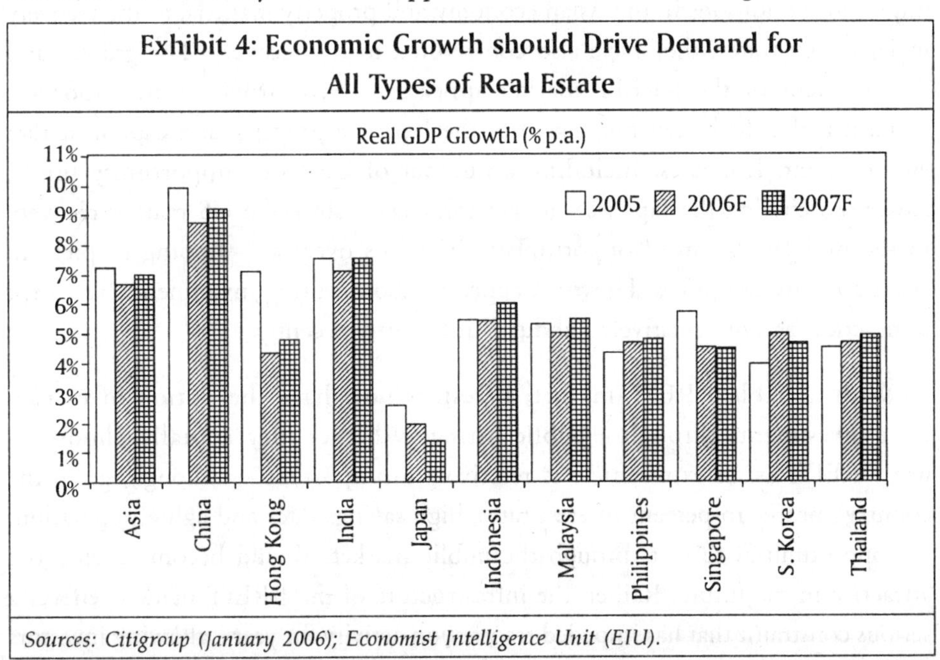

Sources: Citigroup (January 2006); Economist Intelligence Unit (EIU).

[11] *Bloomberg.com*, September 20, 2005.

or India. Strong and diverse economic growth should lead to increasing demand for all types of real estate – offices for a growing professional services sector, industrial and retail to support increasing trade and consumption, and residential assets to accommodate the expanding population with more and better housing – and a wide range of opportunities for investors.

Government authorities throughout Asia also have shown a keen interest in seeing REITs succeed and, in some countries, are actively encouraging their growth. Continued refinements to the S-REIT structure and last year's revisions to the Hong Kong REIT in particular should encourage more developers, property firms, and corporate and government owners to consider using REITs to move some of their stabilized real estate holdings off their balance sheets, thereby freeing up capital that can be reinvested into core activities or used to reduce debt.

Government interest stems at least in part from the positive effects that REITs have provided to investors and to the real estate industry as a whole in countries such as Australia and the US. While REITs clearly have benefited from the improving conditions in the Asian economy and property markets, as the recovery in Japan illustrates, they have also contributed to the recovery. The growth and development of the J-REIT market appears to have provided an important ingredient that had been missing from the Japanese property and capital market environment. Investors, including a number of US-based opportunity funds, have been circling the Japanese market for years – since the US market recovery in the mid-1990s forced opportunistic investors overseas – hoping to pick up assets at distressed prices. However, concerns about exiting investments have kept transaction activity relatively subdued until fairly recently.

With a viable J-REIT market, investors now have the option of exiting their investments through a public listing. Whether they actually choose to use J-REITs as an exit vehicle is relatively unimportant – although, given the country's near-zero-percent interest rates, high savings rates and aging population, the opportunities to exit through the public markets should become even more attractive in the future. Rather, the infrastructure of the J-REIT market relieves a serious constraint that has impeded transaction activity for years, allowing investors to buy assets with greater confidence. As the J-REIT market has grown and the opportunities for exiting investments through a public listing have become more attractive, transaction activity in the Japanese market has increased.

REITs have also provided investors with an attractive opportunity that satisfies their demand for yield and security, yet allows them to participate in the ongoing recovery and long-term growth of the Asian economy and property markets. The expected growth and urbanization of the populations in emerging Asian countries will create tremendous demand for real estate, particularly in urban centers. Between 2000 and 2005, for example, China's urban population increased by about 75 million, or by an amount equal to roughly one-quarter of the entire US population and three times the size of Australia.[12] Such large-scale urbanization demands more and better quality office space, shops and homes, which, directly or indirectly, provide a potential source of income (rent) for investors that, increasingly, can be accessed through REITs. Although China is an admittedly extreme example, similar growth stories are playing out on a smaller scale elsewhere in Asia, with similar consequences for the property markets, as the region becomes more important as a source of goods and capital and as a consumer market.

As Exhibit 5 makes very clear, the ability to tap into income-generating assets will become more important over the next decade or so. Globally, the percentage

Exhibit 5: Aging Population and Increasing Demand for Secure, Stable Cash Yields

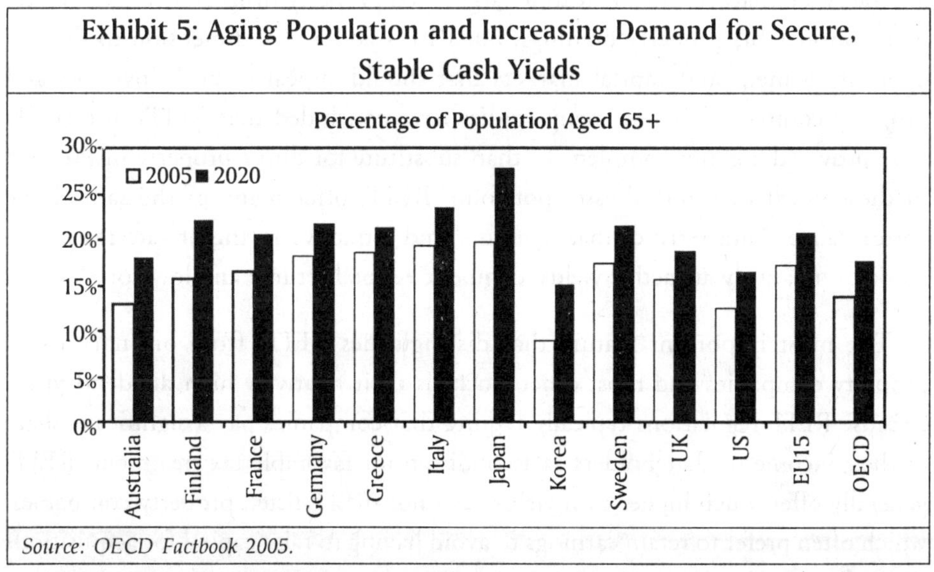

Source: OECD Factbook 2005.

12 Economist Intelligence Unit (EIU).

of the population age 65 and over will increase significantly during the next two decades, placing a tremendous burden on pension schemes around the world. Asia is not exempt from these trends. While Asia's population is growing rapidly, it is also aging. By 2020, more than 27% of Japan's population will be age 65 or older, the highest of any OECD country. In fact, over the next 15 years, Japan's population is forecast to fall slightly below the 123.5 million recorded in 1990. China's population will also age rapidly over the next several decades due to the government's one-child policy and improving life expectancy. Its population is forecast to peak sometime between 2030 and 2040.

The aging world population has profound implications for the global economy and for investment markets in particular. As the population ages, demand for secure, yield-oriented investments, such as real estate, will grow significantly. With institutional and individual investors being relatively underweight in real estate in their investment portfolios, compared with stocks and bonds, REITs stand a good chance of capturing more than their fair share of increasing allocations to higher-yielding investments, especially as the global REIT market continues to develop and mature.

Portfolio Implications and Future Trends

Several Asian markets already feature large listed property firms and conglomerates with considerable property holdings, but REITs add a new dimension to the real estate investment and capital markets that should appeal to both investors and property companies. While many studies have concluded that REITs historically have provided a better complement than substitute for direct property investment in the context of a mixed-asset portfolio, REITs offer many of the same basic performance characteristics that investors find attractive in the private real estate market – relatively attractive yields, competitive total returns and low correlations.

The most important feature that distinguishes REITs from ordinary listed property companies and most other stocks is their relatively high dividend yield. Because REIT regulations typically require that companies pay a significant share of their income to shareholders as a condition for favorable tax treatment, REITs generally offer much higher cash yields than non-REIT listed property companies, which often prefer to retain earnings to avoid having to raise capital for acquisitions and other activities.

Exhibit 6: REIT Yield Spreads Remain Attractive

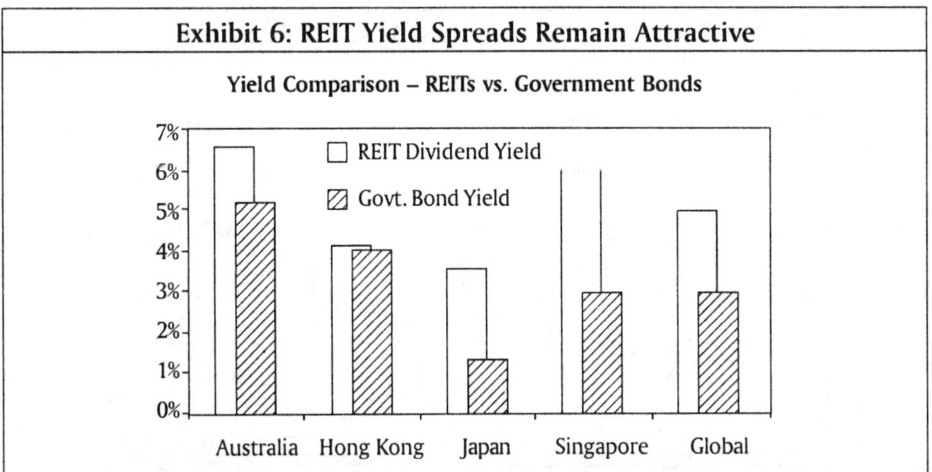

Note: Hong Kong REIT yield based on reported dividend yield for *Fortune* REIT at year-end and estimated dividend for Link REIT at year-end closing share price.

Sources: S&P/Citigroup BMI REIT Index; Bloomberg (Merrill Lynch Global Government Bond indexes); data as of year-end 2005.

Falling property yields and rising long-term interest rates have narrowed the spread between REITs and long-term government bonds in recent years, but yield spreads remain positive and relatively attractive in many Asian markets (see Exhibit 6). The contrast is most striking in Japan and Singapore. At year-end 2005, J-REITs and S-REITs offered spreads of about 220 bps and 300 bps, respectively, over government bonds. But yield spreads between non-REIT listed property firms and government bonds were barely positive in Singapore and were slightly negative in Japan.

As the global rally in REIT shares over the last several years has shown, investor sentiment can be a powerful driver in the investment markets. Exhibit 7 illustrates the effects of the sudden change in investor sentiment in spring 2000, when the tech bubble burst and investors rotated out of growth and into high-yielding value investments. After struggling during the late 1990s through the peak of the tech boom and dot-com mania, global REIT total returns (on a trailing 12-month basis) turned positive in May 2000 and have been so ever since, consistently outperforming stocks and bonds. More recently, despite the strong recovery in the broader stock market and lower yields, investors have not abandoned REITs.

Exhibit 7: Demand for Yield has Driven Healthy Returns

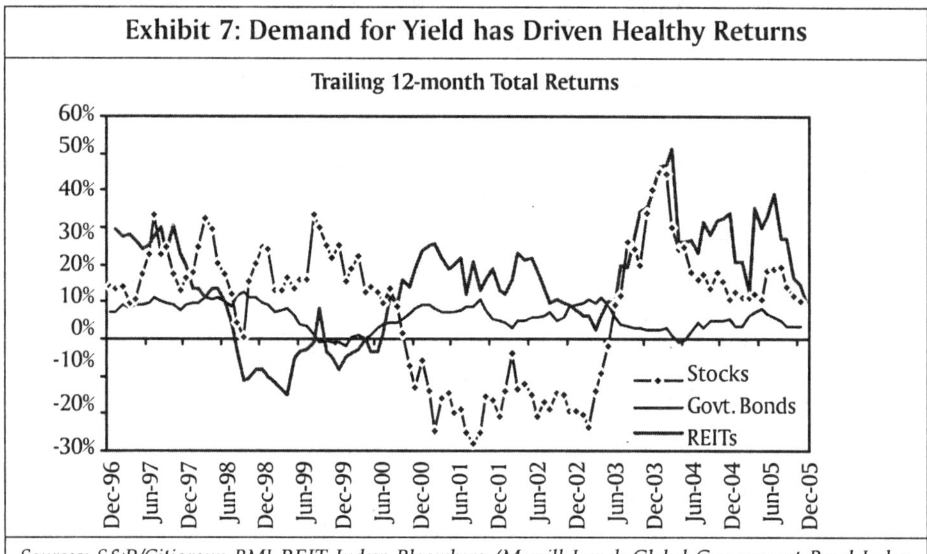

Sources: S&P/Citigroup BMI REIT Index; Bloomberg (Merrill Lynch Global Government Bond Index, MSCI World equity index); data as of year-end 2005.

Exhibit 8 further shows how Asian REITs have outperformed stocks and bonds in the Asia Pacific region recently. Although the sharp rebound in the Asian stock markets over the last two years has narrowed the performance gap, REITs have outperformed stocks and bonds over three-, five- and 10-year periods ending December 2005. And on a risk-adjusted basis, REIT returns are even more attractive. REIT returns will be more volatile than private market returns, particularly over the near term, due to fundamental differences between the two

Exhibit 8: Competitive Absolute and Risk-Adjusted Returns

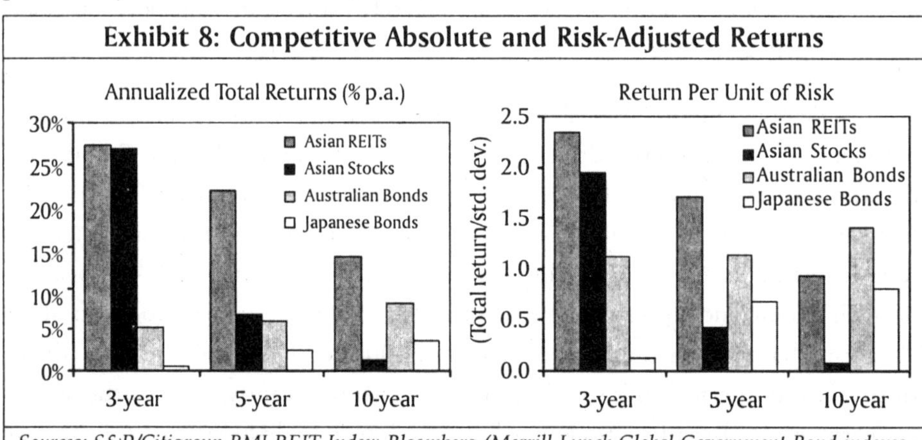

Sources: S&P/Citigroup BMI REIT Index; Bloomberg (Merrill Lynch Global Government Bond indexes, MSCI Pacific equity index); data as of year-end 2005.

markets. However, over the longer term, REITs have offered competitive absolute returns and attractive risk-adjusted returns.

Exhibit 9: Modest Correlations Highlight Diversification Benefits

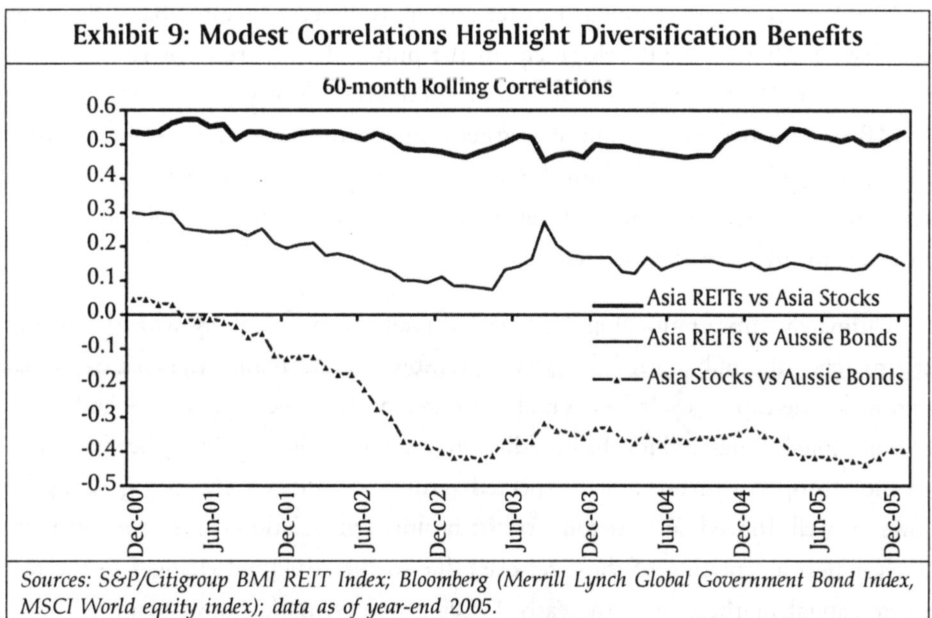

Sources: S&P/Citigroup BMI REIT Index; Bloomberg (Merrill Lynch Global Government Bond Index, MSCI World equity index); data as of year-end 2005.

Historically, perhaps the most compelling argument for including private real estate in a mixed-asset portfolio, however, has been for diversification. As Exhibit 9 shows, REITs also offer some of the diversification benefits that private real estate provides in a mixed-asset portfolio. Correlations between REITs and stocks have drifted higher in recent years, but they remain relatively low (between 0.5 and 0.6), while bond correlations are even lower. The lack of correlation with bonds is particularly interesting given the relatively strong yield-orientation of both asset classes. However, it suggests that investors can reduce the risk in their portfolios by including REITs alongside stocks and bonds. Moreover, although not shown here, the correlations between listed property performance in different countries also tends to be much lower than those for the broader equities market due to the local nature of real estate demand, which implies that the benefits from a global allocation in listed property will be greater.

From a broader real estate industry perspective, the development of REITs and a more liquid, vibrant global REIT market is an important milestone in the increasing sophistication of the global real estate capital markets. REITs obviously expand the industry's access to capital, complementing traditional private equity and debt sources with a much broader and more diverse investor base. But they also have facilitated the development of the public debt market for real estate in the form of REIT corporate bonds and commercial mortgage-backed securities (CMBS). The real estate capital markets, therefore, have become more finely segmented, which should allow for more efficient pricing of risk and a better alignment between investors' risk-reward preferences and the vehicles they choose in order to invest in the asset class.

Ultimately, more rational and efficient capital allocation, along with the greater transparency the public capital markets promote, should reduce the cost of capital and make the capital cycle less volatile. While a more stable capital cycle and lower cost of capital should reduce the liquidity premium that historically has been attached to most property investments, expected returns should, all else being equal, be lower as well. Indeed, at least some of the healthy appreciation gains in recent years likely reflect a repricing of the asset class due to the structural changes in the real estate capital markets since the early-1990s property market downturn.

The global REIT market is still evolving, however, which means that the vehicles themselves and the market dynamics will change as well. The development of the Australian LPT and US REIT market may provide some insights into how the newer REIT vehicles and markets will develop. Both markets have changed dramatically since LPTs and REITs were first introduced, and they are continuing to evolve as the global REIT market develops. Although external management arrangements are still common in Australia, more LPTs are moving toward dedicated internal management teams that have become the standard in the US REIT market. A similar evolution may very well play out in the newer REIT markets over time. Most of the new REIT vehicles in Asia are externally advised by management teams that often provide similar services to other vehicles. For now, investors do not seem overly concerned about potential conflicts of interest that can arise with an external management structure. However, as the markets develop, internal management may become a more important differentiating factor between REITs competing for investor capital.

Similarly, LPTs and US REITs have grown more specialized over the last decade or so, with more companies focusing on a single property type. Although large, diversified companies exist in both countries, most companies now focus exclusively on a particular sector, such as retail or office. Several forces have helped to drive the specialization trend. However, for investors, the emergence of large, focused companies makes it much easier to construct diversified portfolios with the best operators and management teams in each sector, and then to rebalance portfolio weightings as the relative attractiveness of different property types changes.

Scale has also become much more important in both Australia and the US, which has led to consolidation in both countries, but particularly in Australia. With the high public ownership penetration rate in Australia, LPTs have had little choice but to consolidate to continue to grow their portfolios. Since 1999, the number of LPTs has fallen from more than 60 trusts to about 37 at year-end 2005. The consolidation trend has produced significantly larger LPTs. At year-end 2005, 14 of the 31 LPTs in the BMI REIT Index had available equity market capitalizations of US$1 billion or more. The drive for scale and the constrained domestic market has also led more LPTs to invest outside Australia.

Although similar trends are evident in the US REIT market, only a handful of REITs have grown large enough that international investment is essential to their future growth. Several US REITs, however, have expanded outside the US market for strategic reasons. A few retail and industrial REITs, for example, are actively investing in Asia and Europe in part to better meet their tenants' global real estate needs. The globalization trend illustrates the changing nature of REITs and LPTs and the potential value that the platforms themselves might add for investors.

Finally, the increasing sophistication of the Australian and US real estate capital markets has led to a proliferation of new structured investment products, both equity and debt, that expand companies' access to capital and investors' access to real estate investment opportunities. LPTs and US REITs have more opportunity to optimize their capital structures to obtain the lowest cost of capital and to more effectively match assets and liabilities.

While the evolution of the new REIT vehicles in Asia is likely to mirror the development of the Australian and US markets in many respects, differences between REIT regimes will undoubtedly remain part of the investment landscape. Structural differences in areas such as taxation, leverage and permitted activities, such as development, will cause variation in performance and growth rates, for example. But investors should also be aware of more subtle differences, like the quality of the assets in REIT portfolios. In Australia and the US, LPTs and REITs invest primarily in institutional-quality assets. However, this may not always be the case, particularly in some of the newer REIT markets.

Closing Thoughts

The development of REITs in Asia and Europe is transforming the real estate investment and capital markets. For the real estate industry generally, REITs promise to improve transparency, liquidity and the industry's access to capital, while creating a more dynamic and competitive property market that should encourage more professionalism and best practices throughout the industry. For investors, the new vehicles improve both their access to property investments throughout Asia (and Europe) and their ability to develop and manage global real estate portfolios. While we do not expect REITs or direct property investments will continue to deliver the outsized gains that investors have enjoyed in recent years, powerful near-term and long-term economic, property market and demographic forces should continue to drive the growth and development of the global REIT market.

(Philip Conner is a Principal in the Investment Research department of Prudential Real Estate Investors. He is also a member of the Pension Real Estate Association (PREA) and the National Council of Real Estate Investment Fiduciaries (NCREIF). He can be reached at philip.conner@prudential.com

Marc Halle is a Managing Director for Prudential Real Estate Investors, He can be reached at marc.halle@prudential.com).

14

Real Estate Investment Trusts in Japan

Stuart Porter and Jan-Erik Vehse

Japan was the first REIT market to emerge in Asia and has rapidly advanced to be the third largest REIT market in a few years, in asset terms behind US and Australian listed property trusts. The J-REIT market is likely to continue growing in the medium term. The article briefly outlines the J-REIT market in Japan and describes the J-REIT structure and their listing requirements.

As a foretaste for the potential of UK REITs for investors and asset managers, this article briefly outlines the J-REIT market in Japan, which has grown exponentially over the five years since inception, providing a diversified alternative real estate asset class for retail and institutional investors, and contributing to the upturn in the Japanese real estate market.

What are REITs?

Real Estate Investment Trusts ("REITs") are investment trusts with real estate as their underlying assets. Income is generated by rents and sale proceeds and distributed to investors in the form of dividends. Investors receive investment certificates (equivalent to share certificates), which can be traded like shares.

The policy behind REITs is that they create new financing sources and increase the liquidity and efficiency of the real estate market. They allow for investment diversification, are readily tradable investments under professional management, and seek to produce annual returns in the form of a stable flow of dividends.

Japan rapidly advanced to be the third largest REIT market in only a few years, in asset terms behind only the US (established since 1960) and Australian listed property trusts (since 1971). Japan was the first REIT market to emerge in Asia, and REITs have since been adopted more widely in Singapore, Hong Kong, Malaysia, Thailand and Korea.

What are J-REITs?

The Japanese REIT ("J-REITs") investment vehicle was modeled on US REITs. Like the US REIT, distributions paid to investors are, under qualifying conditions, deductible from its taxable income, thereby providing a tax-efficient flow-through investment vehicle for investors.

Revisions in May 2000 (effective from 1 November 2000) to the *Investment Trust and Investment Corporation Law* permitted investment trusts to invest in real estate. Shortly thereafter, effective from September 2001, the Tokyo Stock Exchange ("TSE") created a system for trading J-REITs. The first two J-REITs (Nippon Building Fund and Japan Real Estate Investment Corporation) were listed in September 2001, and the market has grown rapidly since, with a total value of listed J-REITs of more than JPY3.2 trillion by March 2006 and forecasted to top JPY4 trillion by year end.

Currently, there are 32 listed J-REITs, among them four are listed in 2006 (with a total of 13 listed in 2005) with many more in the pipeline; 30 listed on the TSE and one each on the Osaka and Jasdaq stock exchanges. However, the size of the newer J-REITs does tend to be smaller than the early market entrants.

The first J-REITs invested mainly in office buildings, but the third J-REIT (Japan Retail Fund), listed in 2002, invested in commercial buildings and J-REITs now, as a class, mark the continuing segmentation and diversification of the overall real estate market, extending coverage to residential, commercial, logistics and hotel properties. Major investors are local banks, individual investors and foreign

Figure 1: J-REIT Market Capitalisation

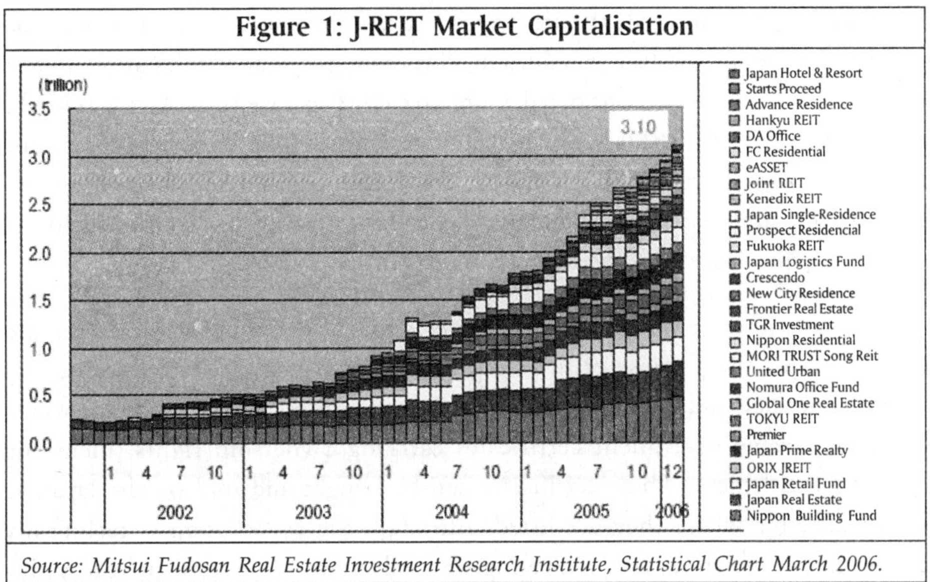

Source: Mitsui Fudosan Real Estate Investment Research Institute, Statistical Chart March 2006.

institutional investors, attracted by the high dividend yield. Apart from sheer growth, the next stage is witnessing the establishment and promotion of "fund of fund" and global REITs.

Setting up a J-REIT

J-REITs are highly regulated and take approximately one year to establish. The first step is to establish an asset management company and acquire a *Building Lots and Building Transactions Agent Licence* and a *Discretionary Transaction Agent Licence* from the National Land and Transportation Ministry. Once obtained, the asset management company must apply for registration with the Financial Services Agency ("FSA"). During this preliminary stage, properties are often assembled using interim vehicles for subsequent transfer to the J-REIT, or transferred from fund vehicles that may have achieved above par returns and wish to arrange an exit from one class of investors to create an asset class for more retail and institutional investor demand and risk profile.

J-REIT Structure

Under the *Investment Trust Law* ("ITL"), a J-REIT may be established in the form of a contract or company-type investment trust. Whilst certificates of both types are tradable on the TSE, J-REITs are exclusively the corporate type. When the first J-REITs were formed, the trust type was administratively cumbersome and more expensive to establish. In addition, corporate governance rules applicable to the corporate type were considered more attractive to investors. As a result, the first publicly-listed J-REITs were all corporate type, despite the trust type having certain tax advantages. Although the tax law has since been amended to unravel some of the administrative requirements, business practice has continued to use corporate types since it is the accepted norm in the market.

The basic premise for the corporate type is that a special purpose corporation, established for the purpose of investing in and managing real estate assets, uses investors' money and third party funding to buy real estate, in return for which investors receive investment certificates carrying ownership rights, including dividend entitlement. These certificates can be bought and sold on the Japanese stock exchange where they are listed. Although the corporation is technically responsible for owning and managing the real estate properties, in reality this function is sub-contracted to a third party manager.

Custody of assets, more precisely custody of certificate of beneficiary and hard assets, is carried out by trust banks on behalf of the investment corporation. Other administrative duties, such as registration of investment certificate holders

Figure 2: J-REIT Structure

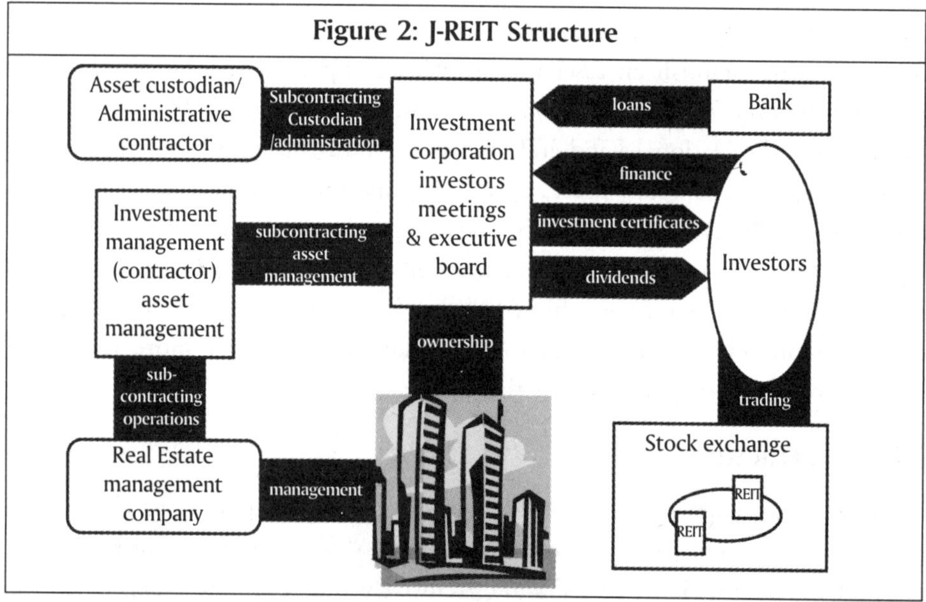

and issue of new certificates, are handled by investment trusts and securities companies, respectively, on behalf of the investment corporation. Real estate management companies handle all aspects of the direct management of the real estate assets, including physical management of the real estate properties and handling rental contracts and invoices (usually physical management is handled by property management companies).

Listing Requirements

Given that investors in J-REITs are doing so as a substitute for direct investment in real estate, the main focus of the TSE's J-REIT listing criteria is on the nature and proportion of real estate assets under management (AUM). The main requirements are summarised in Figure 3.

Figure 3: Listing Requirements

AUM	Distribution of units
• At least 75% of total AUM invested in real estate	• At least 4,000 units to be listed
• Must be real estate related, cash or highly-liquid cash equivalents	• At least 1,000 holders
• At least 50% income producing with likely holding period exceeding one year	• Ten largest investors may hold no more than 75% of units
• Total NBV at least JPY 1 billion and gross book value at least JPY 5 billion	
• Net assets per share unit at least JPY 50,000	

Attractiveness of J-REITs

The attractiveness of J-REITs among domestic and foreign investors is generally due to:

- Credibility of sponsors;
- Comfort from strict regulation;
- High yields compared to bond interest;
- Return stability; and
- Opportunity to invest in a diversified Japanese real estate portfolio.

Performance of J-REIT Market

Average yields are still well above bond yields, but have shrunk from a peak of more than 6% in 2002 to currently 3.5%, a spread below 200 bps. The following chart depicts the yield comparison between J-REITs and Japanese government bonds ("JGBs") over the last four and a half years.

Figure 4: J-REIT Index, Estimated Dividend Yields and Comparison to 10-year Government Bonds

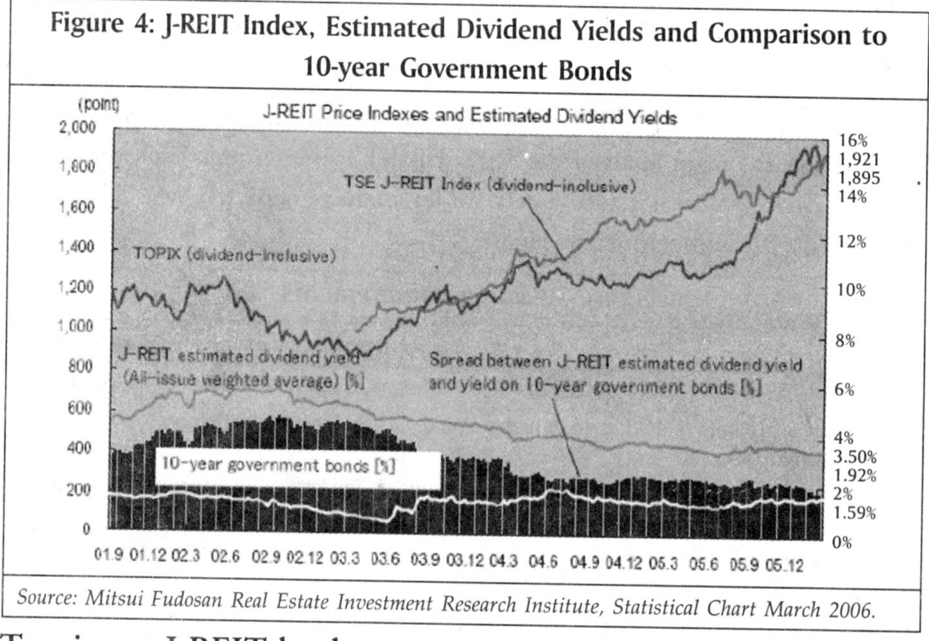

Source: Mitsui Fudosan Real Estate Investment Research Institute, Statistical Chart March 2006.

Taxation at J-REIT level

J-REITs are not flow-through vehicles in the traditional sense where income is only taxed at the shareholder level. A J-REIT is taxable like any other Japanese corporation; however, the effective taxation resembles a flow-through vehicle, as deductibility of distributed dividends (albeit subject to detailed requirements) reduces the REIT tax liability of corporation tax to virtually zero. There are transfer taxes that may be applicable on the purchase of real estate, although there are concessionary rates for J-REITs and often by purchasing beneficiary interests in land and building through trust certificates, the imposition of transfer taxes is minimised.

Taxation at J-REIT Investor Level for Foreign Investors

Foreign investors who do not have a presence in Japan are generally subject to Japanese taxation in J-REITs as follows:

Figure 5: Main Requirements for Dividend Deductibility

Main requirements	Main continuing requirements
• Registration under the *Investment Corporation Law* • Public offering in Japan (form and amount of investment unit) • Total initial issue value at the set up of JREIT should be publicly traded and at least JPY 100m; or shares held by at least 50 investors or solely by qualified institutional investors ("QIIs") at every fiscal period end • Shares mainly offered in Japan • Fiscal period not exceeding one year	• Distribute more than 90% of distributable income • Avoid family company characterisation • Generally not hold 50% or more of equity of another company • Not receive loans from parties other than QIIs

- Withholding tax on dividends from REITs (currently 7% but scheduled to rise to 15% on or after 1 April 2008); and
- Taxation at the rate of 30% for corporations and 15% for individuals on capital gains on disposals (by reporting and filing Japanese tax returns) if investors and related parties' holding exceed 5% of the listed J-REIT.

Investors resident in jurisdictions with a double tax treaty with Japan may be entitled to exemptions and reductions from the above Japanese taxes depending on the precise terms of the double tax treaty and whether the investor is duly entitled.

Outlook

The J-REIT market is likely to continue growing in the medium term. The impact of J-REITs on the real estate market has manifested itself (in conjunction with the large and expanding unlisted real estate funds investing in Japan) in intensifying competition to acquire properties, contributing to rising prices, especially in central Tokyo, and driving down yields. J-REITs and other real estate investors in Japan have responded to these challenges by investing in development properties and increasing investment in new asset types or properties outside Tokyo. Real estate asset managers have been able to capitalise on the appeal of J-REITs, and earn profits on disposals to J-REITs and ongoing management fees on the J-REIT itself.

Now that the Bank of Japan has started to phase out its zero interest rate policy (known as quantitative easing), pressure on yields has started to materialise, especially for highly leveraged investments. However, these effects are being compensated by higher property and rental pricing due to Japan's strong economic recovery.

Disclaimer

Lessons for Japan from US REITs

– G Sushuma

The outburst of the bubble economy in 1992 had decreased the land prices in Japan by 18%.[1] Commercial banks that provided land loans were affected by the sudden decline in the prices. To strengthen the commercial banks, the Japanese government had restricted the investment types in Japan and directed most of the savings to bank deposits. Further, to help recovery of the real estate industry the Japanese government enacted laws to create real estate investment trusts in 2001 on the lines of United States.

J-REIT – An Introduction

In September 2001, the REIT market in Japan made its first move with two listed J-REITs. J-REIT is a company that deals with real estate properties and gives certificates to the investors similar to the stock issued by a company and listed and traded in public exchanges. Ninety percent[2] of the profit of the J-REIT is distributed to the investors as dividends and the dividends paid can be deducted from the taxable income of the company.

J-REITs can be classified into two basic types:

- Contract Style – Under this type, a separate corporation is being formed to invest and manage the real estate.
- Corporate Style – In case of Intermediated Contract Style, the fund managers manage the assets possessed by the investment bank as distinguished from the Direct Contract Style of REIT, wherein the investment bank owns and manages the real estate assets.

Evaluation of J-REIT

The Japanese REITs are based on US REIT structure and are similar to them in terms of investment and dividend distribution. The US REIT was started in 1960, and now after forty seven years of its existence and various amendments to the laws governing them they are most complex and provide strong protection to the investors. The J-REITs are governed by the four laws and provide very less protection when compared with US REIT. With regard to the operations, US REIT allows ownership, management and development whereas J-REITs allow leasing properties. All professional services in US are internal whereas in Japan it is outsourced. The market size of both the REITs is shown in Table 1.

Table 1: Comparison of REIT Market Size between Japan and US

	J-REIT	US REIT
No. of listed REITs (approximately)	40	200
REIT market size (Trillion Yen)	2.8	42.8
Share of stock market capitalization	0.5%	3%

Source: Compiled from Japan's Growing REIT Industry and Related Additional Financial Reporting and Regulatory Guidance, www.pwc.com

Lessons for Japan

In Japan, the laws governing the REIT market do not facilitate its expansion. By comparing the J-REIT and US REIT, it is evident that the policy makers have not implemented polices prevailing in the US market in its entirety. Changes have been made with reference to the shareholders diversification, operations, etc. However, the Japanese government should amend the rules

1 "The J-REIT – An emerging market for residential and commercial mortgage securitization in Japan", *www.realtor.org*

2 "Japanese Real Estate Investment Trusts: Champagne Bubbles or Price Bubble?" September 2005.

Contd...

Contd...

governing REIT to make their investment trust to be effective. For this purpose the government should carry on research to identify the impact of different investment types and dividend levels on the market and to understand the requirements of the investors.

(G Sushuma is a Research Associate, Icfai Business School Research Center, Chennai. She can be reached at sushumag@gmail.com).

References

1. A Comparison of REITs in Three Countries.
2. Characteristics of J-REIT assets, STB Research Institute.
3. "ETFs and REITs in Japan: Innovation and Steps for the Future Growth", Nomura Institute of Capital Markets Research.
4. "Japanese Real Estate Investment Trusts: Champagne Bubbles or Price Bubble?" September 2005.
5. "The J-REIT – An emerging market for residential and commercial mortgage securitization in Japan", *www.realtor.org.*

15

China – Many Opportunities, Unique Risks*

Youguo Liang and M Shayne Arcilla

The abolition of the state-sponsored housing system in the '90s and the introduction of land-lease rights helped spur an investment market for real estate over the past 10 years. China holds many risks for real estate investors, including the lack of legal tradition and judicial independence and government corruption, underdeveloped banking and capital markets, currency control and an opaque market. China also has unique risks arising from state monopoly on land ownership, uncertainties associated with evolving rules and regulations.

Executive Summary

- Since China's adoption of its open-door policy in 1978, real GDP has grown 9.7% per year. Last year, China overtook the UK as the fourth-largest economy in the world.
- China is experiencing slow population growth, at about 0.6% per year. But massive urbanization will expand the urban population by more than

* This report was first published in the Spring 2007 issue of the *Wharton Real Estate Review*.

one-third over the next 10 years, with annual increases projected to be more than 19 million.

- China's middle class and affluent households now compose less than one-quarter of all urban households, but their share will rise substantially over the next decade.
- Until now, foreign investors have been investing mainly in Beijing, Shanghai, Guangzhou and Shenzhen, the Tier I cities. Tier II cities and the advanced economic areas anchored by Tier I cities will provide attractive investment opportunities, especially in retail and residential, as urbanization occurs, incomes rise and the middle class expands.
- The downside risks to China's future growth should not be overlooked. Severe environmental issues, the increasing income gap between rich and poor, and external political tensions could slow or derail economic growth.
- Investors also face risks arising from China's deficient legal system, underdeveloped contract law, and cronyism and corruption in government. Foreign currency control, the government's monopoly on land supply and frequent rule changes are additional hurdles that investors need to overcome.

Introduction

The rapid economic development of the People's Republic of China began in 1978 with the introduction of open-door reforms, which ultimately integrated China's economy into the world market via trade and foreign investment. Since then, China's economy has experienced explosive growth in exports and manufacturing, propelling the country's transition from a rigidly planned, primarily state-owned system to a market economy with the majority of economic output produced by a booming private sector.

Moreover, the abolition of the state-sponsored housing system in the '90s and the introduction of land-lease rights helped spur an investment market for real estate over the past 10 years. As continued high economic growth and massive urbanization push more households into the ranks of the middle class, the number of institutional-quality real estate and investment opportunities will rise across all sectors.

Exhibit 1 shows a snapshot of China. With 1.3 billion people, China is the most populous nation, representing 20% of the world's residents. According to China's official statistics, the majority of its citizens live in rural areas, where life has not changed substantially since the first emperor united the country in 221 B.C. More relevant to real estate investing, however, are urban residents and their purchasing power. Although only 43% of the population lives in urban areas, the urban population still amounts to 562 million, forming 189 million urban households. China's overall population growth has slowed to a current rate of 0.6% per year, less than the US growth rate of 0.8%. But its urban population will continue to expand five to six times faster due to the intense urbanization of the rural population. Relative to other emerging countries, China has a small household size (2.98 people in urban areas). The median household income for urban residents, which has been growing at about 10% per year, was $4,200 in 2005.

Exhibit 1: Snapshot of China

	Total	Urban
Population (Millions)	1,308	562
Growth Rate	0.6%	3.6%
Urbanization Rate	43%	
Median Age	32.7 years	
Life Expectancy at Birth	72.6 years	
Literacy Rate	90.9%	
Households (Millions)	389	189
Household Size (Persons)	3.36	2.98
Median HH Income (US$)		4,200
GDP (US$ Trillion)	2.2	2.0
GDP (PPP, US$ Trillion)	8.9	
Agriculture Share	12.4%	
Industry and Construction	47.3%	
Services	40.3%	
GDP Per Capita (US$)	1,740	3,550
GDP Per Capita (PPP, US$)	6,800	13,900
Inflation Rate	1.8%	

Sources: Bureau of Statistics of China; Pramerica Real Estate Investors.

China's 2005 GDP reached $2.2 trillion, after gaining 9.9% from the previous year, pushing it past the UK as the world's fourth-largest economy, after the US, Japan and Germany. Calculated in terms of purchasing power parity (PPP), China's GDP totaled $8.9 trillion, making it the second-largest economy. Yet, despite the country's sizeable wealth, it is still the world's largest developing nation, with a per capita income of only $1,740. However, the GDP per capita for urban residents is $3,550, with 20% of urban areas already reaching $5,000.

China's high literacy rate will continue to support the country's development. Thanks to a compulsory nine-year educational system, China's population stands well ahead of its developing peers in terms of education, with nearly 91% of its adult population (ages 15 and over) completing the government's education requirement.

Strong Economic Growth

As shown in Exhibit 2, China managed to achieve a real GDP growth averaging 9.7% since 1978, the start of economic reform. A low economic base and a relatively well-educated and disciplined labor force powered its initial growth. Beginning in the early '90s, massive foreign direct investments (FDI) attracted to China's lowcost and productive work force further injected vitality into the expanding economy. In addition, a massive internal population shift into urban areas has been feeding the nation's burgeoning private enterprises, especially in coastal areas.

Exhibit 2: China's Real GDP Growth

Source: International Institute of Finance.

China's performance hasn't always been stellar, with the country experiencing three periods of sub-par growth since 1978. Internal politics and economic weakness in major developing markets dragged down China's growth in the early '80s. Later, the Tiananmen Square incident in 1989 caused the deceleration in 1990. Finally, the Asian financial crisis led to a period of relatively slower growth (but still healthy in absolute terms) in the late '90s.

Recent data from China's National Bureau of Statistics shows that the nation's economy has yet to slow, as real GDP grew at an annualized rate of 11.3% in 2Q06. This exceeded China's long-term average of 9.7% and translate to an annualized real GDP growth rate of 10.9% for the first half of 2006. China's economic expansion will gradually slow to a more sustainable level, but China's growth is expected to remain in the high single digits for the next 10 years.

Exhibit 3 shows a ranking of a select group of countries according to their strongest 20-year period of real GDP growth. While emerging market peers India and Turkey expanded at an annual pace of 6.0% and 5.6%, respectively, during their strongest 20-year periods, their growth rates are less than China's 10.0% annual growth rate between 1982 and 2002. Even Japan's annual growth rate of 8.4% between 1955 and 1975 is smaller than China's recent 20-year track record.

Exhibit 3: Strongest 20-Year Growth of Real GDP for Select Economies

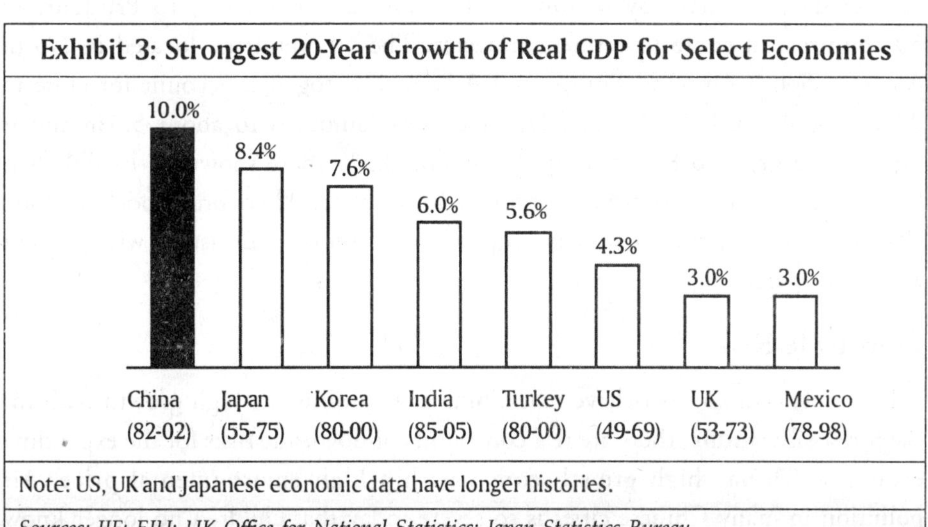

Note: US, UK and Japanese economic data have longer histories.

Sources: IIF; EIU; UK Office for National Statistics; Japan Statistics Bureau.

The US and UK are models of mature, developed economies, whose respective annual growth rates of 4.3% and 3.0% during their booming periods provide the benchmark for sustainable economic growth at which emerging markets should eventually converge.

Medium-term projections show that China could overtake Japan as the second-largest economy after the US by 2015. The rationale for this baseline forecast is China's expected annual growth rate of 7% over the next decade, plus a 2% Chinese yuan appreciation, while Japan expands at an annual pace of 1.3%. These growth assumptions are in line with the most recent forecasts from EIU. At these growth rates, China's GDP will reach $5.3 trillion in 2015, surpassing Japan's $5.2 trillion (all in 2005 dollars).

Exhibit 4 displays a range of possibilities for the size of Japan and China's economies. The assumed GDP growth rate for Japan is 1 to 2%, with the most likely forecast being 1.3%. China's GDP growth rate in dollars is projected to be 8 to 10% (6 to 8% GDP growth, plus 2% currency appreciation), with a baseline forecast of 9%. China's GDP will likely catch up with Japan's between 2014 and 2016.

China's projected growth over the next decade should compel investors to increase their portfolio allocations in Chinese investments. Exhibit 5 shows projected GDP share by region in 2005 and 2015, relative to Prudential's 50-country real estate investment universe. The 50 countries, located in North America, South America, Europe and Asia Pacific, together account for close to 97% of global GDP. China's GDP share now amounts to about 5.3% and is expected to grow to 8 to 9% by 2015. The 8.3% share shown in Exhibit 5 is based on EIU's most recent forecast for all 50 countries. Therefore, model portfolio allocations should rise to similar proportions to remain consistent with current allocation percentages.

Downside Risks

While most economists believe that China can continue its high growth path for the foreseeable future, there are real constraints or downside risks for the expanding economy. China's high growth comes with a high environmental price. Air pollution in many Chinese cities is so severe today that children no longer know that sky's natural color is blue. Pollution to ground water and soil is equally

Exhibit 4: Racing for the Title of "Second-Largest Economy"

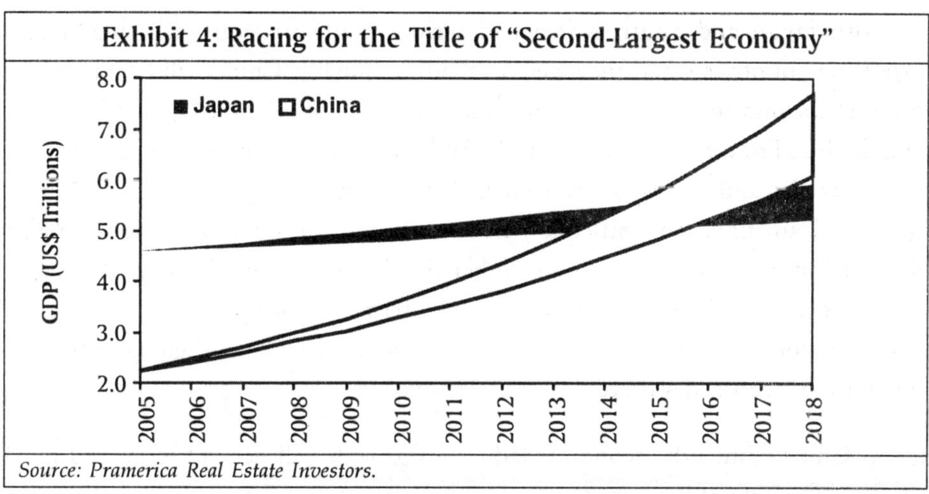

Source: Pramerica Real Estate Investors.

Exhibit 5: China's GDP Share: 2005 vs. 2015

	2005	2015
Asia Pacific excluding China	20.0%	29.2%
China	5.3%	8.3%
Europe	36.8%	33.7%
Latin America	5.3%	5.0%
US/Canada	32.6%	32.1%

Source: EIU.

severe but even more expensive to mitigate. It is unclear as to whether China's environmental condition has permanently impaired its ability to grow, but we do know that as a society grows in wealth, it also values its natural environment more. China may decide that slower but more sustainable growth is indeed a better path to prosperity.

China's strong growth has increased the living standards of the vast majority of its people, transforming a society with shared poverty to uneven wealth for many. But the income gaps between urban and rural residents, and between the urban rich and poor, have reached unhealthy and even alarming levels. These tensions, if not managed properly, could erupt any time, disrupting growth-friendly economic policies and delaying further economic and political reforms. In the most extreme scenario, the widening gap between rich and poor, coupled with a deteriorating social safety net, could cause large upheavals.

Both Japan and South Korea had serious trade friction with their major exporting countries when they were expanding quickly. China will encounter far more challenges in managing both trade and political relationships with the US and the EU. From the perspective of the West, China poses more problems because of its size, its authoritarian government led by a nominally communist political party and an inherited unification issue with Taiwan. China's economy highly depends on exports to the US and other developed nations. Mishaps on major, sensitive external matters would surely trim China's growth. A military confrontation with Taiwan, while extremely unlikely in an era of global economic integration, would devastate China's economy.

As China climbs the economic ladder, its growth will depend more and more on the softer side of its economy, such as human resources, the efficient allocation of capital and transparent government. China has always valued education, but with its intense focus on short-term economic growth, the government has not been emphasizing basic education as much as in the past, especially in the countryside. While access to higher education has vastly expanded, the quality of college education needs equally vast improvement to meet the needs of an advanced economy. China's banking and capital markets lag behind its own economic development and are far from being globally competitive. The government, while well known for efficiency in orchestrating large-scale projects, has serious corruption problems and is opaque in policy deliberations. China's future growth critically depends on the improvement of these softer factors.

Massive Urbanization

Rapid urbanization is the hallmark of developing economies, with fully industrialized nations having urbanization rates of at least 75%. From the current urbanization rate of 43%, it will take China 25 years or more before most of its citizens become urban dwellers. The massive urbanization that occurred over the past 20 years will surely continue and even accelerate as long as the economy continues to expand.

Exhibit 6 shows China's population growth and urbanization trends over the past 10 years. China is experiencing slow population growth, resulting from the one-child policy enacted in the '70s. The policy almost immediately reduced

Exhibit 6: High Growth in Urban Population

	Population (millions)	Growth (millions)	Growth Rate	Urban Population (millions)	Growth (millions)	Growth Rate	Urbanization Rate	Yearly Change
1995	1,211			352			29.0%	
1996	1,224	12.7	1.0%	373	21.3	6.1%	30.5%	1.4%
1997	1,236	12.4	1.0%	394	21.5	5.8%	31.9%	1.4%
1998	1,248	11.3	0.9%	416	21.6	5.5%	33.4%	1.4%
1999	1,258	10.3	0.8%	437	21.4	5.1%	34.8%	1.4%
2000	1,267	9.6	0.8%	459	21.6	4.9%	36.2%	1.4%
2001	1,276	8.8	0.7%	481	21.6	4.7%	37.7%	1.4%
2002	1,285	8.3	0.6%	502	21.5	4.5%	39.1%	1.4%
2003	1,292	7.7	0.6%	524	21.6	4.3%	40.5%	1.4%
2004	1,300	7.6	0.6%	543	19.1	3.6%	41.8%	1.2%
2005	1,308	7.7	0.6%	562	19.3	3.6%	43.0%	1.2%
10-Year Avg.		9.6	0.8%		21.0	4.8%		1.4%

Source: China Statistical Yearbook.

the birth rate from more than four to 1.7 per woman. Population growth averaged only 0.8% per year over the past 10 years and now stands at only 0.6%. But the sheer size of the population still ensured 9.6 million more Chinese every year for the past 10 years. Demographers believe that the current low population growth rate of 0.6% will persist for the next 10 to 15 years.

The growth of China's urban population is both a driving force behind and a consequence of rapid economic development. As the nation gradually shifted from a centrally planned regime to one resembling market-based economies, improving economic conditions prompted the government to relax laws restricting internal migration, which were prevalent during the early stages of urbanization (1950-1982). The increased leniency of migration controls dramatically expanded the pace of urban population growth, as young farmers flowed into the cities, especially along the eastern and southern seaboards, in search of employment opportunities and a better life. Over the past 10 years, the urban population grew by 21 million per year, at an average annual rate of 4.8%. By 2005, urban residents totaled 562 million, accounting for 43% of the population.

China's urban population is projected to grow at an average of about 3%, or 19.3 million, per year over the next decade (see Exhibit 7). By 2015, urban residents will number 755 million, accounting for 54.4% of the total population. The urbanization rate is expected to rise by 1.1% per year. Also, the annual increase of nearly 20 million people should translate into demand for 12 million new jobs per year.

Exhibit 7: Projected Urban Population in 10 Years

	2005	2015	Annual Increase	Annualized Rate
Total Population (million)	1,308	1,388	8.1	0.6%
Urban Population (million)	562	755	19.3	3.0%
Urbanization Rate	43.0%	54.4%	1.1%	
Urban Households (million)	189	272	8.3	3.7%
Household Size	2.98	2.78	2 bps decline	

Sources: EIU; National Bureau of Statistics of China; Pramerica Real Estate Investors.

In the meantime, the combined effects of a growing urban population and smaller household size will fuel the growth of China's urban households by 8.3 million, or 3.7%, per year over the next decade. Sheer population growth will add 6.7 million new households and a projected reduction of household size from 2.98 to 2.78 over 10 years will add another 1.6 million per year. By 2015, the number of China's urban households will reach 272 million, 2.2 times the projected US household number.

(For reference, the average US household size was 2.98 in 1976, 2.78 in 1983 and 2.67 in 2005. The US now has 110 million households, almost all urban, which will rise to 126 million by 2015, according to Moody's Economy.com.)

The implications of rising numbers of urban households are most apparent for residential development. Applying a very conservative obsolescence rate of 2.5% to existing housing stock, demand for residential homes will be 13 million units per year – 8.3 million new households plus 4.7 million replacement homes. (US demand for homes is likely to be 1.5 to two million units per year for the next decade.) China needs to develop eight times as many homes as the US per year to meet its demand.

While China's urbanization is widespread, real estate investment opportunities will mainly concentrate in large cities and more developed regions, where relative income is high and the growth potential is above average. One way to analyze China's real estate market is the "3+Xs" framework: three advanced economic regions and 10 to 15 Tier II cities (see Exhibit 8).

Exhibit 8: Major Urban Centers and Advanced Economic Areas

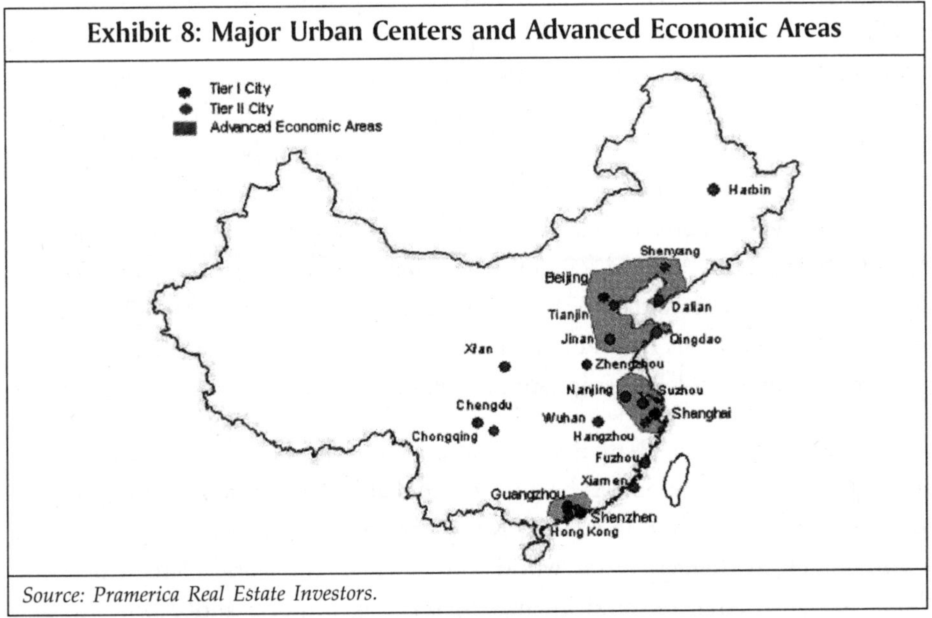

Source: Pramerica Real Estate Investors.

China has four Tier I cities – Beijing, Shanghai, Guangzhou and Shenzhen. They have advanced infrastructure, the highest incomes and the largest stock of institutional-quality real estate. As a result, they have received most of the foreign investments in real estate over the past five years.

As income grows, residential and retail developments are spreading into large economic areas spearheaded by the Tier I cities. The three advanced economic areas shown in Exhibit 8 are large in economic scale, well connected through highways and rail, have high per-capita GDP and are leading China into the era of the middle class.

The Bohai Pan area, in the north, has become the third driver of China's economic development after the Yangtze and Pearl River deltas. Anchored by the nation's capital, Beijing, the region comprises Tianjin and the Shandong, Hebei and Liaoning provinces. Its economic development has benefited mainly from Shandong and Liaoning's traditional advantages in heavy industry, while Tianjin profits from its large, busy port and the inflow of high-tech industries and foreign capital. The area's other key cities are Dalian, Shenyang, Jinan and Qingdao.

The Yangtze River delta, anchored by Shanghai, continues to enjoy its status as China's financial, trade and industrial center. This region comprises Shanghai, Zhejiang province and Jiangsu province and contains 74 cities, 15 of which have populations of more than one million. The key cities include Nanjing, China's capital between 1910 and 1949; Hangzhou, capital of Zhejiang province; and Suzhou, an industrial city west of Shanghai. Shanghai hosts one of China's two stock exchanges (Shenzhen has the other, much smaller, one). The American Association of Port Authorities ranked Shanghai as the world's second-busiest port in 2004, with more than 378 million tons of cargo passing through annually. With the opening of the new Yangshan deepwater port in 2006, Shanghai probably has become the global leader in shipping volume.

Further south is the Pearl River delta, anchored by Hong Kong, Guangzhou and Shenzhen. This region has become the global hub for manufacturing, thanks to China's low-cost labor and Hong Kong's management experience. Port traffic is also among the highest in the world, with three of the world's largest ports (in Hong Kong, Guangzhou and Shenzhen) relaying imports and exports to and from every part of the globe.

Beyond these three advanced economic areas are Tier II cities such as Wuhan and Zhengzhou in central China; Fuzhou and Xiamen across the strait from Taiwan; Chongqing, Chengdu and Xi'an in the west; and Harbin in the northeast. Xiamen and Fuzhou benefit from inflows of Taiwanese investments. Wuhan has historically been central China's commercial hub and center of higher education. Chongqing, Chengdu and Xi'an have all benefited from the government's "Go West" policy, which encouraged a greater inflow of foreign investment to western China as part of an effort to develop the hinterland.

Rising Middle Class

Concomitant with the urbanization of China's people is the creation of a new middle class. Strong economic growth in the recent past transformed the economy from an impoverished, but largely egalitarian, society into one with distinct income classes. By global standards, China's middle class is still small relative to its population. But the country's income level has reached an inflection point, which marks the start of the middle class's 10- to 20-year rise toward social and economic dominance.

The McKinsey Global Institute classifies China's urban households into five income classes: global affluent, with an annual income of at least 200,000 yuan ($40,000); mass affluent, with 100,000 to 200,000 yuan ($12,500 to $40,000); upper middle class, with 40,000 to 100,000 yuan ($5,000 to $12,500); lower middle class, with 25,000 to 40,000 yuan ($3,125 to $5,000); and poor, with less than 25,000 yuan ($3,125). These numbers seem low compared with incomes in developed countries such as the US or Japan, but a $5,000 income in China would ensure a lifestyle of at least $20,000 on a purchasing power parity basis.

Chinese global affluent and mass affluent households have the purchasing power for luxury homes and cars, and Western high-end consumer goods. The upper middle class can afford a professionally built home and a car. The lower middle class can afford a quality home or a car, but not both. The urban poor probably can only live in a subsidized and often substandard home.

Exhibit 9 shows the distribution of China's urban households by income, as projected by the McKinsey Global Institute at the start of 2006. In 1995, the vast majority of China's urban households were poor, and the lower middle class and above formed only 7.1% of total urban households. In 2005, poor urban households fell to 77.3%, and the share of the lower middle class and above rose to 22.7%. By 2015, the urban poor will shrink to only 23.2% of all urban households; the lower middle class will have a share of 49.7%, and the upper middle class and above a share of 27.1%. By 2025, the upper middle class will be the dominant income group, with a share of 59.4%, with the poor having a share of only 9.7% and the global affluent and mass affluent an 11% share.

The forecasts assume a GDP growth rate of about 7% and a GDP per capita growth of 6.5% per year. But the forecast does not consider the possibility of a rising yuan – China has a large trade surplus, and its currency reserve is near $1 trillion. Any appreciation of the currency is likely to speed China's transformation into a middle-class society.

Exhibit 9: Urban Households by Income

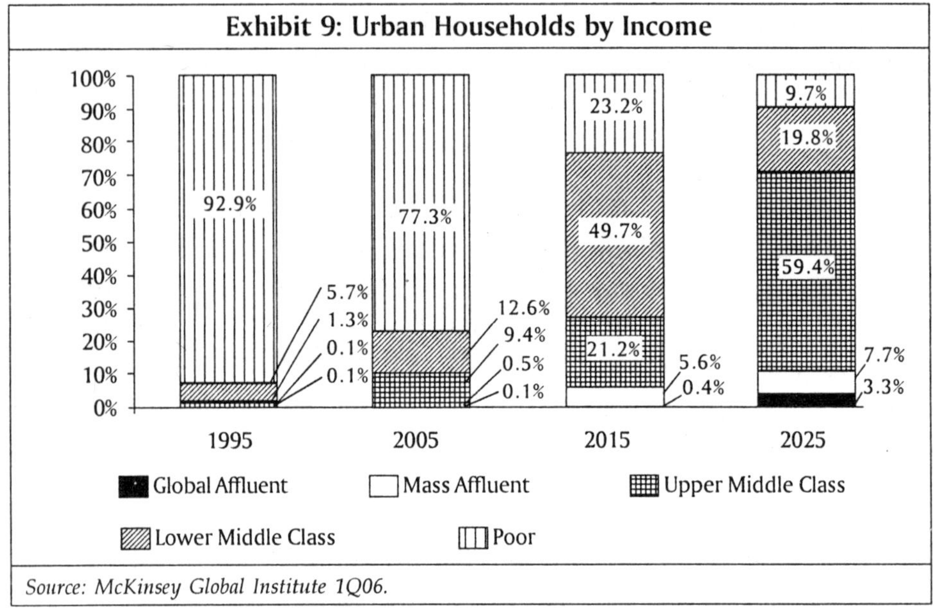

Source: McKinsey Global Institute 1Q06.

Exhibit 10 translates the percentage distribution into numbers of households. Affluent and upper middle class households are projected to grow from 19 million in 2005 to 74 million in 2015, a yearly rise of 5.5 million, at an annual rate of 14.6%. Total middle class (lower middle class and above) households are projected to increase by 166 million households, or 16.6 million, at 17.1% per year, reaching 209 million households by 2015. China's urban middle class and above are projected to grow to account for 76.9% of total urban households in 10 years, pulling millions out of substandard living. In the following decade, middle class and above households are projected to reach 327 million, of which 255 million will be upper middle class and above.

Exhibit 10: Projected Middle Class Households (millions)

	2005	2015	2025
Urban Households	189	272	362
Upper Middle Class and Above	19	74	255
Lower Middle Class	24	135	72
Total Middle Class and Above	43	209	327
Share of Urban Households	22.6%	76.9%	90.2%

Sources: Pramerica Real Estate Investors; McKinsey Global Institute.

Global Economic Integration

Political instability and underdeveloped markets are among the many risks that foreign investors face in developing nations such as China. Yet as these developing economies enter an era of increased international participation through trade and investment, which then fuels rapid economic development, the need to comply with global standards and policies provides a strong force for socio-political stabilization.

Exhibit 11 shows the dramatic rise in China's net FDI since the early '80s. By 2005, FDI reached $67.8 billion. With a large labor pool, increasing skill levels and an agglomeration of related suppliers, China has become the global manufacturing hub for textiles, furniture, electronics, computers and machine tools. Since the early '90s, China has been the preferred destination for multinationals to outsource production. The influx of foreign capital brought with it related technologies and management expertise, and deepened the links between China and the global economy.

Exhibit 11: China's Foreign Direct Investment

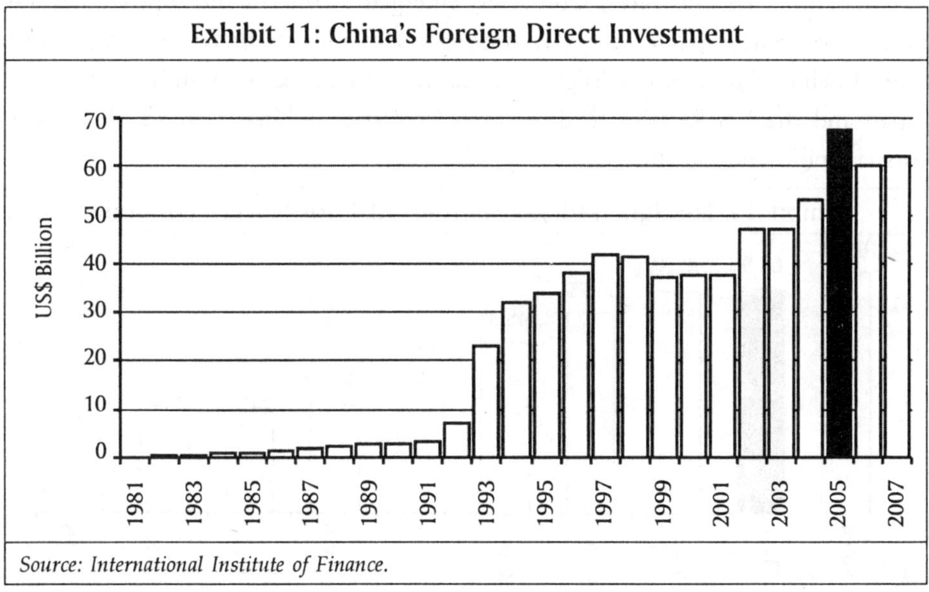

Source: International Institute of Finance.

Besides foreign investment in China's markets, exports have also been one of the main reasons for China's rapid economic growth (see Exhibit 12). China's foreign trade rose from $474.3 billion in 2000 to $1,422 billion in 2005 – an annual growth rate of 25%. By 2005, China's total trade volume rose to 63.9% of its national GDP and is projected to grow to 75% by 2008.

Exhibit 12: China's Foreign Trade as Share of GDP

Source: International Institute of Finance.

As Exhibit 13 illustrates, China has emerged as one of the top-tier nations ranked by trade relative to GDP. Among select industrialized nations, China ranked behind South Korea, slightly ahead of Germany, and far ahead of the UK, Japan and the US Relative to developing countries, China is ahead of Mexico, Russia, India and Brazil.

Exhibit 13: Foreign Trade as Share of GDP for Select Economies

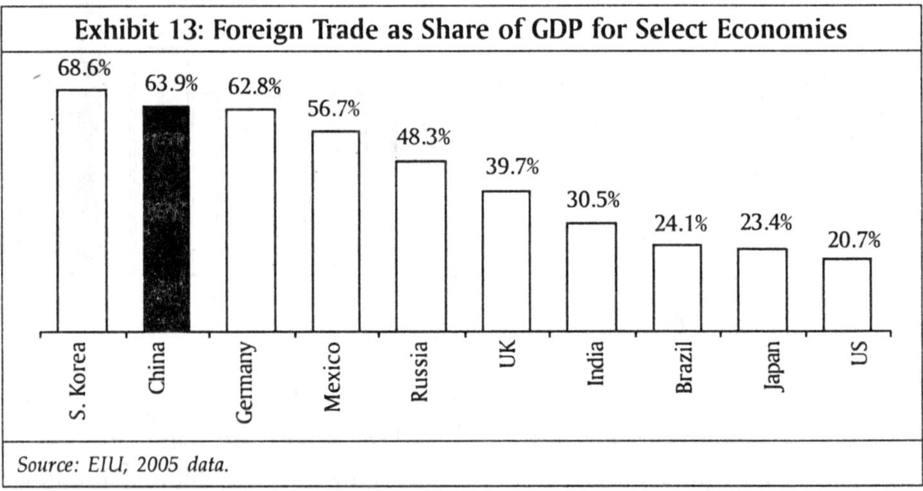

Source: EIU, 2005 data.

Besides fueling the Chinese economy, foreign trade and investment have led to a growing interdependence between China and its trading partners. In 2005, China's largest trading partners were the EU, the US and Japan (see Exhibit 14).

The US was the biggest importer of Chinese goods, with a total volume of $162.9 billion. Japan continued to be China's biggest source of imports, with a total import volume of $100.5 billion. China has also maintained a large and fastgrowing trade relationship with its Asian neighbors. The Association of Southeast Asian Nations (ASEAN) exchanged a total volume of $130.4 billion with China in 2005, while South Korea's total trade with China reached $111.9 billion.

Exhibit 14: China's Major Trading Partners (US$ Billion)

	Total	Exports	Imports
European Union	217.3	143.7	73.6
US	211.6	162.9	48.7
Japan	184.5	84.0	100.5
Hong Kong	136.7	124.5	12.2
Assoc. of Southeast Asian Nations	130.4	55.4	75.0
South Korea	111.9	35.1	76.8
Taiwan	91.2	16.5	74.7
Russia	29.1	13.2	15.9

Source: Bureau of Statistics of China, 2005 data.

For investors, the close links between China and its major trade and investment partners are an imbedded insurance against any irrational political and economic changes. While it is difficult to measure political risks in an emerging economy, China's overwhelming economic integration into the global economy is a strong force for future economic stability and political moderation.

Emergence of Institutional Players

For foreign real estate investors going to China, a reliable and reputable partner is one of the critical factors for success. Most foreign investors demand value-added to opportunistic returns when investing in China. Development, therefore, is often critical to achieve the required rates of return. For those with lower return hurdles, development may be an effective way of acquiring high-quality assets, given the limited stock available for sale in the market.

Fortunately, after 20 years of growth, the Chinese domestic real estate development community has matured in skill and increased in size. Today many Chinese developers have established reputable brands and critical mass. A recent report, released in March 2006, identified China's top 100 real estate developers (the majority also have asset-management capabilities) in terms of size, growth potential, profitability and comprehensive strength.

These 100 firms had total combined assets of 608 billion yuan ($76 billion) in 2005, amounting to about 3.3% of the nation's GDP. Seven companies controlled about 33.4% of these assets, with a combined asset total of 203 billion yuan ($25 billion). Of the top 100 firms, China Vanke, China Overseas Land & Investment (COLI) and Hopson Development stood at the top, with the highest comprehensive strength. Exhibit 15 shows information on these three companies.

Exhibit 15: China's Top Three Real Estate Developers

	China Vanke	COLI	Hopson Devel.
Stock Exchange	Shenzhen	Hong Kong	Hong Kong
Market Capitalization (US$ Billion)	2.97	4.10	2.40
ROE	16.3%	13.9%	14.8%
Credit Rating	Investment Grade	BBB-/Baa3	BB+/Ba1
Sales Volume (US$ Billion)	1.74	1.23	0.81
Floor Space Sold (mil. sq. m.)	2.32	1.21	1.01
Land Reserve (mil. sq. m.)	12.09	10.75	12.95

Notes: Overall market strength ranking per "China Real Estate Top 10 Research 2005" for Chinese developers. Market capitalization as of July 27, 2006. China Vanke's credit rating estimated by Pramerica Real Estate Investors. Other information is based on respective 2005 annual reports.

Hurdle Rates of Return

China's overall development cannot hide the fact that, from an investor's perspective, it is still an emerging market. But China is taking the steps needed to mitigate its issues. The government's economic and financial reform measures continue to support strong growth, while the country's inefficient capital markets are expected to improve as China allows increased foreign ownership of its financial institutions. Thus, China's overall risk profile has been steadily improving. In July 2006, Standard & Poor's upgraded China's credit rating to A from A–. This places China in the same rank as South Korea, Saudi Arabia and Chile, reflecting more confidence in the country's finances. Also, China's large foreign-exchange reserves and ongoing reform, along with the economic liberalization of its industries, will consolidate its position as a leader in emerging markets.

Exhibit 16 shows the most recent country-risk rankings from Institutional Investor and Euromoney. Per Institutional Investor, China's country risk is below that of industrialized countries but ahead of major developing economies, including Poland, Mexico, Russia, India and Brazil. Euromoney ranked China below Poland and Mexico but ahead of the other three BRIC countries (Brazil, Russia and India).

Exhibit 16: Country Risk Rankings, March 2006

Country	Instit. Investor	Euromoney
UK	94.1	92.2
US	93.5	96.7
Canada	93.2	92.2
Germany	92.8	90.1
Singapore	88.9	87.9
Japan	85.3	90.1
Taiwan	79.1	81.4
Hong Kong	78.7	82.7
S. Korea	76.7	69.9
China	**69.8**	**61.7**
Poland	68.2	66.3
Mexico	65.7	63.2
Russia	62.1	54.7
India	57.1	56.5
Brazil	52.1	50.5
Turkey	48.4	50.2

Notes: Institutional Investor ranks countries' credit risk. Euromoney ranks overall country risk. Scores out of 100 (100 = least risk).

Given China's emerging-market risk profile, investors often consider what return is needed to compensate them for the risks. Exhibit 17 shows Prudential's risk-return matrix by country risk and investment risk. The average emerging-market risk premium relative to developed countries is about 4.5%, estimated from historical stock market returns for investable emerging markets. Thus, as an emerging market, China should be expected to return somewhere between 12% on core investments and 19.5% on opportunistic investments to compensate for its inherent risks.

Exhibit 17: Risk-Return Matrix

Country Risk	Investment Risk		
	Core	Value-Added	Opportunistic
Emerging	12.0%	14.5%	19.5%
Maturing	9.0%	11.5%	16.5%
Developed	7.5%	10.0%	15.0%

Source: Pramerica Real Estate Investors.

Investor Challenges

As an emerging economy, China holds many risks for real estate investors, including the lack of a reputable legal system, underdeveloped contract law, cronyism and government corruption, underdeveloped banking and capital markets, currency control and an opaque market. These risks are not necessarily unique to China, but China's lack of legal tradition and judicial independence indeed stands out even among developing countries. Another example is China's rigid foreign currency control, which makes money flows in and out of the country more difficult and less predictable, and the deployment of money less efficient.

While the World Bank ranks China ahead of other developing markets such as Brazil, India, Mexico and Russia in terms of political stability and government effectiveness, China is behind Brazil, India and Mexico in terms of rule of law and corruption. Exhibit 18 shows the rankings of a select group of countries by regulatory quality, rule of law and control of corruption, according to a recent World Bank governance study of 209 countries and economic entities.

Exhibit 18: Percentile Ranking of Governance Indicators (0-100)

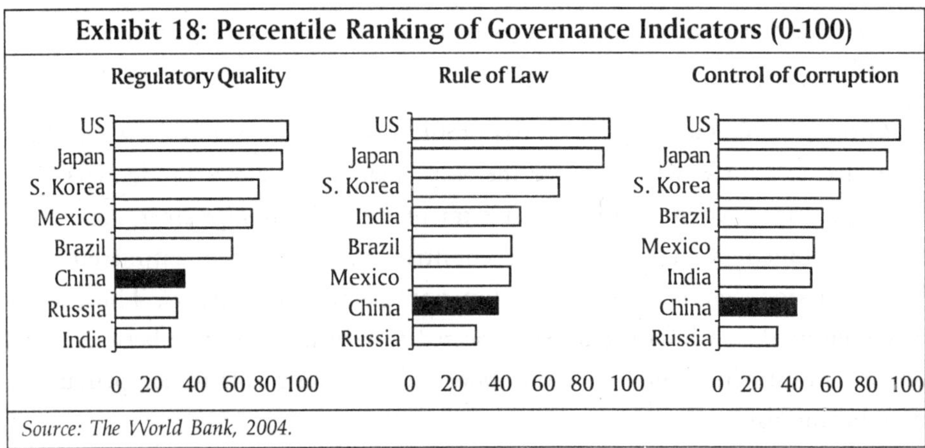

Source: The World Bank, 2004.

China is in the 35th percentile in terms of regulatory quality, indicating a high probability of policies deterring market development. It ranks behind Mexico and Brazil but ahead of Russia and India. In terms of rule of law, China's score is higher at 41, but China is still behind India, Brazil and Mexico. China is weak in managing government corruption as well, as it ranks only ahead of Russia, with a score of 39.

In addition to major governance issues, China also has unique risks arising from land ownership. All land in China is state-owned; users can only obtain leasing rights. Ownership of leasehold properties in itself is not a risk, as leasehold is common in the US and other developed countries. A state monopoly on land supply, however, gives disproportional power to the government in regulating the industry.

China's economy is growing fast, which creates high demand for institutional-quality real estate. But rules and regulations are evolving quickly as well, creating high uncertainty for investors, especially long-term ones. Most past rule changes, however, were in favor of investors, as China improves its capital markets and raises efficiency in the real estate industry. But occasionally rule changes may be detrimental. For example, Chinese academic circles and think tanks have been discussing the introduction of property tax for residential and commercial real estate. The imposition of property taxation is not a problem for investors in itself. The problem comes with the uncertainty – when, how much and on what properties. Recently there have been discussions on restricting foreign investment in real estate as a means of cooling the economy. If serious restrictions were to be imposed, foreign investors would have difficulty accessing this fastgrowing market.

Closing Thoughts

China is in the midst of a rapid economic expansion expected to persist over the next two decades. From an investor's perspective, China presents enormous opportunities as many urban areas are reaching a GDP per capita of $5,000, at which level mass demand for institutional-quality real estate emerges.

Three fundamental forces will ensure significant growth of institutional-quality real estate in China for the next decade. First, strong economic growth and massive urbanization are projected to add 20 million urban residents and form more than eight million urban households per year. Second, China has reached an inflection point on income, where further growth will drastically increase the size of the middle class – by 2015, the number of middle class households and above is projected to expand fivefold to 209 million. Third, the market share of institutional-quality developers will likely continue to rise as an increasing amount of higher-quality space is developed.

As China continues to progress, foreign investors will likely continue to expand their geographic interests in order to participate in China's growth. In recent years, four Tier I cities – Beijing, Shanghai, Guangzhou and Shenzhen – have been the main focus of foreign investors. Other major urban centers and secondary cities in advanced economic areas – most notably the Pearl River delta anchored by Hong Kong, the Yangtze River delta anchored by Shanghai and the Bohai Pan area anchored by Beijing – are emerging as promising venues for future investment, especially in the retail and residential sectors.

(Youguo Liang is the Managing Director of Investment Research and a member of the Investment Committee and Management Committee of Prudential Real Estate Investors. Liang is a CFA charter holder, the President of the American Real Estate Society and international editor of Real Estate Finance. He can be reached at youguo.liang@prudential.com

M Shayne Arcilla is a member of the Penn State Investment Association and was a mentor for the Smeal Business School. She can be reached at shayne.arcilla@ prudential.com).

16

Middle East Capital Flows and the Allure of Real Estate

Anwar Elgonemy

Middle East investors have long been net exporters of capital, and a large proportion of these outflows have traditionally been directed into real estate markets outside the region. Interest in Middle East real estate investment is starting to flow from traditional destinations like Europe and the US to look at opportunities closer to home. The property market in the Middle East is worth an estimated $150 billion.

The Allure of Real Estate

Real estate has the allure of a safe-harbor investment in times of volatility. Three years of poor equity market returns have reminded investors of the risks of being overweight in equities, plus changes in monetary policy in European markets have lowered the cost of debt leading to a renewed interest in the real estate sector. Financial institutions are also eager to increase their exposure to a sector that has a weak correlation with the volatility of stocks and bonds.

The rise in popularity of real estate as an investment in bear markets has not been overlooked by financial institutions in the Middle East. The array of real

---

estate investment funds based on international property in Europe, and increasingly within the Middle East, has jump-started a niche that previously catered largely to direct real estate investment by affluent individuals and families.

The recent bear markets have seen investors focus on the preservation of capital. Pension funds in Europe typically have between 5% and 10% of their portfolio in real estate, but because of low interest rates and volatility in equity markets, these investors have reassessed their portfolios and have given real estate a higher weighting in recent years. This sentiment is now the same in the Middle East, where investors are looking for diversification and a credible instrument to get into.

Capital Outflows

Middle East investors have long been net exporters of capital, and a large proportion of these outflows have traditionally been directed into real estate markets outside the region.

According to the Arab Monetary Fund (AMF), capital outflows from the Gulf Cooperation Council (GCC)[1] during the past 10 years amount to approximately $240 billion although the vast majority of this is in non real estate assets. More than 60% of these outflows emanated from Saudi Arabia, and real estate markets in the US and Europe were traditionally the prime beneficiaries of Arab capital seeking overseas opportunities. Although recent figures show a flight of capital away from the US since 9/11, some markets, such as the UK, are still very popular with Middle Eastern investors. According to a report by US think-tank, The Council on Foreign Relations, Arab investors (mainly Saudis) have pulled close to $200 billion out of the US since 9/11, and have reinvested much of that capital into the EU, the UK and the GCC countries.

Europe is Where the Money's Going

Middle East investment in the UK market has always been ubiquitous. The UK has traditionally been seen as a safe haven for Arab funds, and with interest rates in the UK currently at 4.75%, investors have been taking advantage of arbitrage between real estate yields of around 7% and low borrowing rates. What is new is the interest in the EU countries.

---

1 Includes Saudi Arabia, Bahrain, Kuwait, Oman, Qatar and the United Arab Emirates (UAE).

Europe continues to attract the attention of real estate funds in the Middle East, despite the opening of the property markets in the Middle East itself. For the most part, investment into real estate in continental Europe has so far been targeted at commercial buildings; especially city-center office buildings, warehousing and storage assets, with high-end hotel investments attracting capital as well. In London, on the other hand, luxury residential properties have been the most popular choice.

A trust linked to Saudi Prince Al Waleed bin Talal, along with the Bank of Scotland and Canada's Fairmont Hotels & Resorts, recently formed a joint venture (JV) to invest in luxury European hotels, kicking-off the partnership by acquiring the Monte Carlo Grand Hotel in Monaco. The hotels acquired will be managed by Fairmont, and Bank of Scotland will provide debt financing for the projects; Cedar Capital Partners serves as manager and investment adviser for the JV. The JV has a $1.5 billion bank roll, of which the Bank will fund 50%; Prince Alwaleed's Kingdom Hotels International and Fairmont will each contribute 25% to the partnership.

The Growing Role of Middle East Banks in Real Estate

Up until now, Middle East capital has been investing in UK real estate via small, mostly family syndicates. However, Middle East banks have been getting much more involved in the creation and syndication of funds that buy into UK and European real estate.

For example, the Albait UK Real Estate Fund is a commercial real estate fund co-sponsored by Kuwait-based Global Securities House and ABC International Bank, the international arm of the Arab Banking Group. Credit Suisse Property Investment Management is the real estate manager of this Shariah-compliant[2] fund that allows Islamic investors to invest in commercial real estate in the UK. The co-sponsors raised up to £100 million for the fund, £40 million of which was structured in equity. An actual fund structure is offered over a class of assets, with the debt arranged in the UK; ABC International Bank and Global Securities House are currently seeking marketing equity from Middle East investors.

---

[2] Financial products engineered like conventional instruments, but are governed by basic Islamic principles. Islamic banking is defined as banking operations carried on in line with Islamic principles that prohibit usury. Interest is therefore often replaced by involvement in the venture by temporarily owning the output from the business and on selling it at a predetermined profit.

The First Islamic Investment Bank (FIIB) is another bank that is targeting property asset classes, which are underwritten wholly by the bank. The assets are then packaged into tax efficient structures, and units are syndicated to high net worth individuals (HNWIs), and other institutional investors in the Middle East. With assets on both sides of the Atlantic, FIIB is seeing a renewed interest in euro-denominated assets as opposed to dollar-based assets.

Capital Inflows

Interest in Middle East real estate investment is starting to flow from traditional destinations like Europe and the US to look at opportunities closer to home. The property market in the Middle East is worth an estimated $150 billion, and there is already an unprecedented real estate phenomena taking place in Dubai, with massive projects such as The Palm, The World, Dubailand and the Dubai International Financial Center (DIFC). The property market in UAE, is projected to be worth some $50 billion by 2010, up from its current level of $30 billion.

In neighboring Abu Dhabi, where the ruling Al Nahyan family's $3 billion, 400-room Emirates Palace hotel recently opened, the Abu Dhabi Tourism Authority (ADTA) is playing a significant role in the lodging investment arena. Doha, Qatar is also on the verge of becoming a center for regional business, attributed to a combination of new initiatives from the Qatari government and the country's natural wealth.

Lebanon is another country that is reaping benefits from the withdrawal of Arab funds from the US. There has been a marked upturn in real estate sales since 2001, especially in the newly rebuilt Beirut central business district area. Approximately 50% of the flats and commercial spaces that Solidere, the Lebanese property group, is developing have already been sold to Arab nationals from outside Lebanon.

Prince Al Waleed bin Talal has put $400 million into hotel projects in Lebanon, Egypt and Dubai. His $140 million Movenpick resort in Beirut, which opened in 2003, was well received by the market, with all its $300,000 chalets selling prior to opening. The Prince also has plans to develop Four Seasons properties in Beirut, Alexandria and Damascus.

Even the traditionally insular market of Saudi Arabia is opening up to foreign investment. Saudi Arabia's real estate industry is undergoing major growth, with both local and foreign capital competing for opportunities. The National Real Estate Committee of Saudi Arabia estimates that $6 billion was invested in the kingdom's real estate in the last quarter of 2004. The growth is pushing forward the regulation of the industry, which will fuel investment, providing opportunities for small and medium investors.

As highlighted in Figure 1, total net private capital inflows[3] to the Middle East have fluctuated enormously over the last 25 years, with a resurgence of net capital inflows since 2001, a trend that is expected to grow rapidly over the next five years.

Figure 1 provides a summary of real estate ownership regulations in the Middle East, with an emphasis on the GCC. Figure 1 highlights the region's gradually changing ownership environment, with a slight shift towards freehold ownership to attract foreign direct investment.

Figure 1: Total Net Private Capital Inflows – Middle East – 1979-2004

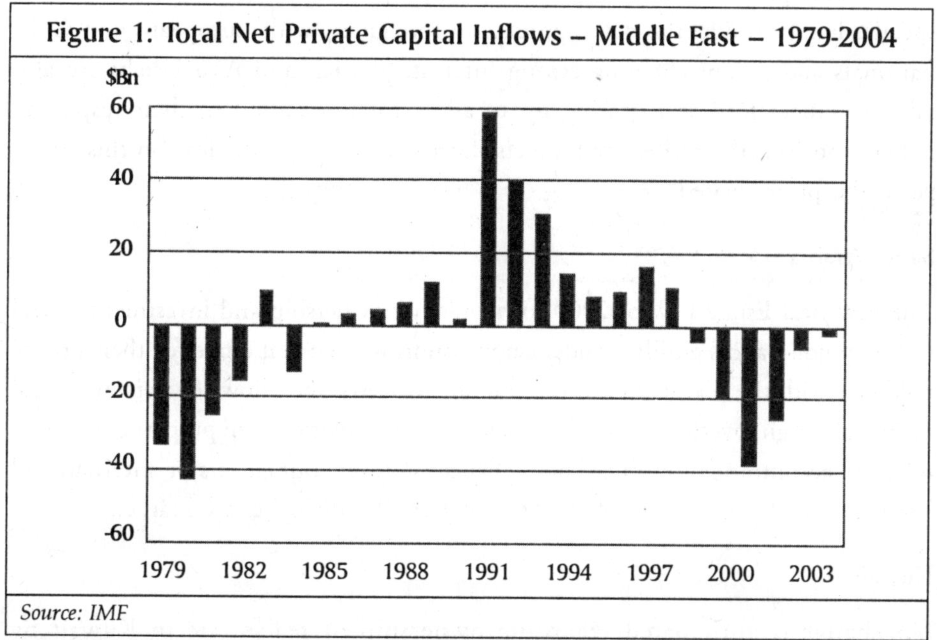

Source: IMF

[3] Comprised of net foreign direct investment (which is the sum of equity capital, reinvestment of earnings, other long-term capital and short-term capital) + net portfolio investments + bank loans.

Ownership Structures

Given the increasing availability in, and popularity of, home real estate markets and the variety of both residential and commercial developments coming on line, domestic real estate assets are expected to become more attractive channels for citizens and national investment groups. However, since freehold ownership is still scarce for foreign investors (i.e., non-GCC), foreign companies such as international hotel corporations are most likely to be interested in non-equity partnerships, licensing contracts and management agreements for the time being.

Summary of Real Estate Ownership Structures in the GCC

UAE

In Dubai, foreign companies and individuals are not permitted to own land or real estate, and all property must be rented or leased (under 999-year structures) for the purposes of running a business. Only the ruling families own the land and opportunities to buy freeholds have historically not existed. However, Dubai has recently pioneered the sale of freehold properties in the GCC, but only in specific luxury residential developments to foreigners, with European, non-GCC nationals and Asians showing strong interest. Sharjah and Abu Dhabi are also taking Dubai's lead and gearing up to allow foreign capital in their respective emirates for specific real estate projects. Legislation is still not clear on this and is yet to be promulgated.

Saudi Arabia

The new Real Estate Law of 2000 for regulating ownership and investment in real estate by non-Saudis entitles resident non-Saudis to own real estate for their private residence with the permission of the Interior Ministry and allows ownership of real estate by foreign investors to conduct their business activities, own properties required for staff accommodation etc. This is expected to encourage major international companies and property developers to enter the Saudi real estate market.

Kuwait

No change is anticipated regarding ownership of real estate in Kuwait by foreigners. Only Kuwaiti nationals can buy property for either self-use or rent/lease. Expatriates coming into the country typically rent out the property for self-use. However, foreign ownership of land is allowed in accordance with Law No. 33/1975, which allows ownership by companies registered in the GCC states. These companies are treated as Kuwaiti nationals with respect to ownership of real estate in Kuwait for commercial and investment purposes.

Oman

The principal legislation governing land ownership in Oman is the Land Law of 1980, which draws clear distinction between the interests and entitlement available to Omanis and non-Omanis. Royal decree 21/2004 expands ownership rights in land to GCC nationals and GCC corporate entities allowing them to own and rent constructed properties and land for residential or investment purposes. Further, in 2004 a decree (not yet ratified) was issued by the Ministry of Housing, Water & Electricity which allows any natural or legal entity to own real estate in designated integrated tourism-related areas, for residential or investment purposes on a freehold basis. Large projects like The Wave, The Muscat golf course project and Al Sawadi tourism projects are expected to benefit. Large sized fully-integrated projects should be developed, as freehold ownership should attract and enhance investments in the real estate sector from foreigners and domestic players.

Qatar

Qatar is opening up to the idea of foreign capital in specific projects. The government has issued a decree that allows non-Qataris to own real estate in three housing projects. The law seeks to allow Qataris and non-Qataris to buy and own real estate of any description in any of the three projects: the proposed Pearl Island, West Bay Lagoon and Al Khor Resort, for a period of 99-years which is further extendable by another 99-years upon expiration. There is a provision of permanent residency and inheritance in the law for buyers. Regulations with regard to these provisions are expected to be passed by the cabinet. However, Qatar has enacted a law which regulates the ownership of real estate and residential units by non-Qataris, with an aim to open up the real estate market to foreign investment.

Bahrain

Legislative decree No. 40 of 1999 allows ownership of Bahraini land by nationals of the member states of the GCC (i.e., non-Bahraini GCC nationals). Further, a decree was passed in 2001 and ratified in 2003 allowing foreigners and foreign investors' 100% ownership of land in predetermined areas, specific projects and tourist developments at Durrat Khaleej al Bahrain, Dannat Hawar and Amwaj Islands. The government is further encouraging investments from international investors, and land will be available for purchase if accompanied by foreign investments in specific sectors.

The Rise of Real Estate Funds and Mortgage-Backed Bonds

National Investor, a UAE investment banking and venture capital company, has launched the first central bank-approved, close-ended real estate fund. The fund capitalizes on investment opportunities in the UAE, as well as other emerging Middle East markets. National Investor has also teamed up with Credit Suisse Asset Management to develop more real estate-related products for individual and institutional investors.

Investment in the real estate market has been a natural progression for Islamic financial institutions (IFIs), and has provided a much needed investment diversification tool. IFIs are already creating real estate funds and have demonstrated innovation in their recent activities in the real estate market.

Islamic banks are increasingly involved in financing large real estate transactions in order to stabilize returns on investment deposits and to improve their balance sheets with relatively secure assets. The past three years have witnessed a rise in the number of investment funds based on real estate transactions. These investment funds tap into a huge market, with pent-up demand for Shariah-compliant European real estate assets estimated to be worth at least $30 billion.

The majority of the IFIs real estate investment products are aimed at HNWIs, and the funds are used to finance assets for capital appreciation, or for the development or acquisition of income-generating assets. These are typically done through special bank deposits or private investment funds.

The development of an Islamic mortgage-backed securities (MBS) market could be warranted, and such securitized real estate transactions will help address previous difficulties faced by IFIs. Securitized real estate transactions will allow IFIs to intermediate in long-term investments, create instruments that can be rolled-over continuously into secondary money markets, and resolve the issue of foreign exchange hedging by creating comparable financial obligations in different currencies.

In the UAE, Dubai Islamic Bank (DIB) has created a joint venture together with Istithmar and the Island Capital Group to launch commercial mortgage-backed securities. These securities will be listed and traded on regional and international markets, including the US and Europe. The JV, named Emirates National Securitization and Finance Corporation, will securitize pools of mortgages and issue them as bonds totaling $1 billion. The mortgages will be kept in a trust vehicle, and once the securitization is complete, the funds will be returned to the banks; the banks can then recycle the capital, further improving liquidity.

These mortgage-backed bonds are expected to boost the local real estate arena, in addition to attracting much needed liquidity into the emerging capital market. The development of the bonds is also expected to smooth-out the development of the ailing mortgage industry in the UAE. Currently, mortgages in Dubai are offered only by a handful of local banks, although this is changing. HSBC has recently entered the mortgage market for Nakheel the local developers for Palm, and will compete with Amlak, the mortgage finance arm of Emaar, which will improve liquidity.

In Summary

The continued popularity of real estate as an asset class should continue unabated. However, it remains to be seen if the tide of capital from the Middle East, traditionally from private direct investors and increasingly through the establishment of real estate funds, will continue to flow into overseas markets. Inexperienced buyers could push up prices locally so that more experienced groups would decide to look outside the region, increasing the outward flows of capital.

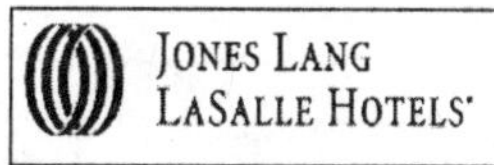

(Anwar Elgonemy represents Jones Lang LaSalle Hotels' investments group in the San Francisco Bay area, is active in lodging sector advisory projects, debt placements and transactions for the firm. He was recently featured in the Cornell Quarterly and The Real Estate Finance Journal, and has been recognized in such media as The Wall Street Journal, The New York Times, The Financial Times, and Time Magazine. ***He can be reached at*** *anwar.elgonemy@am.jll.com).*

Index

F

G

H

I

J

K

L

M

N

O

P

Q

R

S

T

U

V

W

Z